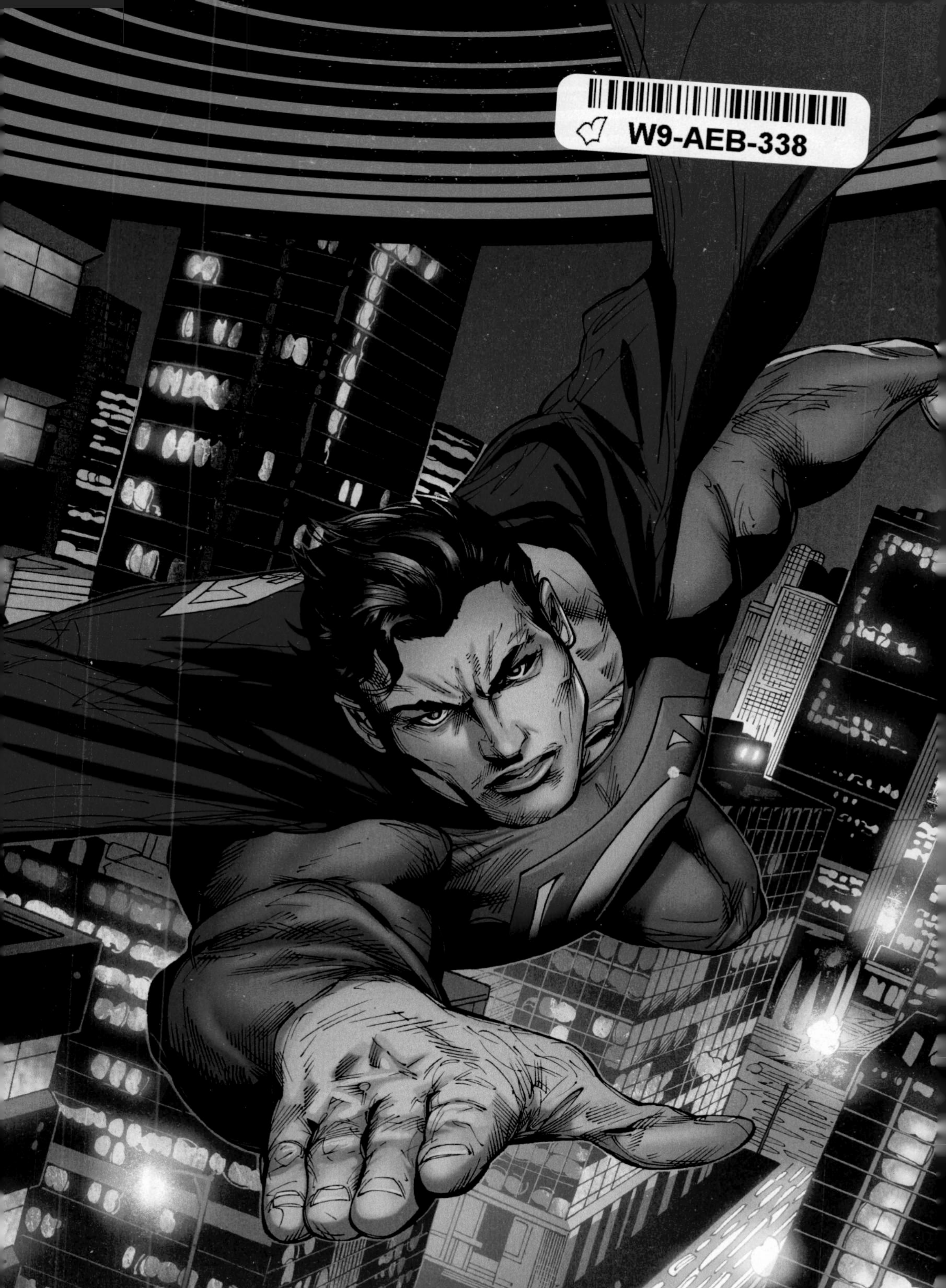

SUPERMAN

VOL.5 HOPES AND FEARS

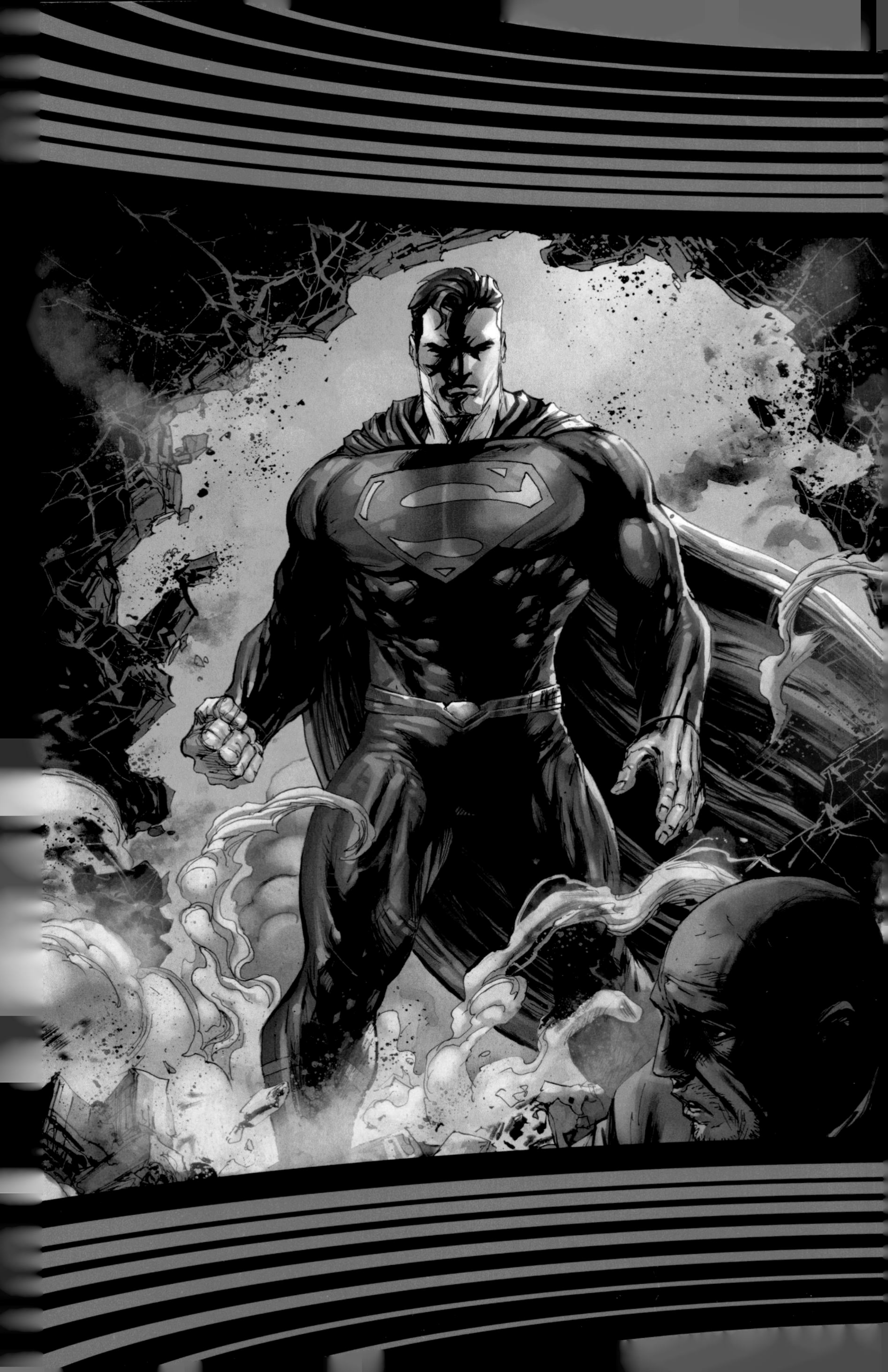

SUPERMAN
VOL.5 HOPES AND FEARS

PETER J. TOMASI * **PATRICK GLEASON** * **KEITH CHAMPAGNE** * **JAMES BONNY**
writers

SCOTT GODLEWSKI * **TYLER KIRKHAM** * **DOUG MAHNKE** * **ED BENES**
PHILIP TAN * **JAIME MENDOZA** * **SCOTT HANNA** * **ROB HUNTER**
artists

GABE ELTAEB * **ARIF PRIANTO** * **WIL QUINTANA**
TONY AVIÑA * **DINEI RIBEIRO** * **TOMEU MOREY** * **SUNNY GHO**
colorists

ROB LEIGH * **DAVE SHARPE**
letterers

LEE WEEKS and BRAD ANDERSON
collection cover artists

LEE WEEKS and BRAD ANDERSON * **RYAN SOOK**
DOUG MAHNKE with JAIME MENDOZA and WIL QUINTANA
IAN CHURCHILL * **TYLER KIRKHAM and ARIF PRIANTO**
original series covers

SUPERMAN created by **JERRY SIEGEL** and **JOE SHUSTER**
SUPERBOY created by **JERRY SIEGEL**
By special arrangement with the Jerry Siegel Family

DEATHSTROKE created by **MARV WOLFMAN** and **GEORGE PÉREZ.**

EDDIE BERGANZA PAUL KAMINSKI Editors – Original Series ✴ **JESSICA CHEN** Associate Editor – Original Series ✴ **ANDREW MARINO** Assistant Editor – Original Series
JEB WOODARD Group Editor – Collected Editions ✴ **ALEX GALER** Editor – Collected Edition
STEVE COOK Design Director – Books ✴ **MONIQUE NARBONETA** Publication Design

BOB HARRAS Senior VP – Editor-in-Chief, DC Comics
PAT McCALLUM Executive Editor, DC Comics

DIANE NELSON President ✴ **DAN DiDIO** Publisher ✴ **JIM LEE** Publisher ✴ **GEOFF JOHNS** President & Chief Creative Officer
AMIT DESAI Executive VP – Business & Marketing Strategy, Direct to Consumer & Global Franchise Management
SAM ADES Senior VP & General Manager, Digital Services ✴ **BOBBIE CHASE** VP & Executive Editor, Young Reader & Talent Development
MARK CHIARELLO Senior VP – Art, Design & Collected Editions ✴ **JOHN CUNNINGHAM** Senior VP – Sales & Trade Marketing
ANNE DePIES Senior VP – Business Strategy, Finance & Administration ✴ **DON FALLETTI** VP – Manufacturing Operations
LAWRENCE GANEM VP – Editorial Administration & Talent Relations ✴ **ALISON GILL** Senior VP – Manufacturing & Operations
HANK KANALZ Senior VP – Editorial Strategy & Administration ✴ **JAY KOGAN** VP – Legal Affairs ✴ **JACK MAHAN** VP – Business Affairs
NICK J. NAPOLITANO VP – Manufacturing Administration ✴ **EDDIE SCANNELL** VP – Consumer Marketing
COURTNEY SIMMONS Senior VP – Publicity & Communications ✴ **JIM (SKI) SOKOLOWSKI** VP – Comic Book Specialty Sales & Trade Marketing
NANCY SPEARS VP – Mass, Book, Digital Sales & Trade Marketing ✴ **MICHELE R. WELLS** VP – Content Strategy

SUPERMAN VOL. 5: HOPES AND FEARS

Published by DC Comics. Compilation and all new material Copyright © 2018 DC Comics. All Rights Reserved.
Originally published in single magazine form in SUPERMAN 27-32. Copyright © 2017 DC Comics.
All Rights Reserved. All characters, their distinctive likenesses and related elements featured in this publication are trademarks of DC Comics.
The stories, characters and incidents featured in this publication are entirely fictional.
DC Comics does not read or accept unsolicited ideas, stories or artwork.

DC Comics, 2900 West Alameda Ave., Burbank, CA 91505
Printed by LSC Communications, Kendallville, IN, USA. 3/9/18. First Printing.
ISBN: 978-1-4012-7729-1

Library of Congress Cataloging-in-Publication Data is available.

PEFC Certified

Printed on paper from
sustainably managed
forests, controlled
sources

PEFC/29-31-337   www.pefc.org

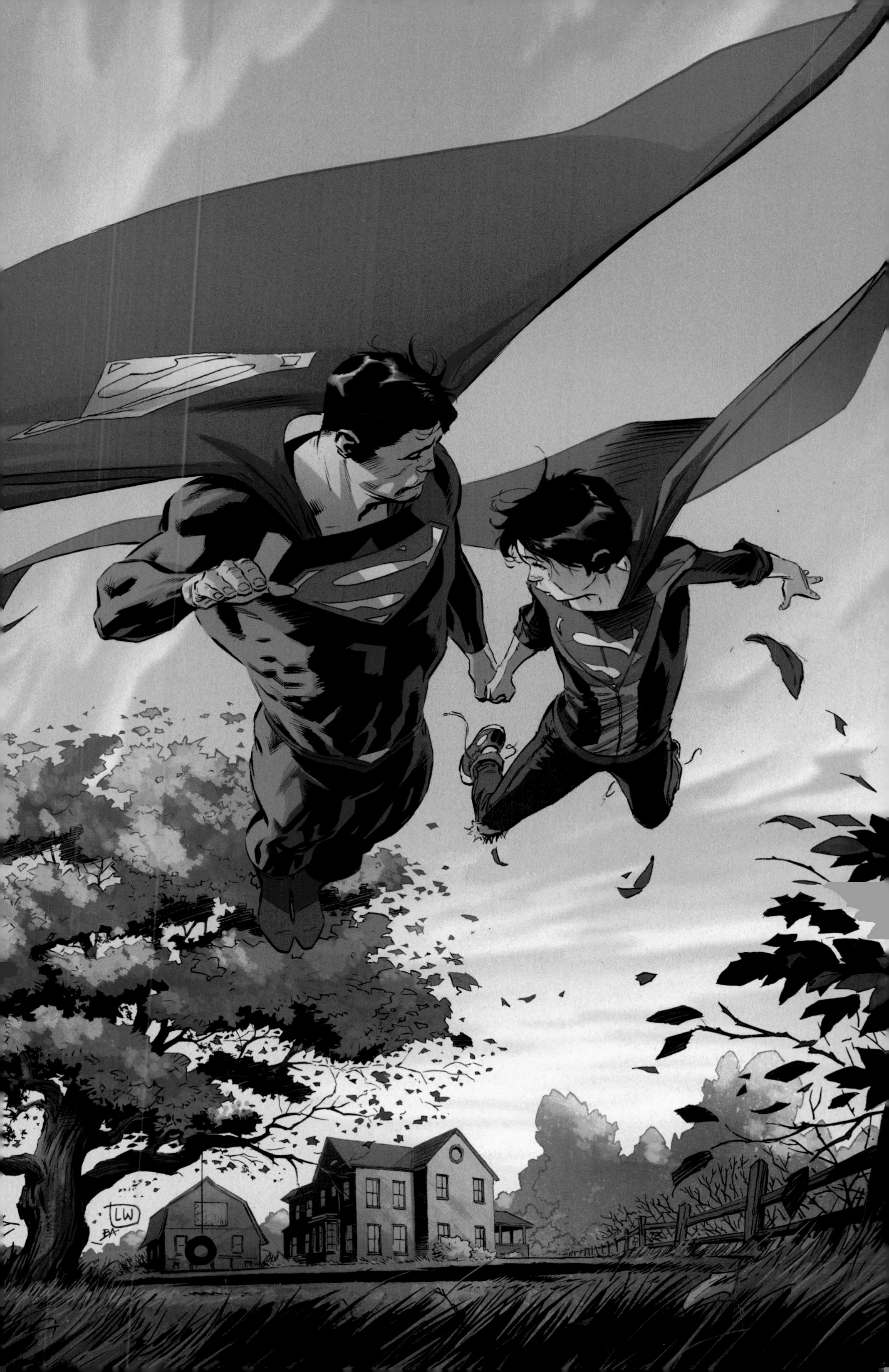

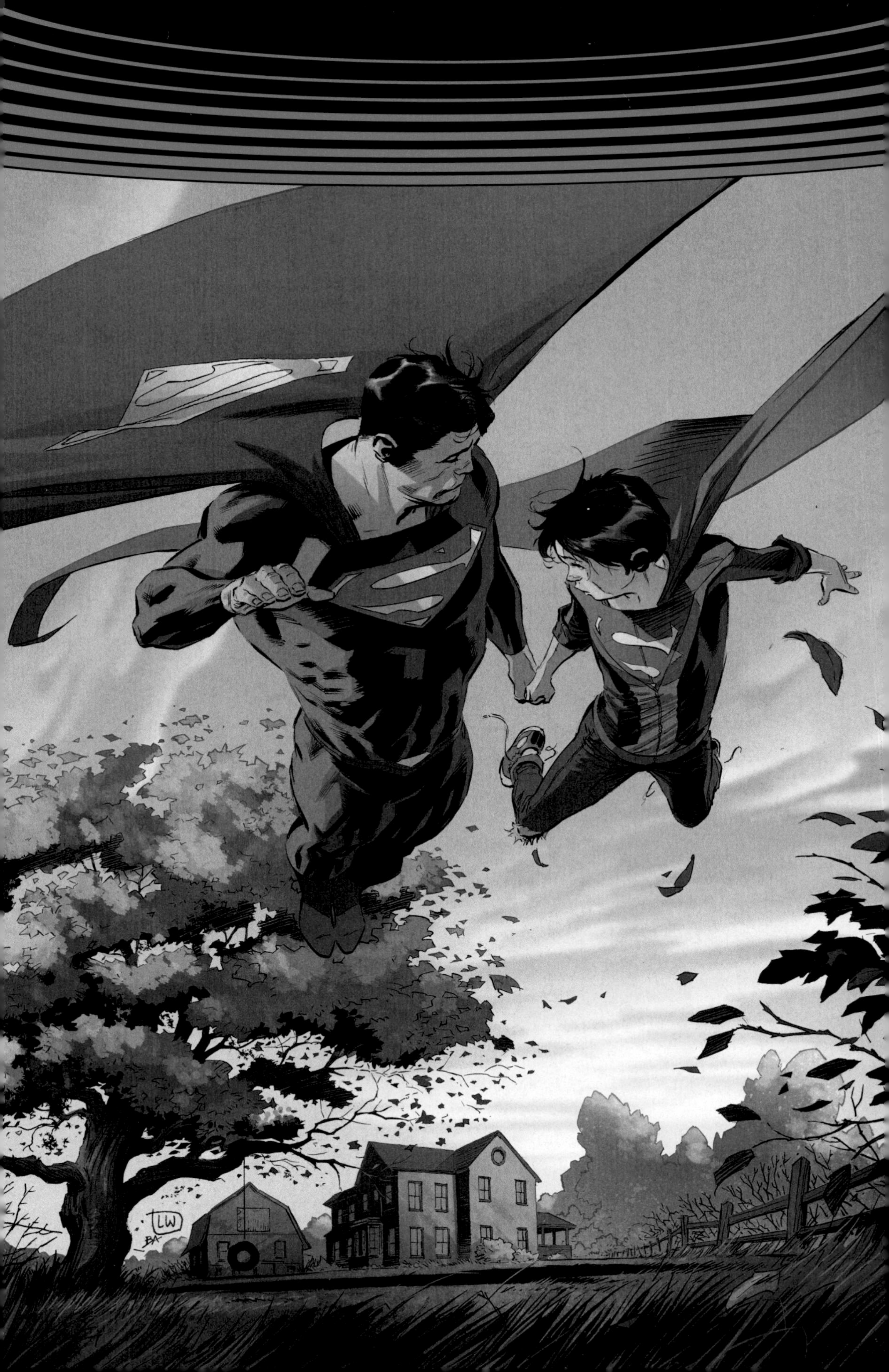

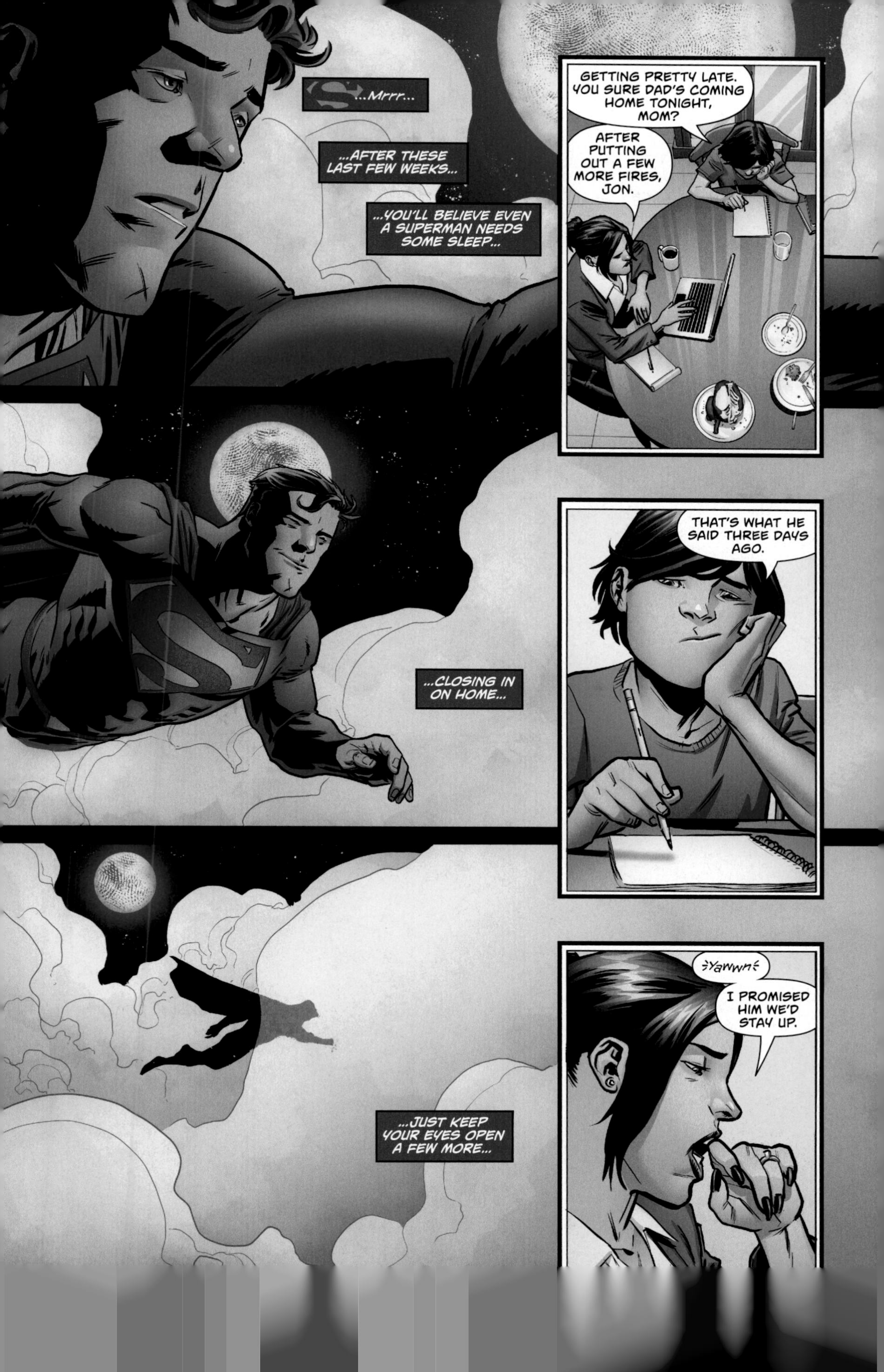
...Mrrr...
...AFTER THESE LAST FEW WEEKS...
...YOU'LL BELIEVE EVEN A SUPERMAN NEEDS SOME SLEEP...
GETTING PRETTY LATE. YOU SURE DAD'S COMING HOME TONIGHT, MOM?
AFTER PUTTING OUT A FEW MORE FIRES, JON.
...CLOSING IN ON HOME...
THAT'S WHAT HE SAID THREE DAYS AGO.
...JUST KEEP YOUR EYES OPEN A FEW MORE...
Yawwn
I PROMISED HIM WE'D STAY UP.

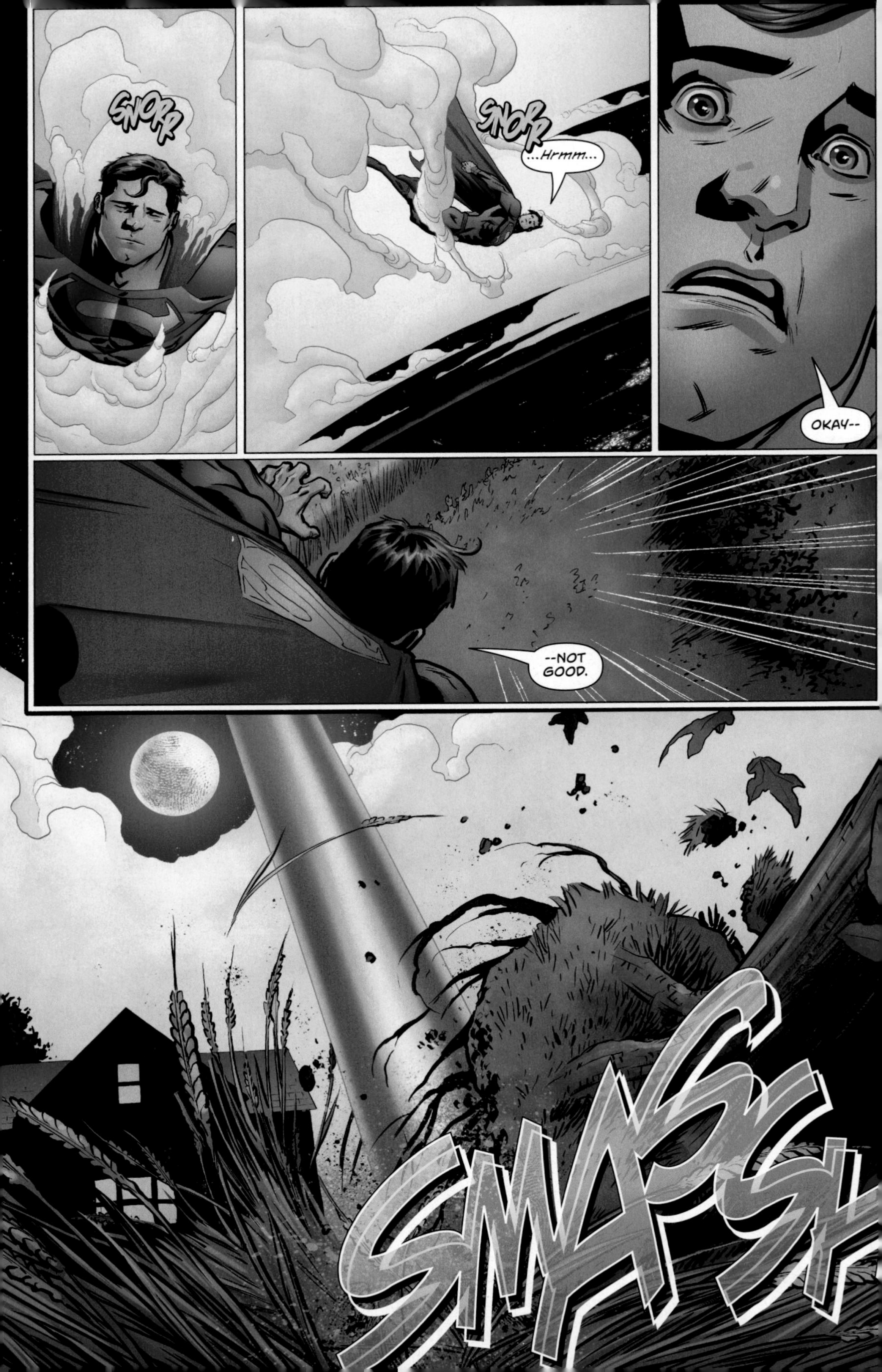
SNORR
SNORR
...Hrmm...
OKAY--
--NOT GOOD.
SMASH

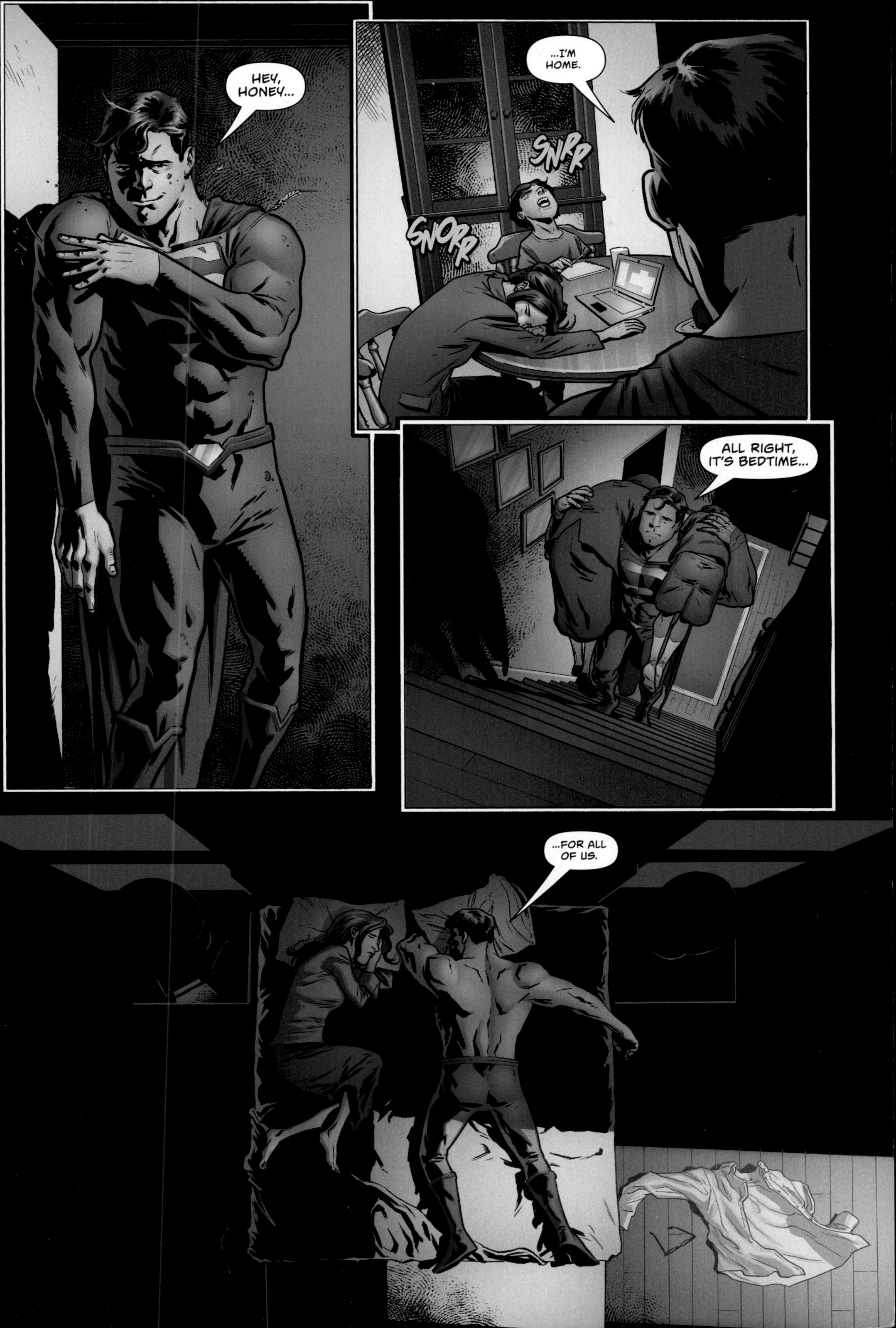
HEY, HONEY...
...I'M HOME.
SNRR
SNORR
ALL RIGHT, IT'S BEDTIME...
...FOR ALL OF US.

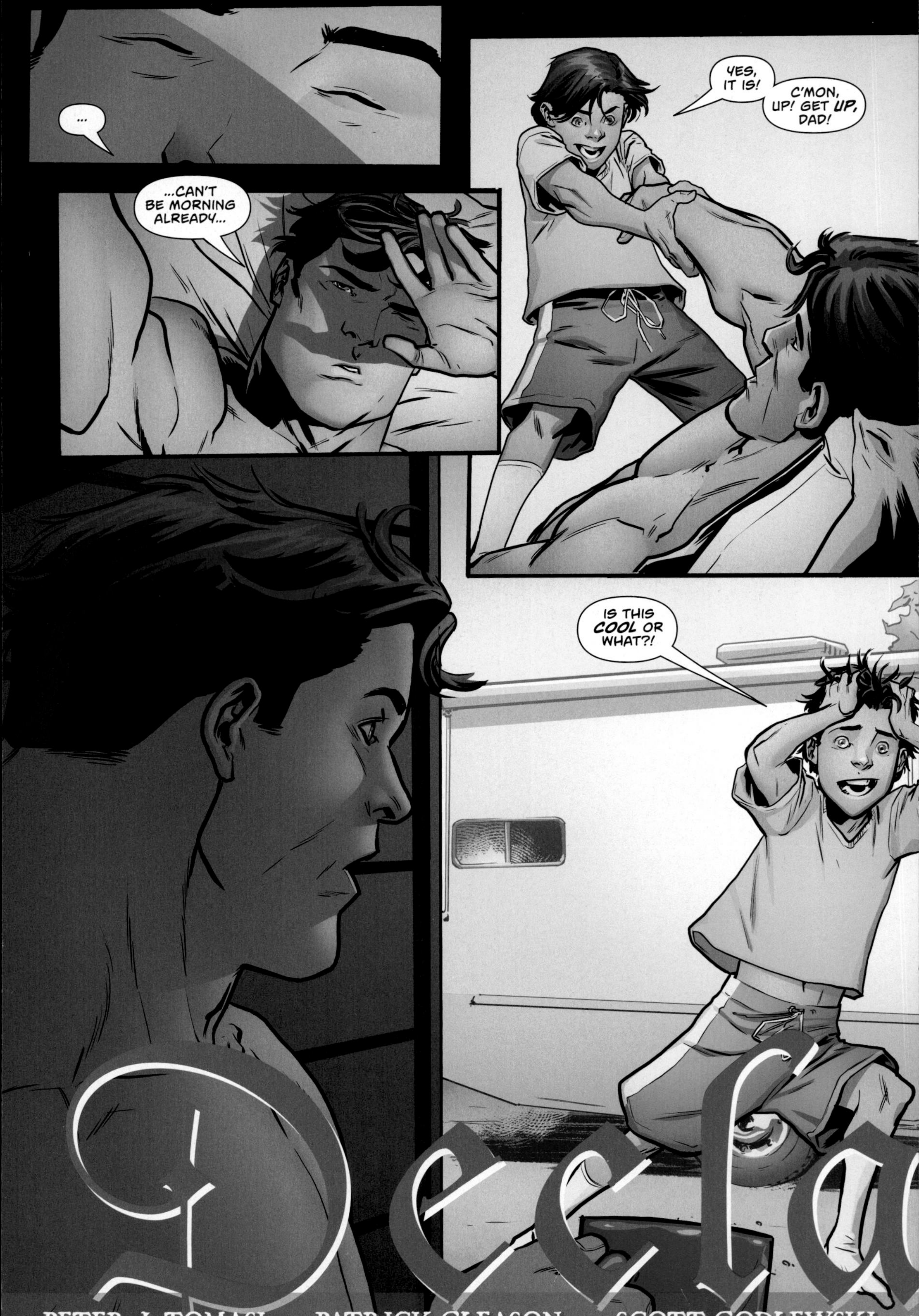
...
...CAN'T BE MORNING ALREADY...
YES, IT IS!
C'MON, UP! GET UP, DAD!
IS THIS COOL OR WHAT?!

PETER J. TOMASI AND PATRICK GLEASON *story* SCOTT GODLEWSKI *artis*
GABE ELTAEB *colorist* ROB LEIGH *letterer* LEE WEEKS AND BRAD ANDERSON *cover*
ANDREW MARINO *assistant editor* EDDIE BERGANZA *editor*

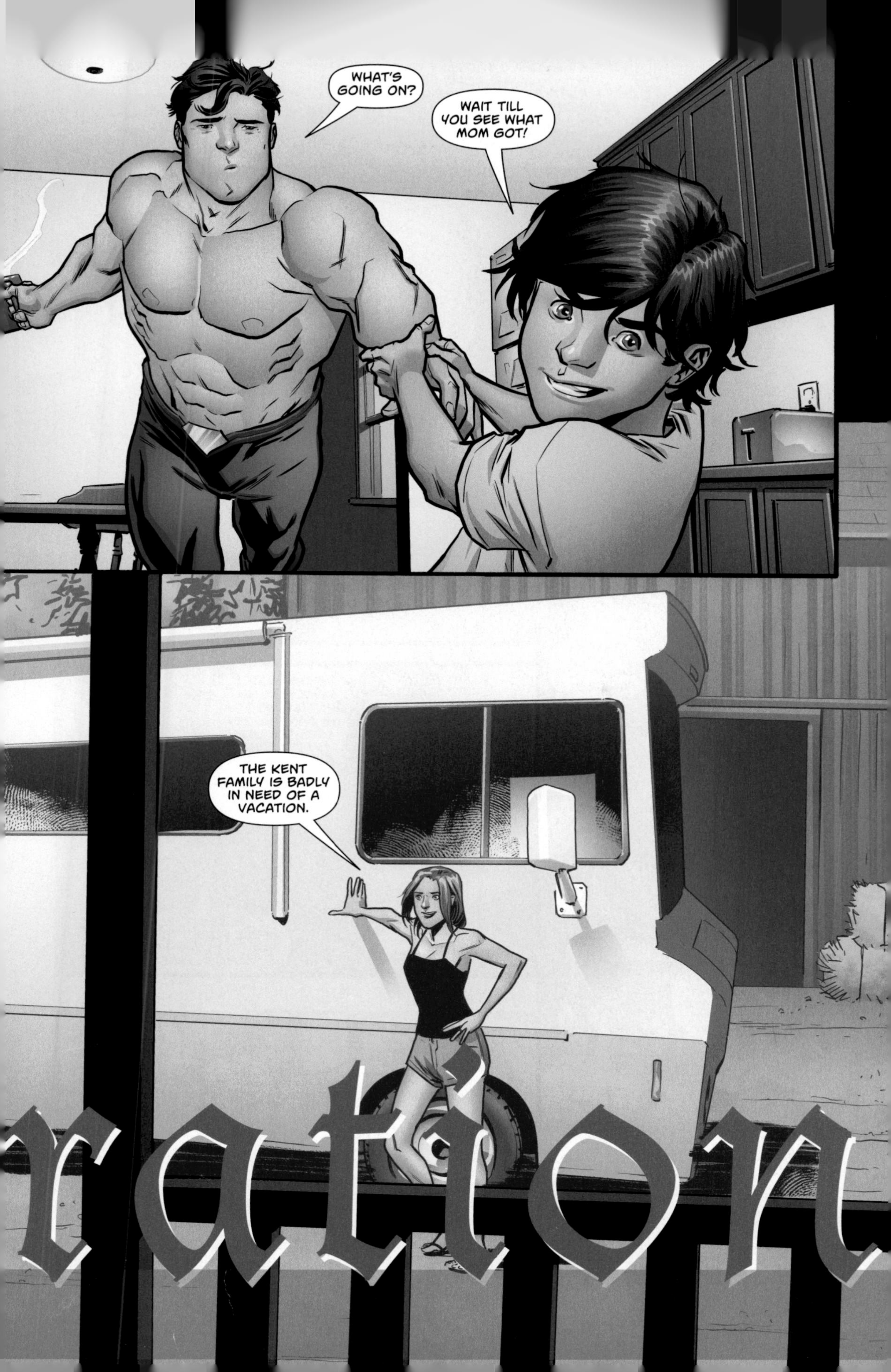
WHAT'S GOING ON?
WAIT TILL YOU SEE WHAT MOM GOT!
THE KENT FAMILY IS BADLY IN NEED OF A VACATION.
ration

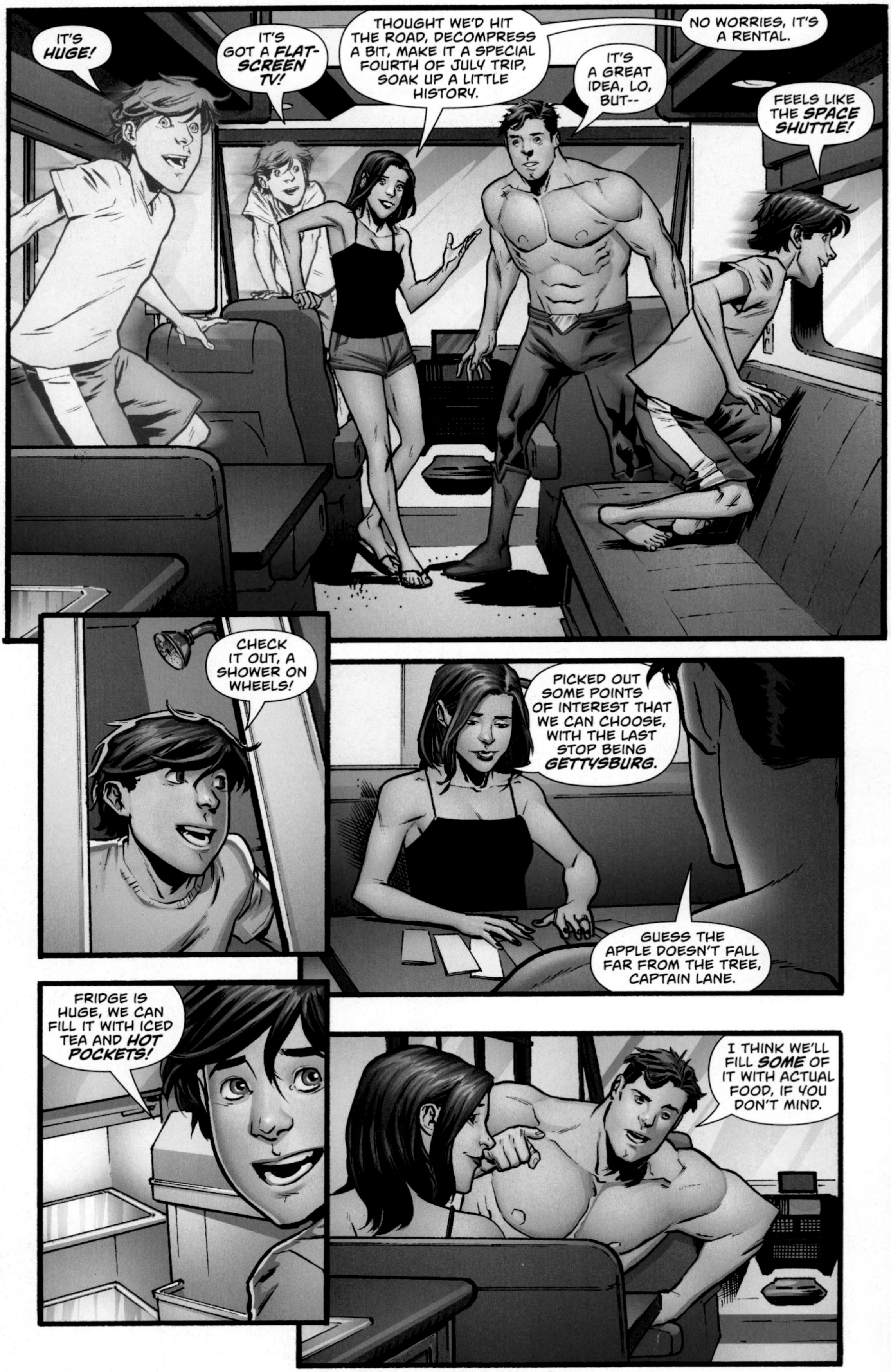
IT'S *HUGE!*
IT'S GOT A *FLAT-SCREEN TV!*
THOUGHT WE'D HIT THE ROAD, DECOMPRESS A BIT, MAKE IT A SPECIAL FOURTH OF JULY TRIP, SOAK UP A LITTLE HISTORY.
IT'S A GREAT IDEA, LO, BUT--
NO WORRIES, IT'S A RENTAL.
FEELS LIKE THE *SPACE SHUTTLE!*
CHECK IT OUT, A SHOWER ON WHEELS!
PICKED OUT SOME POINTS OF INTEREST THAT WE CAN CHOOSE, WITH THE LAST STOP BEING *GETTYSBURG*.
GUESS THE APPLE DOESN'T FALL FAR FROM THE TREE, CAPTAIN LANE.
FRIDGE IS HUGE, WE CAN FILL IT WITH ICED TEA AND *HOT POCKETS!*
I THINK WE'LL FILL *SOME* OF IT WITH ACTUAL FOOD, IF YOU DON'T MIND.

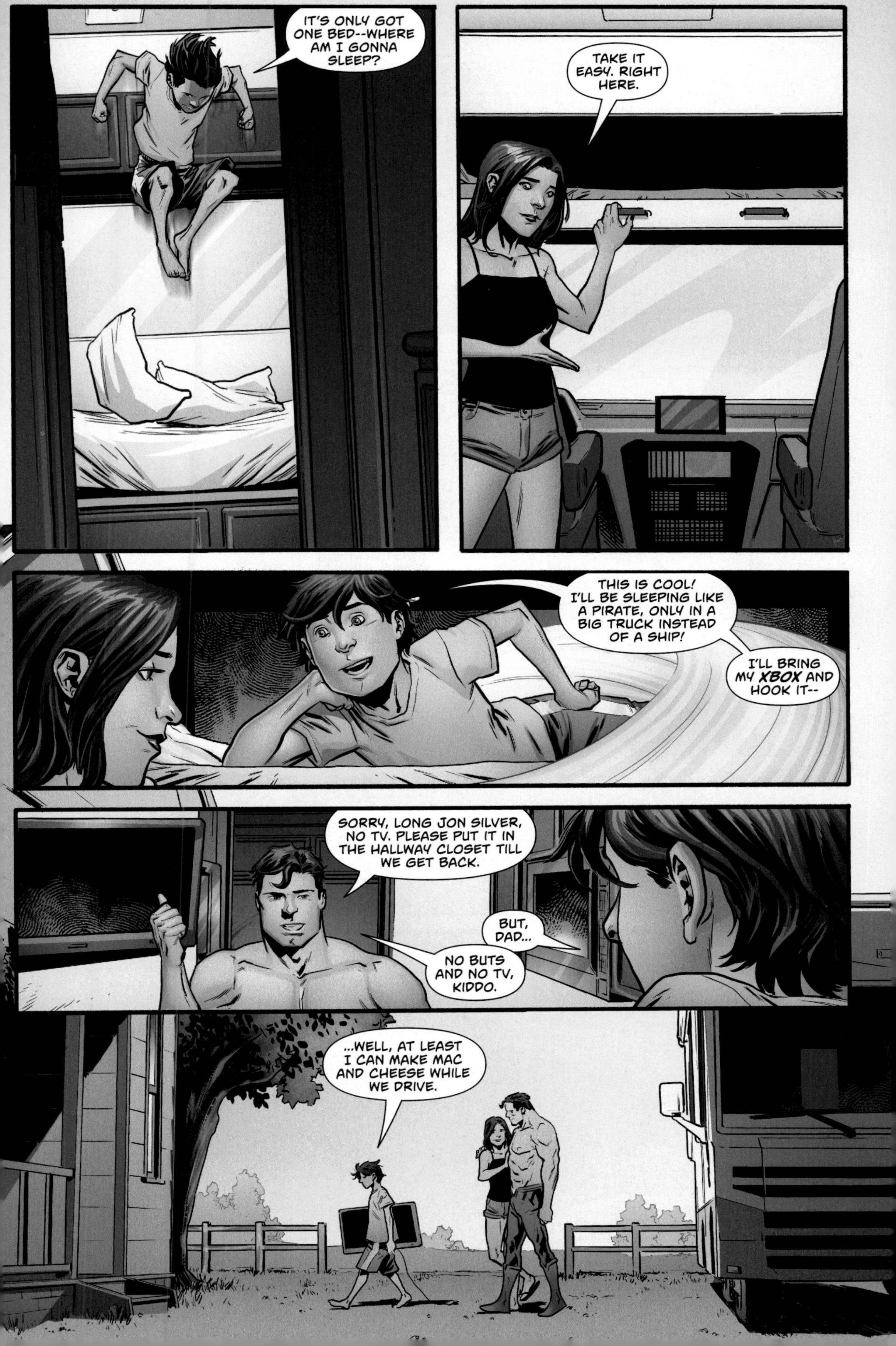
IT'S ONLY GOT ONE BED--WHERE AM I GONNA SLEEP?
TAKE IT EASY. RIGHT HERE.
THIS IS COOL! I'LL BE SLEEPING LIKE A PIRATE, ONLY IN A BIG TRUCK INSTEAD OF A SHIP!
I'LL BRING MY *XBOX* AND HOOK IT--
SORRY, LONG JON SILVER, NO TV. PLEASE PUT IT IN THE HALLWAY CLOSET TILL WE GET BACK.
BUT, DAD...
NO BUTS AND NO TV, KIDDO.
...WELL, AT LEAST I CAN MAKE MAC AND CHEESE WHILE WE DRIVE.

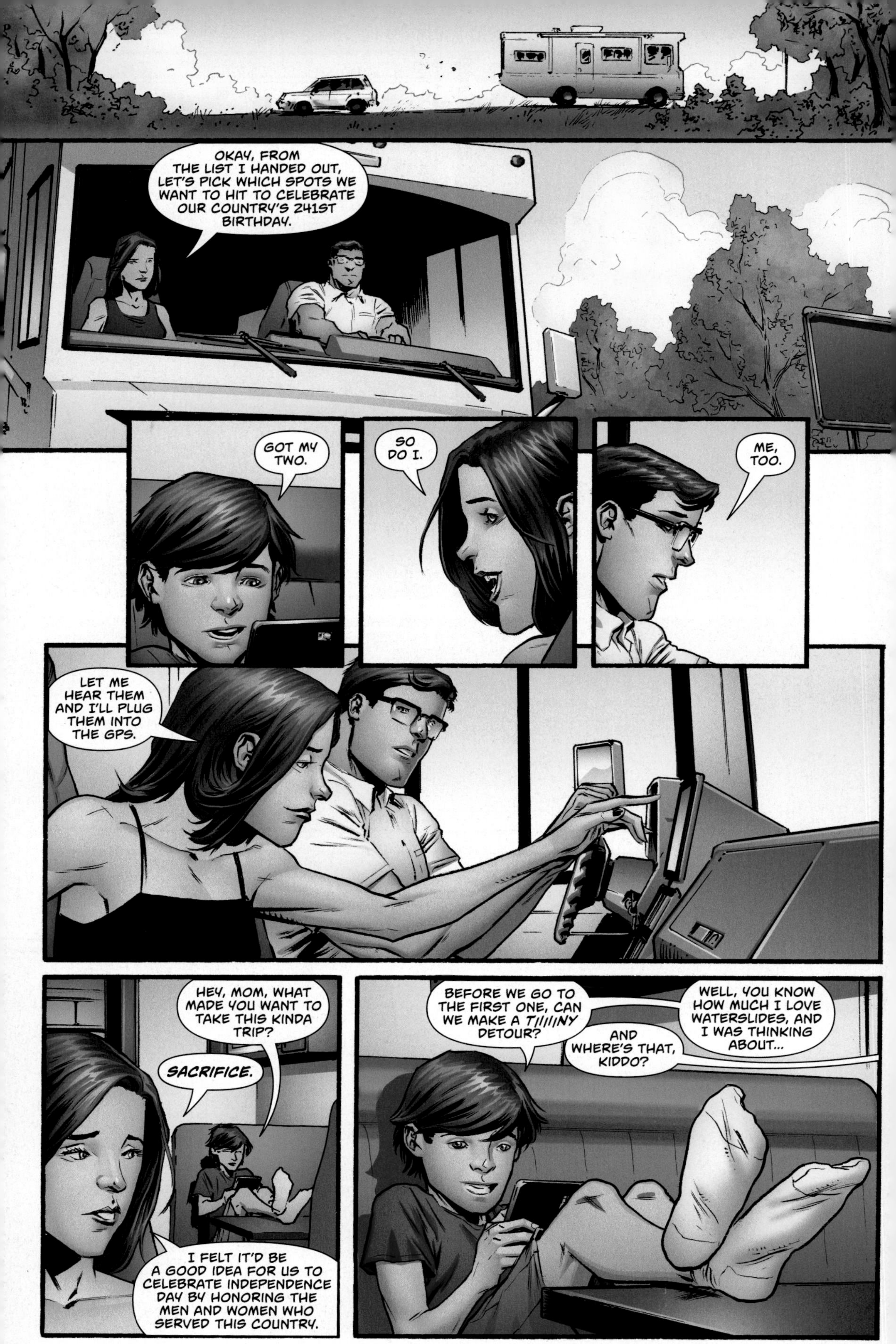
OKAY, FROM THE LIST I HANDED OUT, LET'S PICK WHICH SPOTS WE WANT TO HIT TO CELEBRATE OUR COUNTRY'S 241ST BIRTHDAY.
GOT MY TWO.
SO DO I.
ME, TOO.
LET ME HEAR THEM AND I'LL PLUG THEM INTO THE GPS.
HEY, MOM, WHAT MADE YOU WANT TO TAKE THIS KINDA TRIP?
SACRIFICE.
I FELT IT'D BE A GOOD IDEA FOR US TO CELEBRATE INDEPENDENCE DAY BY HONORING THE MEN AND WOMEN WHO SERVED THIS COUNTRY.
BEFORE WE GO TO THE FIRST ONE, CAN WE MAKE A TIIIIINY DETOUR?
AND WHERE'S THAT, KIDDO?
WELL, YOU KNOW HOW MUCH I LOVE WATERSLIDES, AND I WAS THINKING ABOUT...

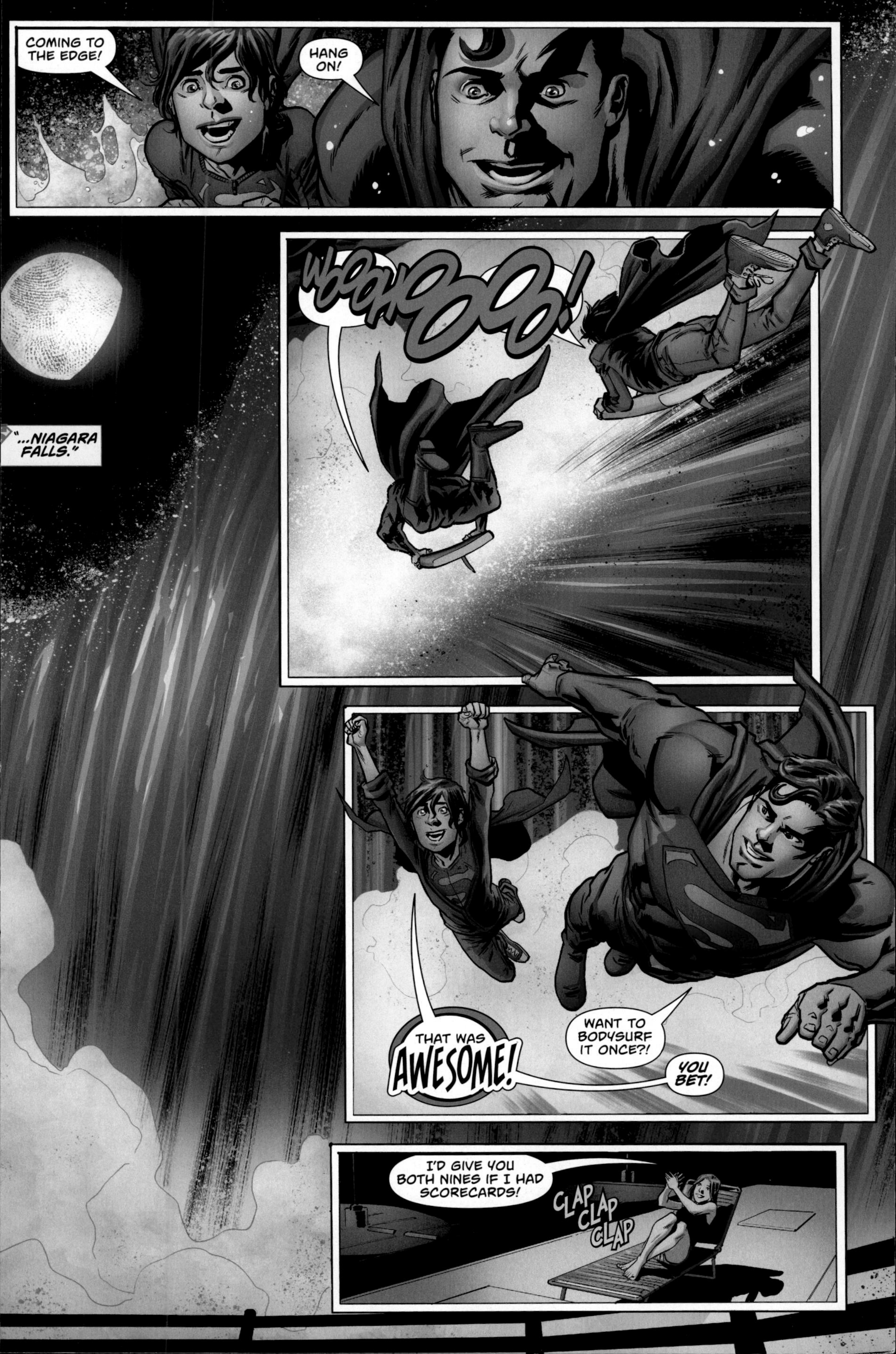

COMING TO THE EDGE!
HANG ON!
WOOOHOOOOO!
"...NIAGARA FALLS."
THAT WAS AWESOME!
WANT TO BODYSURF IT ONCE?!
YOU BET!
I'D GIVE YOU BOTH NINES IF I HAD SCORECARDS!
CLAP CLAP CLAP

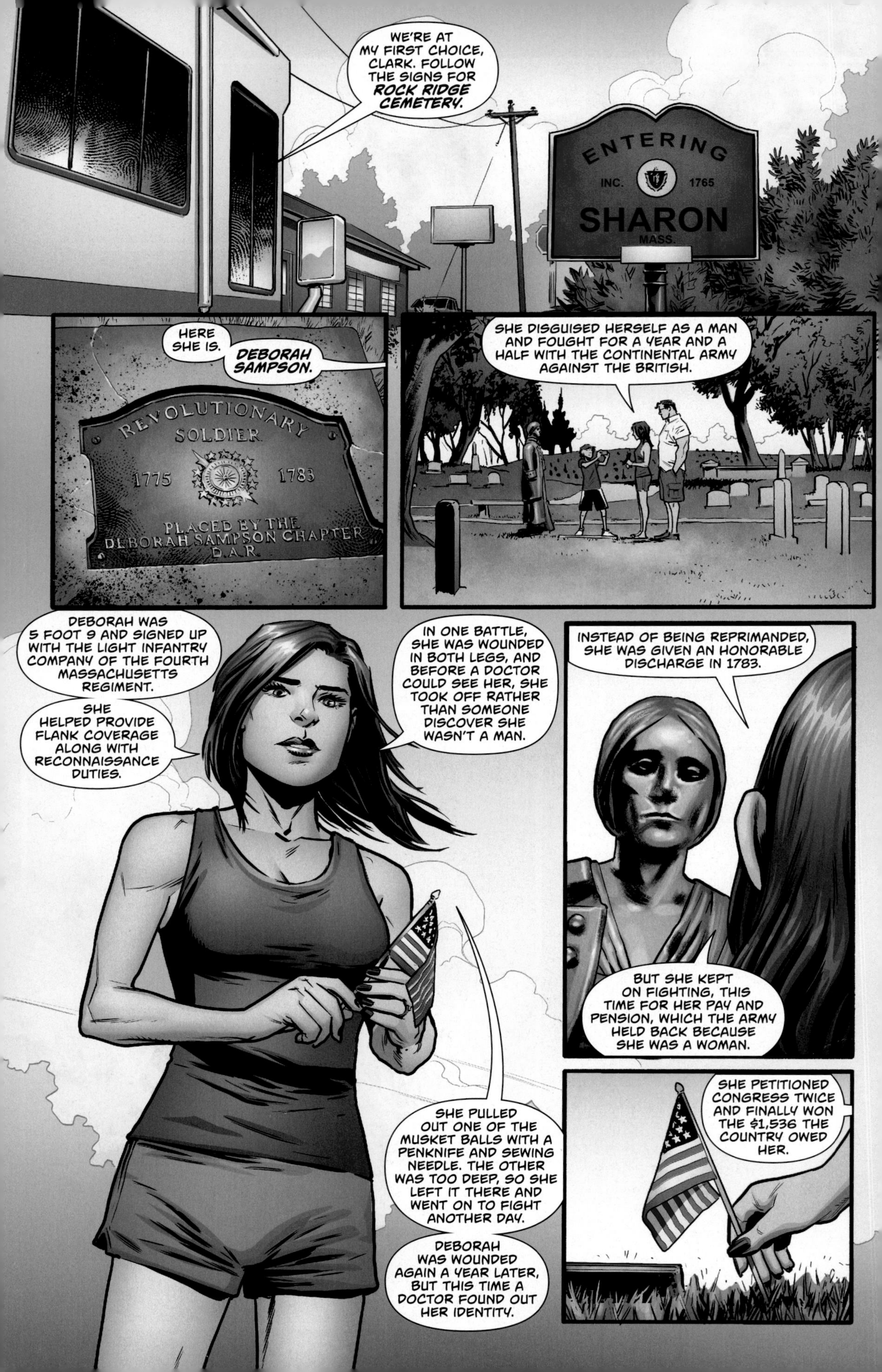

WE'RE AT MY FIRST CHOICE, CLARK. FOLLOW THE SIGNS FOR ROCK RIDGE CEMETERY.
ENTERING
INC. 1765
SHARON
MASS.
HERE SHE IS.
DEBORAH SAMPSON.
REVOLUTIONARY SOLDIER
1775 1783
PLACED BY THE DEBORAH SAMPSON CHAPTER D.A.R.
SHE DISGUISED HERSELF AS A MAN AND FOUGHT FOR A YEAR AND A HALF WITH THE CONTINENTAL ARMY AGAINST THE BRITISH.
DEBORAH WAS 5 FOOT 9 AND SIGNED UP WITH THE LIGHT INFANTRY COMPANY OF THE FOURTH MASSACHUSETTS REGIMENT.
SHE HELPED PROVIDE FLANK COVERAGE ALONG WITH RECONNAISSANCE DUTIES.
IN ONE BATTLE, SHE WAS WOUNDED IN BOTH LEGS, AND BEFORE A DOCTOR COULD SEE HER, SHE TOOK OFF RATHER THAN SOMEONE DISCOVER SHE WASN'T A MAN.
SHE PULLED OUT ONE OF THE MUSKET BALLS WITH A PENKNIFE AND SEWING NEEDLE. THE OTHER WAS TOO DEEP, SO SHE LEFT IT THERE AND WENT ON TO FIGHT ANOTHER DAY.
DEBORAH WAS WOUNDED AGAIN A YEAR LATER, BUT THIS TIME A DOCTOR FOUND OUT HER IDENTITY.
INSTEAD OF BEING REPRIMANDED, SHE WAS GIVEN AN HONORABLE DISCHARGE IN 1783.
BUT SHE KEPT ON FIGHTING, THIS TIME FOR HER PAY AND PENSION, WHICH THE ARMY HELD BACK BECAUSE SHE WAS A WOMAN.
SHE PETITIONED CONGRESS TWICE AND FINALLY WON THE $1,536 THE COUNTRY OWED HER.

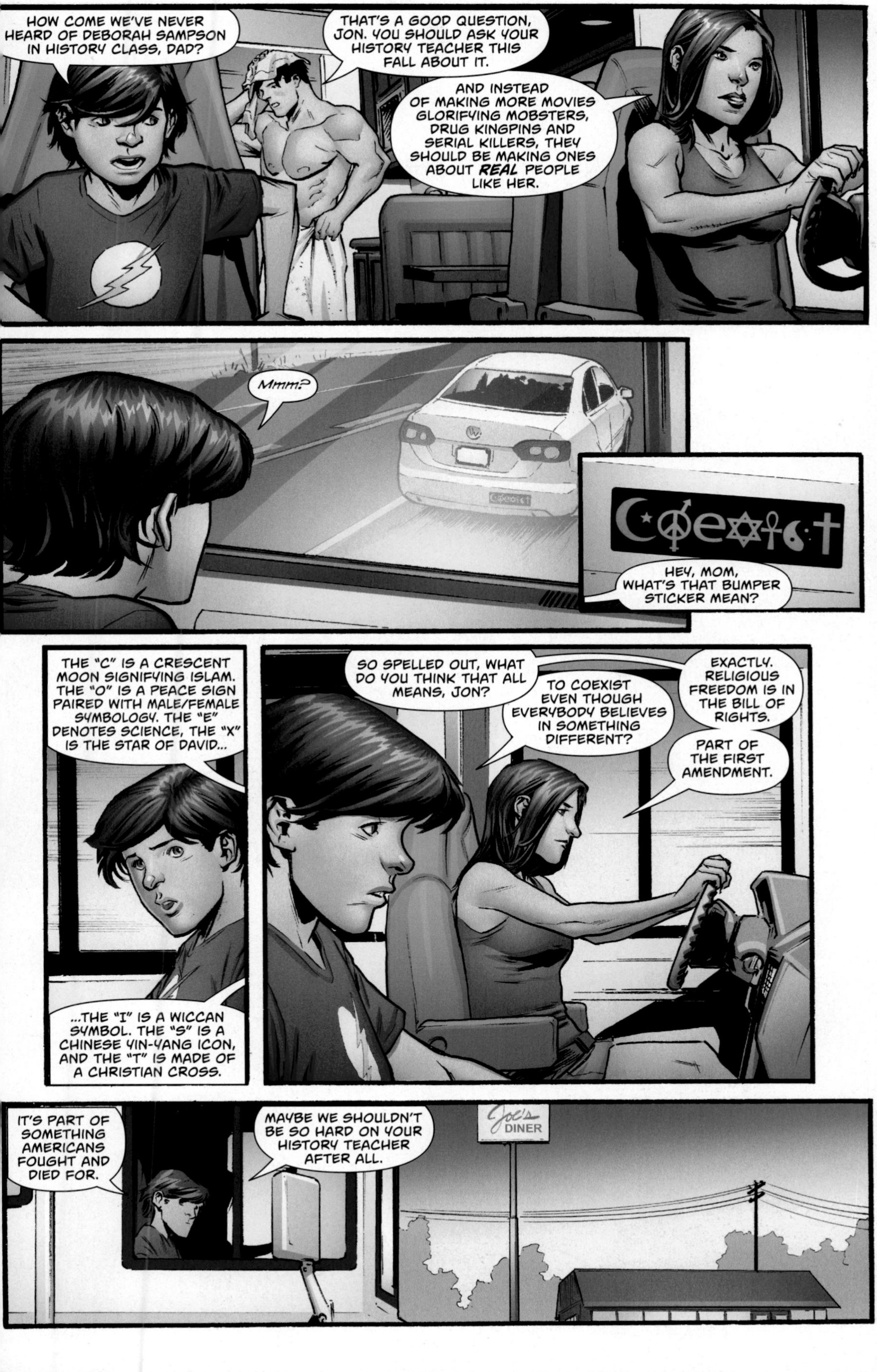
HOW COME WE'VE NEVER HEARD OF DEBORAH SAMPSON IN HISTORY CLASS, DAD?
THAT'S A GOOD QUESTION, JON. YOU SHOULD ASK YOUR HISTORY TEACHER THIS FALL ABOUT IT.
AND INSTEAD OF MAKING MORE MOVIES GLORIFYING MOBSTERS, DRUG KINGPINS AND SERIAL KILLERS, THEY SHOULD BE MAKING ONES ABOUT REAL PEOPLE LIKE HER.
Mmm?
COEXIST
HEY, MOM, WHAT'S THAT BUMPER STICKER MEAN?
THE "C" IS A CRESCENT MOON SIGNIFYING ISLAM. THE "O" IS A PEACE SIGN PAIRED WITH MALE/FEMALE SYMBOLOGY. THE "E" DENOTES SCIENCE, THE "X" IS THE STAR OF DAVID...
...THE "I" IS A WICCAN SYMBOL. THE "S" IS A CHINESE YIN-YANG ICON, AND THE "T" IS MADE OF A CHRISTIAN CROSS.
SO SPELLED OUT, WHAT DO YOU THINK THAT ALL MEANS, JON?
TO COEXIST EVEN THOUGH EVERYBODY BELIEVES IN SOMETHING DIFFERENT?
EXACTLY. RELIGIOUS FREEDOM IS IN THE BILL OF RIGHTS.
PART OF THE FIRST AMENDMENT.
IT'S PART OF SOMETHING AMERICANS FOUGHT AND DIED FOR.
MAYBE WE SHOULDN'T BE SO HARD ON YOUR HISTORY TEACHER AFTER ALL.
Joe's DINER

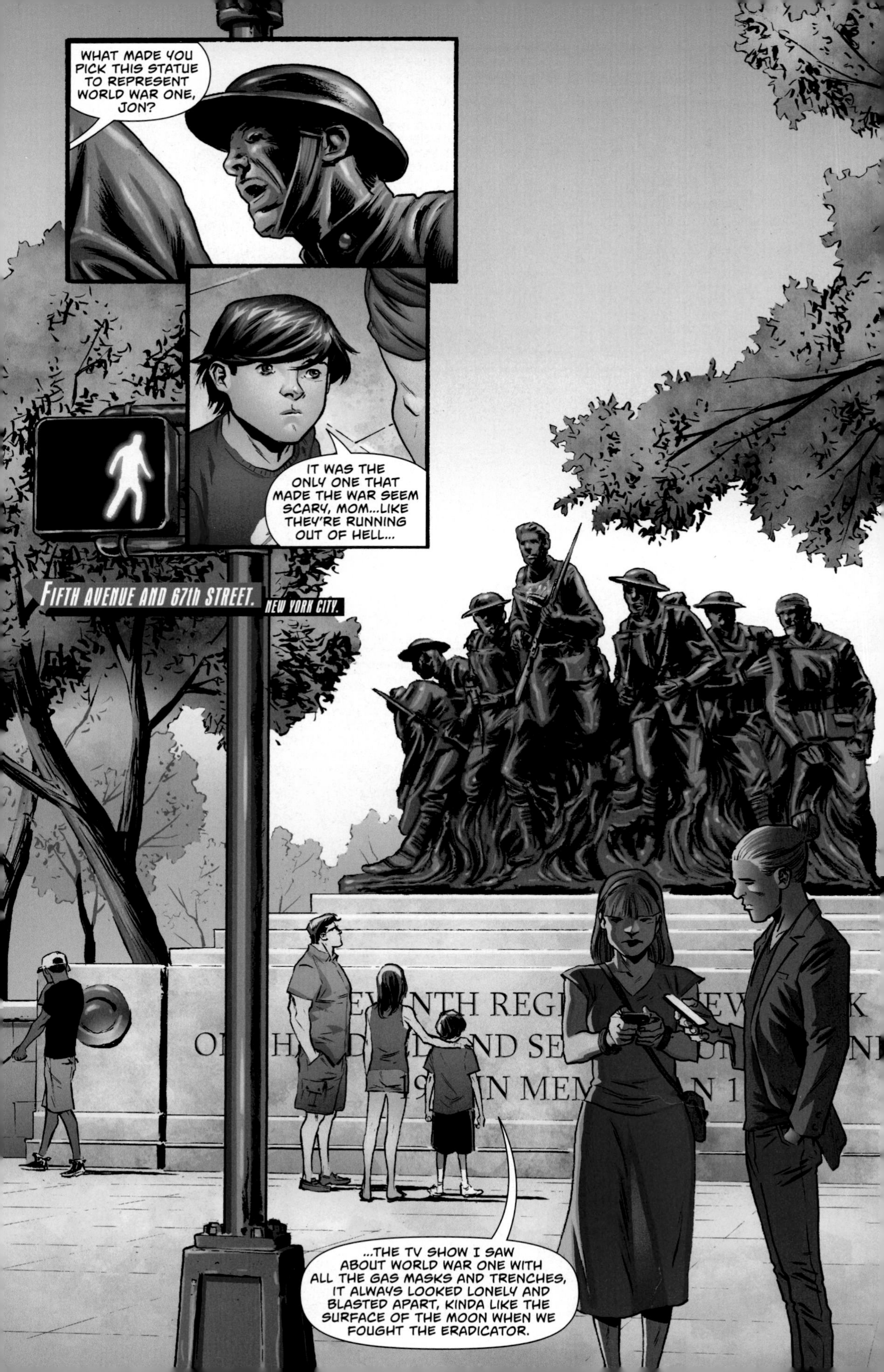
WHAT MADE YOU PICK THIS STATUE TO REPRESENT WORLD WAR ONE, JON?
IT WAS THE ONLY ONE THAT MADE THE WAR SEEM SCARY, MOM...LIKE THEY'RE RUNNING OUT OF HELL...
FIFTH AVENUE AND 67th STREET.
NEW YORK CITY.
...THE TV SHOW I SAW ABOUT WORLD WAR ONE WITH ALL THE GAS MASKS AND TRENCHES, IT ALWAYS LOOKED LONELY AND BLASTED APART, KINDA LIKE THE SURFACE OF THE MOON WHEN WE FOUGHT THE ERADICATOR.

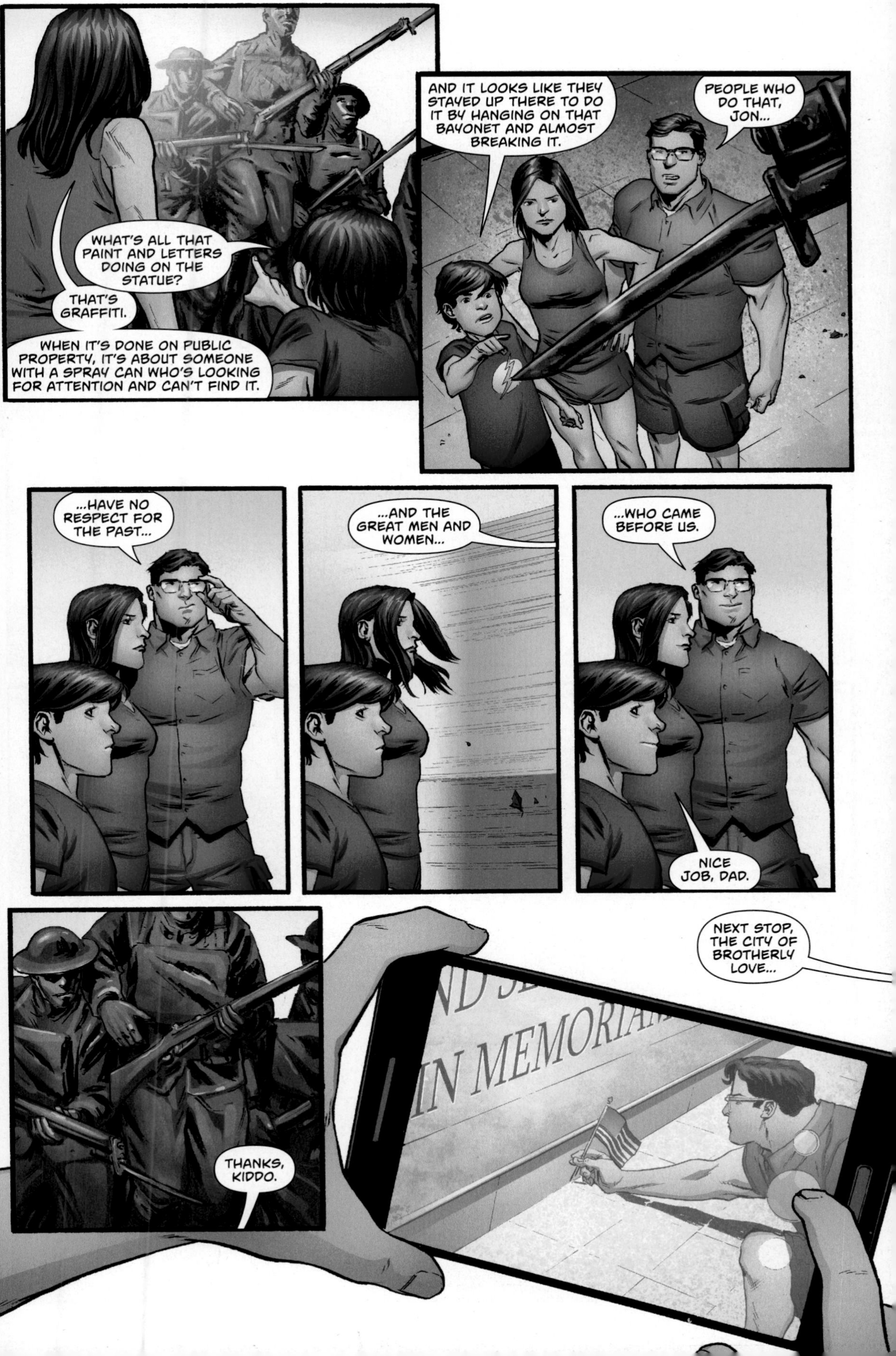
WHAT'S ALL THAT PAINT AND LETTERS DOING ON THE STATUE?
THAT'S GRAFFITI.
WHEN IT'S DONE ON PUBLIC PROPERTY, IT'S ABOUT SOMEONE WITH A SPRAY CAN WHO'S LOOKING FOR ATTENTION AND CAN'T FIND IT.
AND IT LOOKS LIKE THEY STAYED UP THERE TO DO IT BY HANGING ON THAT BAYONET AND ALMOST BREAKING IT.
PEOPLE WHO DO THAT, JON...
...HAVE NO RESPECT FOR THE PAST...
...AND THE GREAT MEN AND WOMEN...
...WHO CAME BEFORE US.
NICE JOB, DAD.
THANKS, KIDDO.
NEXT STOP, THE CITY OF BROTHERLY LOVE...
IN MEMORIAM

"...AND *INDEPENDENCE HALL* IN *PHILADELPHIA.*"

...THE BUILDING WAS FINISHED IN 1753 AND IT BECAME THE MAIN ASSEMBLY PLACE OF THE SECOND CONTINENTAL CONGRESS FROM 1775 TO 1783, AND WAS THE SITE OF THE CONSTITUTIONAL CONVENTION IN THE SUMMER OF 1787.

YEAH, THE PLACE WHERE POLITICIANS DID THE EASY WORK AND NONE OF THE FIGHTING.

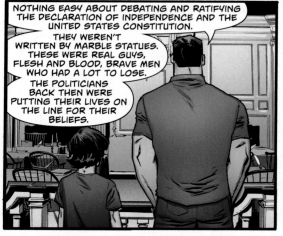

NOTHING EASY ABOUT DEBATING AND RATIFYING THE DECLARATION OF INDEPENDENCE AND THE UNITED STATES CONSTITUTION.

THEY WEREN'T WRITTEN BY MARBLE STATUES. THESE WERE REAL GUYS, FLESH AND BLOOD, BRAVE MEN WHO HAD A LOT TO LOSE.

THE POLITICIANS BACK THEN WERE PUTTING THEIR LIVES ON THE LINE FOR THEIR BELIEFS.

ONCE THEY SIGNED THOSE DOCUMENTS, THEY WERE COMMITTING TREASON. AND THE BRITISH HANGED TREASONOUS MEN.

LIKE JEFFERSON SAID IN THE DECLARATION, THEY WERE PLEDGING THEIR SACRED--

--AND HONOR'S A WORD THAT MEANS A LOT TO A PERSON WHO BELIEVES AND LIVES BY IT, JON.

MAY WANT TO CHECK THE ROOF FOR WATER DAMAGE, RANGER.

DON'T I WISH.

I HAVEN'T SEEN ANY SIGNS OF WATER TROUBLE. WHAT DO YOU HAVE, *X-RAY VISION* OR SOMETHING?

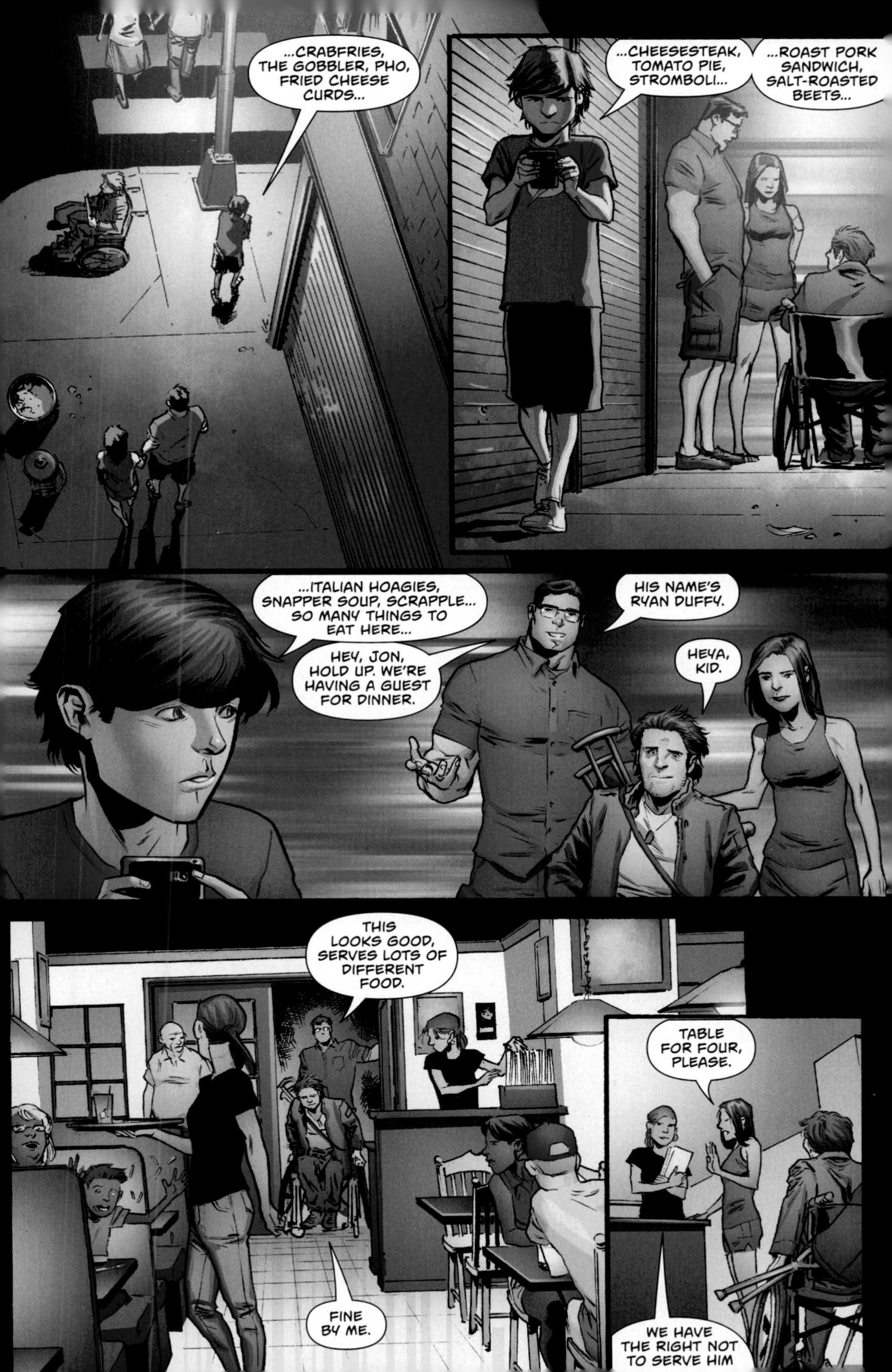
...CRABFRIES, THE GOBBLER, PHO, FRIED CHEESE CURDS...
...CHEESESTEAK, TOMATO PIE, STROMBOLI...
...ROAST PORK SANDWICH, SALT-ROASTED BEETS...
...ITALIAN HOAGIES, SNAPPER SOUP, SCRAPPLE... SO MANY THINGS TO EAT HERE...
HEY, JON, HOLD UP. WE'RE HAVING A GUEST FOR DINNER.
HIS NAME'S RYAN DUFFY.
HEYA, KID.
THIS LOOKS GOOD, SERVES LOTS OF DIFFERENT FOOD.
FINE BY ME.
TABLE FOR FOUR, PLEASE.
WE HAVE THE RIGHT NOT TO SERVE HIM

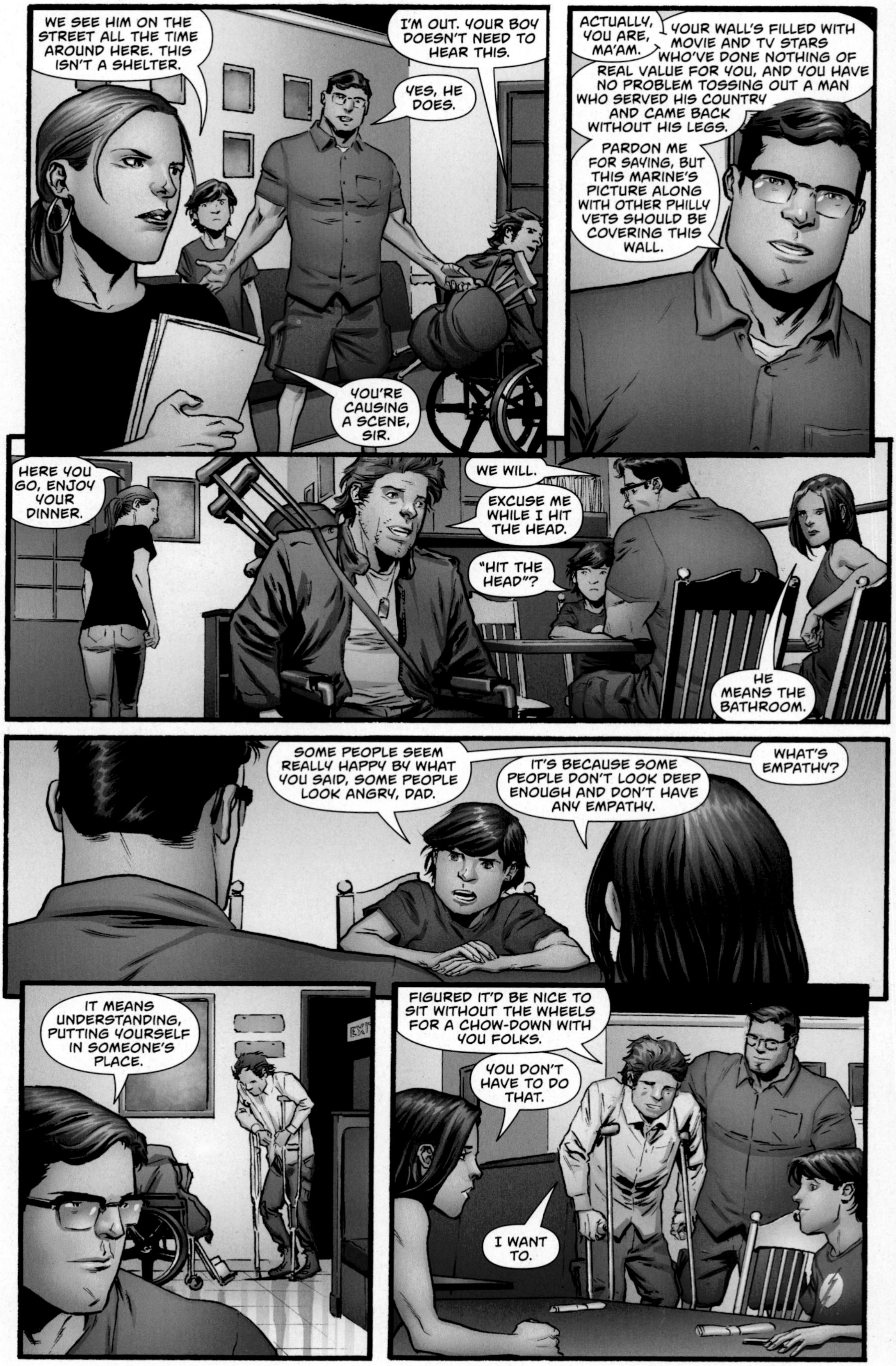
WE SEE HIM ON THE STREET ALL THE TIME AROUND HERE. THIS ISN'T A SHELTER.
I'M OUT. YOUR BOY DOESN'T NEED TO HEAR THIS.
YES, HE DOES.
YOU'RE CAUSING A SCENE, SIR.
ACTUALLY, YOU ARE, MA'AM.
YOUR WALL'S FILLED WITH MOVIE AND TV STARS WHO'VE DONE NOTHING OF REAL VALUE FOR YOU, AND YOU HAVE NO PROBLEM TOSSING OUT A MAN WHO SERVED HIS COUNTRY AND CAME BACK WITHOUT HIS LEGS.
PARDON ME FOR SAYING, BUT THIS MARINE'S PICTURE ALONG WITH OTHER PHILLY VETS SHOULD BE COVERING THIS WALL.
HERE YOU GO, ENJOY YOUR DINNER.
WE WILL.
EXCUSE ME WHILE I HIT THE HEAD.
"HIT THE HEAD"?
HE MEANS THE BATHROOM.
SOME PEOPLE SEEM REALLY HAPPY BY WHAT YOU SAID, SOME PEOPLE LOOK ANGRY, DAD.
IT'S BECAUSE SOME PEOPLE DON'T LOOK DEEP ENOUGH AND DON'T HAVE ANY EMPATHY.
WHAT'S EMPATHY?
IT MEANS UNDERSTANDING, PUTTING YOURSELF IN SOMEONE'S PLACE.
EXIT
FIGURED IT'D BE NICE TO SIT WITHOUT THE WHEELS FOR A CHOW-DOWN WITH YOU FOLKS.
YOU DON'T HAVE TO DO THAT.
I WANT TO.

HEY, MR. DUFFY, WHERE'D YOU GET HURT?

JON, THAT'S NOT A POLITE QUESTION AT DINNER.

THAT'S OKAY, MRS. LANE.

IT WAS AT THE BATTLE OF AL-FAW. I WAS WITH THE 15TH MARINE EXPEDITIONARY UNIT IN ONE OF THE FIRST BATTLES OF THE 2003 IRAQ WAR.

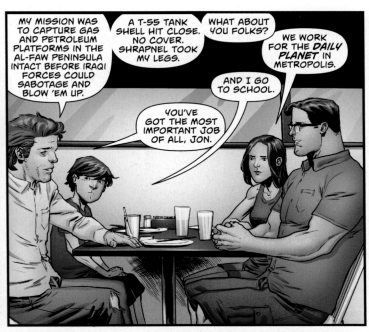

MY MISSION WAS TO CAPTURE GAS AND PETROLEUM PLATFORMS IN THE AL-FAW PENINSULA INTACT BEFORE IRAQI FORCES COULD SABOTAGE AND BLOW 'EM UP.

A T-55 TANK SHELL HIT CLOSE. NO COVER. SHRAPNEL TOOK MY LEGS.

WHAT ABOUT YOU FOLKS?

WE WORK FOR THE *DAILY PLANET* IN METROPOLIS.

AND I GO TO SCHOOL.

YOU'VE GOT THE MOST IMPORTANT JOB OF ALL, JON.

THAT WAS A GREAT DINNER.

GLAD YOU ENJOYED IT.

HEY, YOU! HOLD UP THERE!

HOW DO YA LIKE THAT? HE OFFERED ME A JOB.

DISHWASHER ON WEEKDAYS, STARTING TOMORROW.

THANKS, KENT FAMILY.

NO, THANK YOU, RYAN.

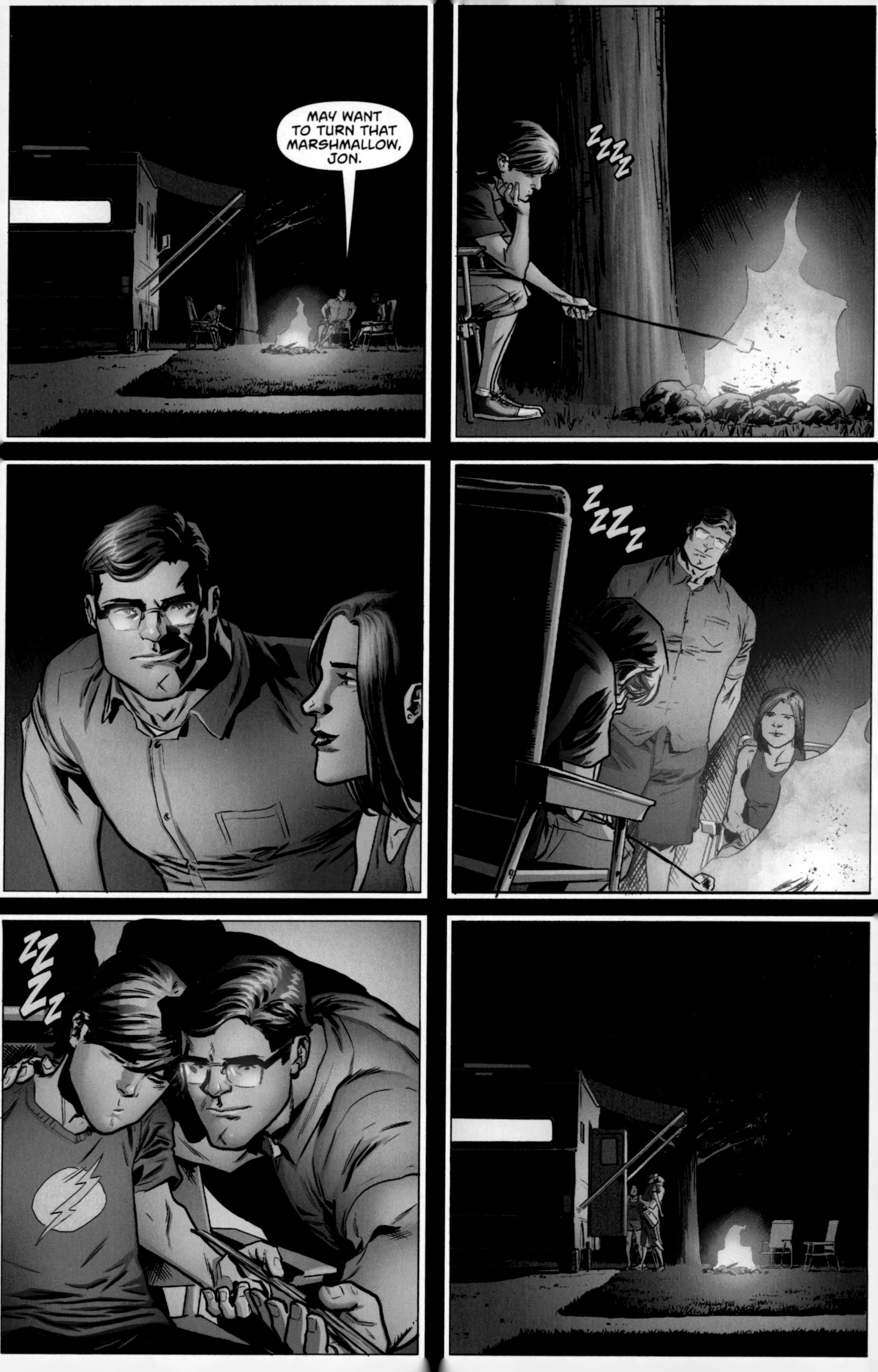
MAY WANT TO TURN THAT MARSHMALLOW, JON.
ZZZZ
ZZZZ
ZZZZ

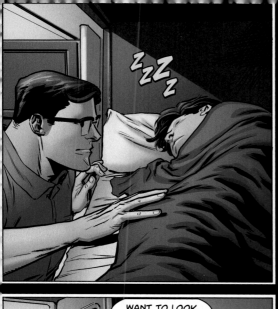

ZZZZ

WANT TO LOOK AT THE STARS AND MAKE OUT?

ABSOLUTELY.

KLINK

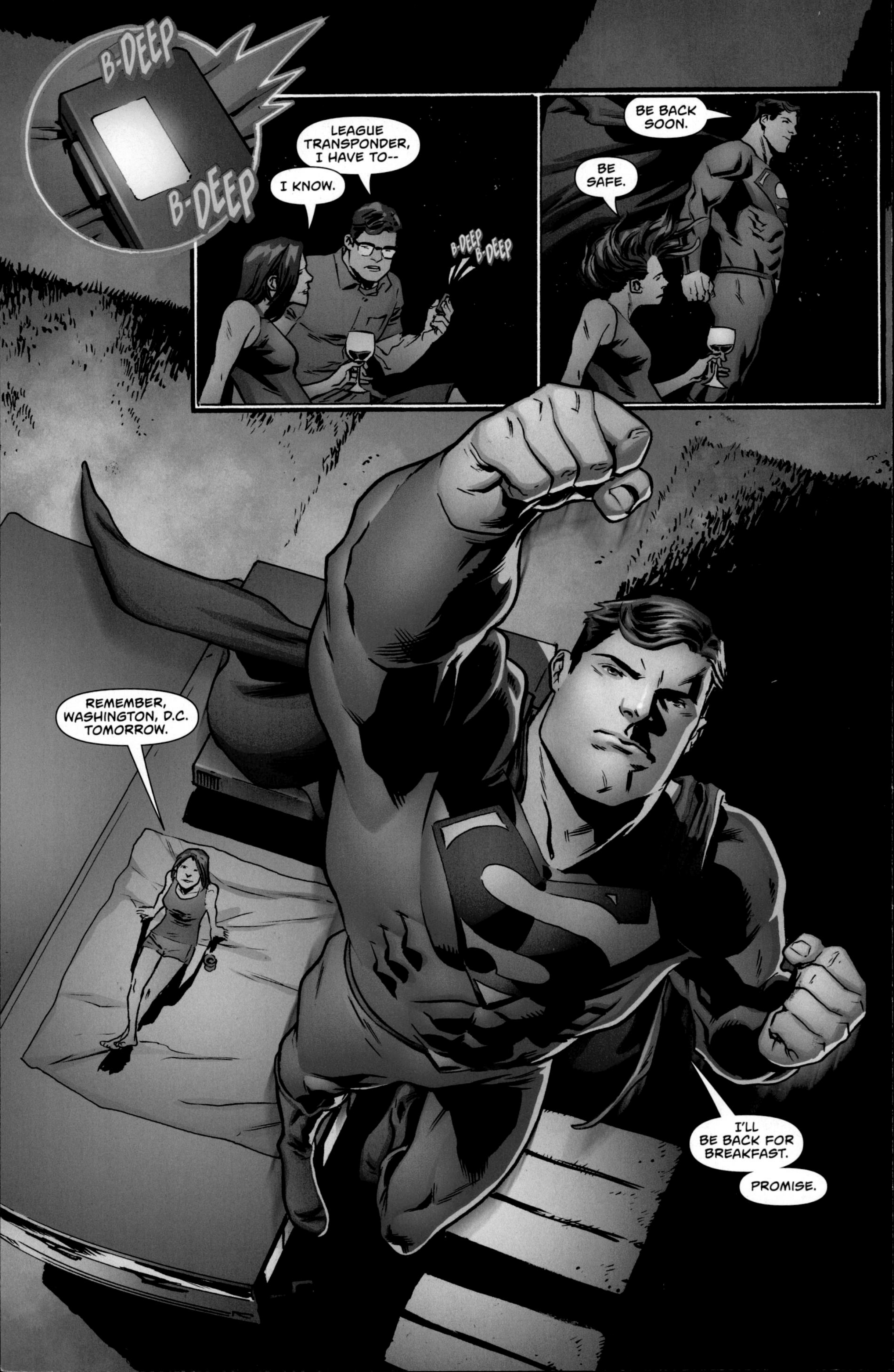
B-DEEP
B-DEEP
LEAGUE TRANSPONDER, I HAVE TO--
I KNOW.
B-DEEP B-DEEP
BE BACK SOON.
BE SAFE.
REMEMBER, WASHINGTON, D.C. TOMORROW.
I'LL BE BACK FOR BREAKFAST.
PROMISE.

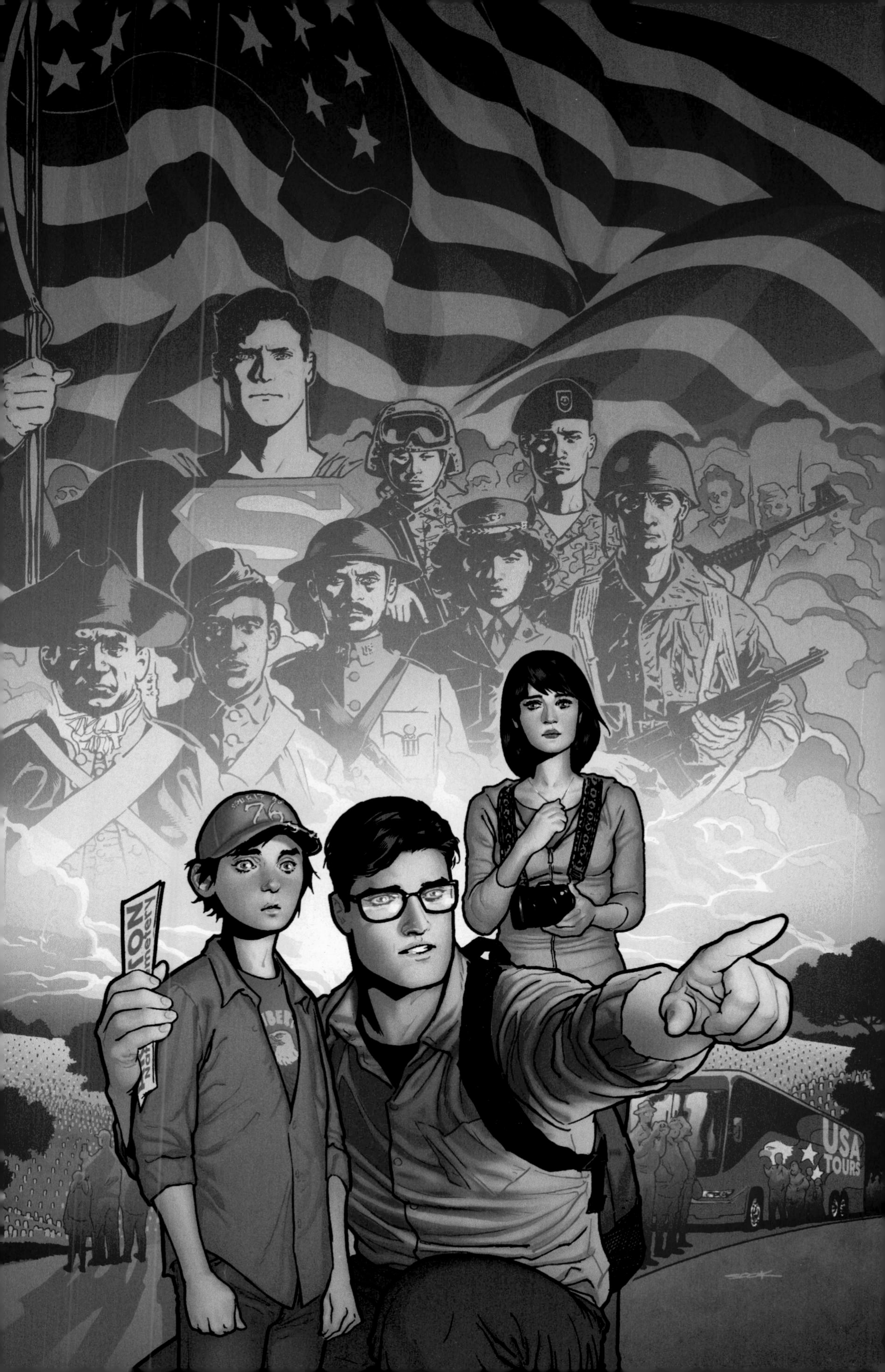
76
USA
TOURS

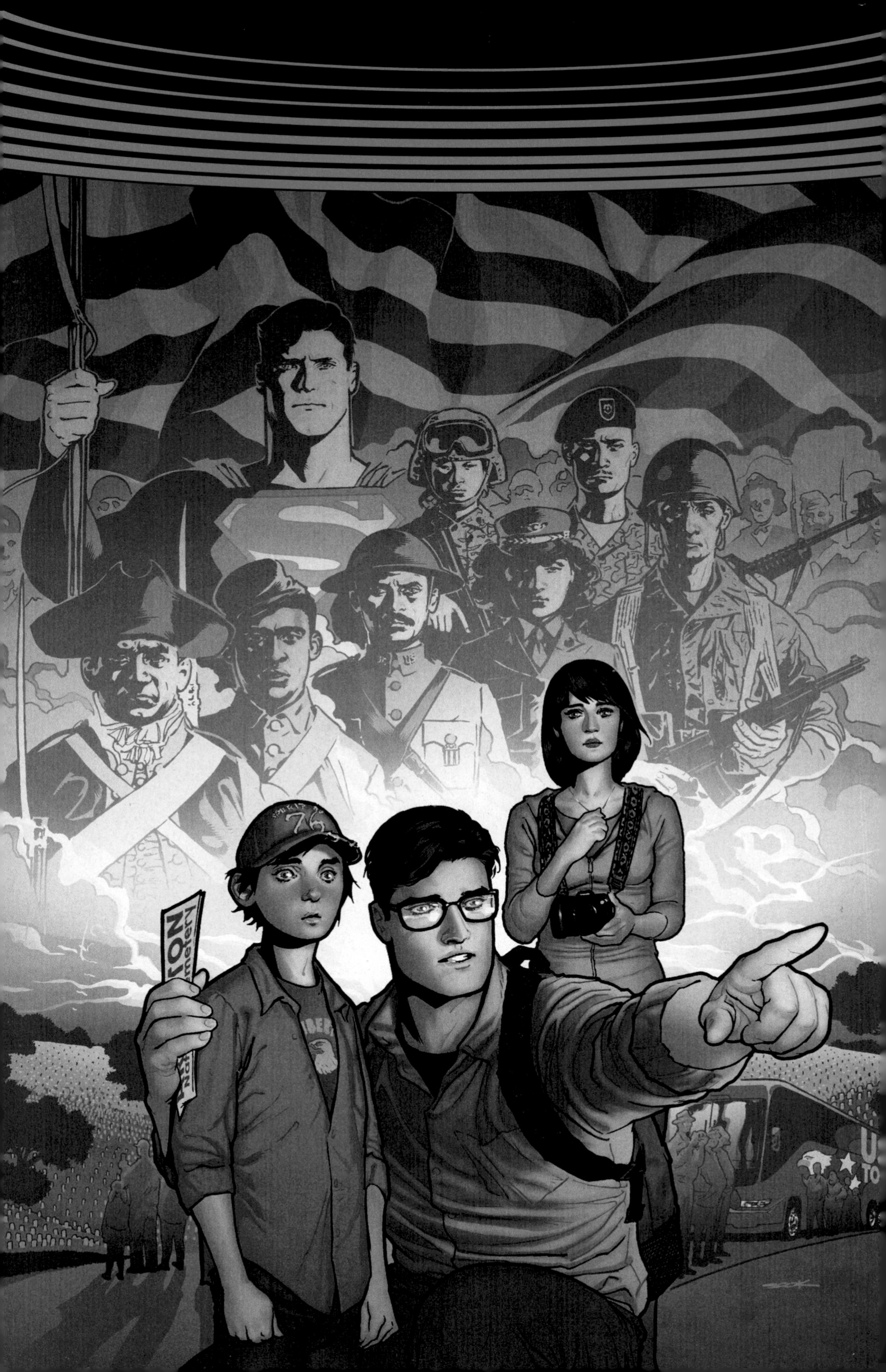

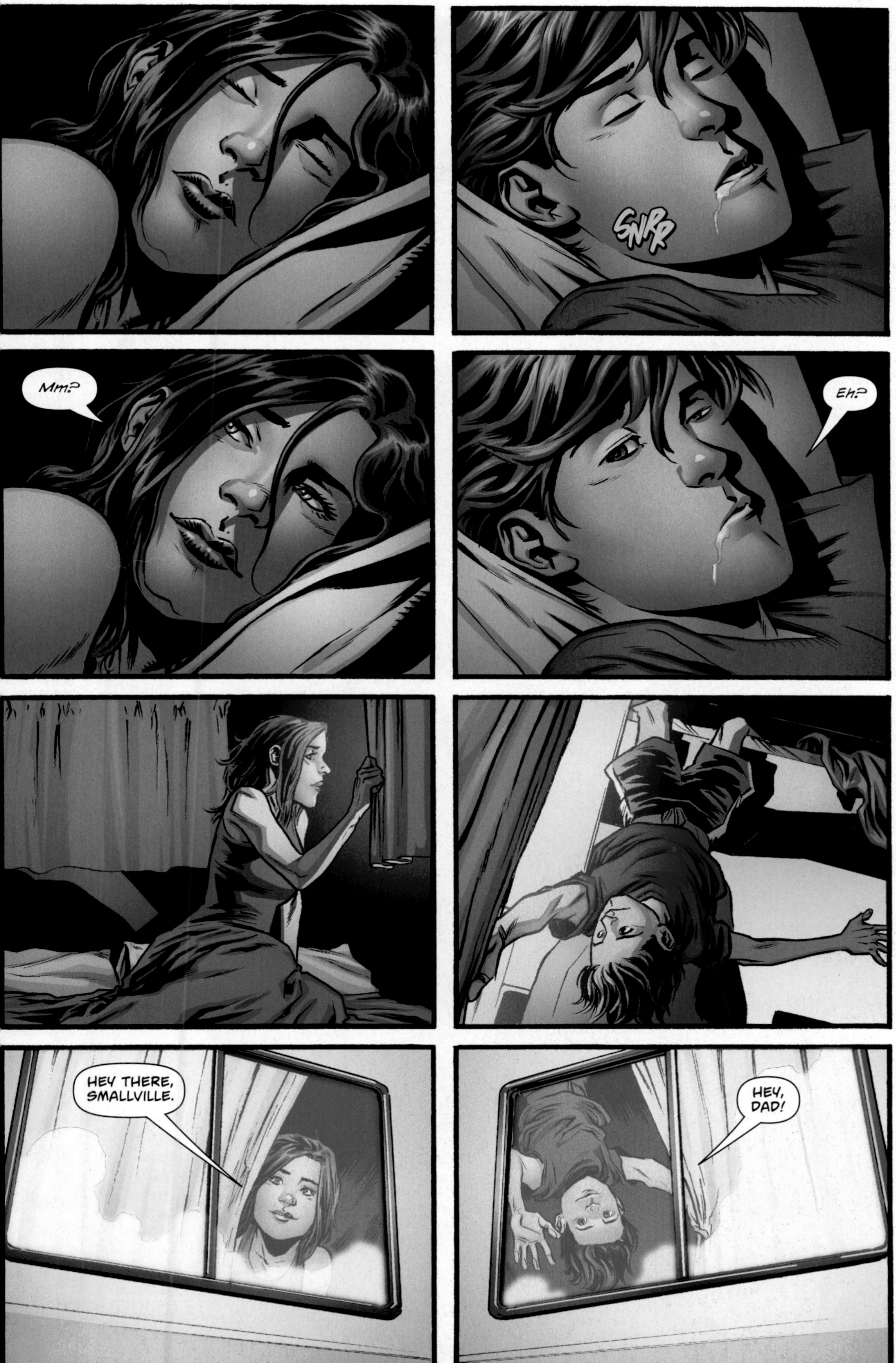
SNRR
Mm?
Eh?
HEY THERE, SMALLVILLE.
HEY, DAD!

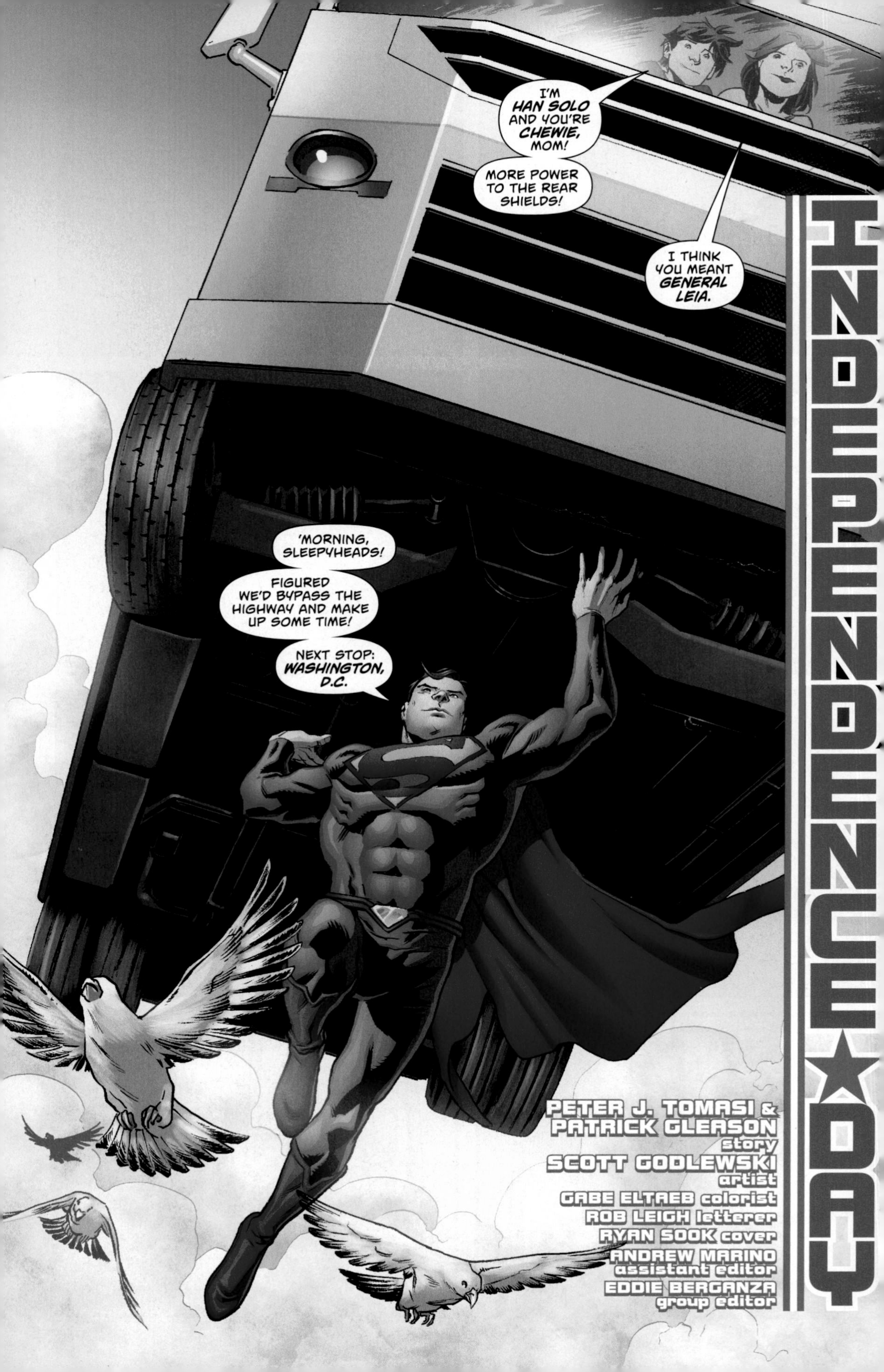

I'M HAN SOLO AND YOU'RE CHEWIE, MOM!
MORE POWER TO THE REAR SHIELDS!
I THINK YOU MEANT GENERAL LEIA.
'MORNING, SLEEPYHEADS!
FIGURED WE'D BYPASS THE HIGHWAY AND MAKE UP SOME TIME!
NEXT STOP: WASHINGTON, D.C.
INDEPENDENCE DAY
PETER J. TOMASI & PATRICK GLEASON story
SCOTT GODLEWSKI artist
GABE ELTAEB colorist
ROB LEIGH letterer
RYAN SOOK cover
ANDREW MARINO assistant editor
EDDIE BERGANZA group editor

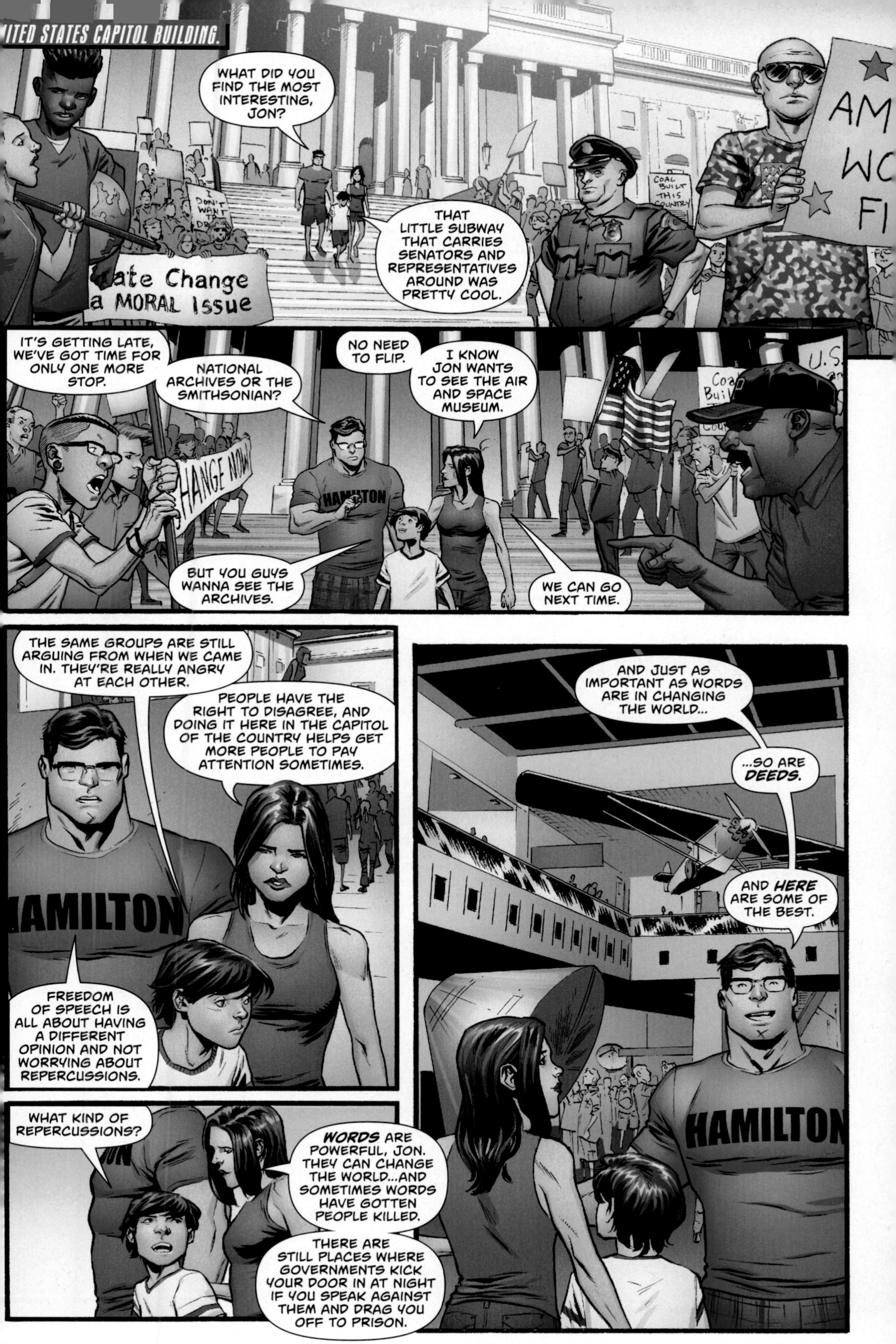
ITED STATES CAPITOL BUILDING.
WHAT DID YOU FIND THE MOST INTERESTING, JON?
THAT LITTLE SUBWAY THAT CARRIES SENATORS AND REPRESENTATIVES AROUND WAS PRETTY COOL.
I DON'T WANT TO DR...
...ate Change a MORAL Issue
COAL BUILT THIS COUNTRY
IT'S GETTING LATE, WE'VE GOT TIME FOR ONLY ONE MORE STOP.
NATIONAL ARCHIVES OR THE SMITHSONIAN?
NO NEED TO FLIP.
I KNOW JON WANTS TO SEE THE AIR AND SPACE MUSEUM.
HANGE NOW!
HAMILTON
BUT YOU GUYS WANNA SEE THE ARCHIVES.
WE CAN GO NEXT TIME.
THE SAME GROUPS ARE STILL ARGUING FROM WHEN WE CAME IN. THEY'RE REALLY ANGRY AT EACH OTHER.
PEOPLE HAVE THE RIGHT TO DISAGREE, AND DOING IT HERE IN THE CAPITOL OF THE COUNTRY HELPS GET MORE PEOPLE TO PAY ATTENTION SOMETIMES.
HAMILTON
FREEDOM OF SPEECH IS ALL ABOUT HAVING A DIFFERENT OPINION AND NOT WORRYING ABOUT REPERCUSSIONS.
WHAT KIND OF REPERCUSSIONS?
WORDS ARE POWERFUL, JON. THEY CAN CHANGE THE WORLD...AND SOMETIMES WORDS HAVE GOTTEN PEOPLE KILLED.
THERE ARE STILL PLACES WHERE GOVERNMENTS KICK YOUR DOOR IN AT NIGHT IF YOU SPEAK AGAINST THEM AND DRAG YOU OFF TO PRISON.
AND JUST AS IMPORTANT AS WORDS ARE IN CHANGING THE WORLD...
...SO ARE DEEDS.
AND HERE ARE SOME OF THE BEST.
HAMILTON

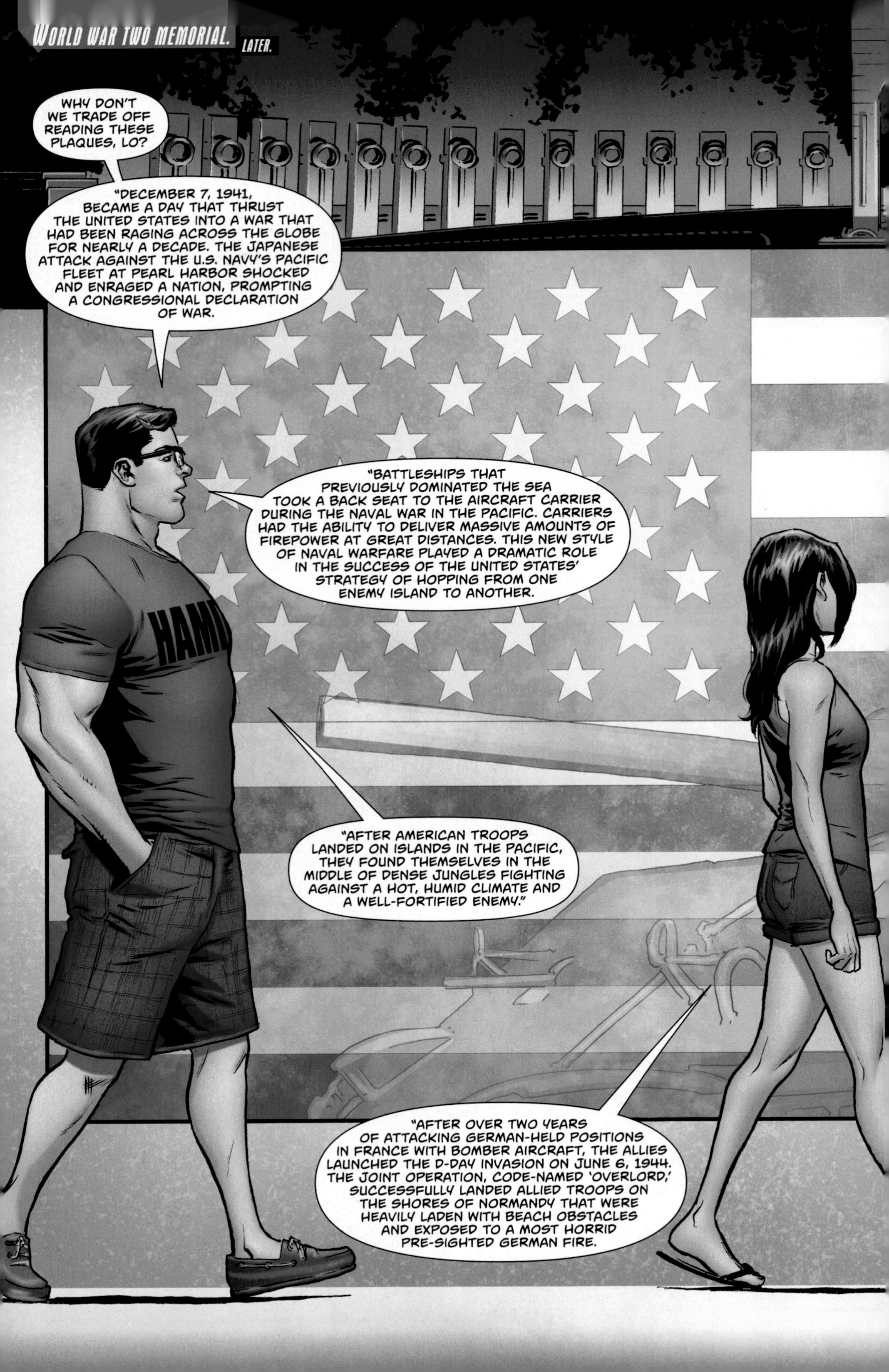
WORLD WAR TWO MEMORIAL. LATER.
WHY DON'T WE TRADE OFF READING THESE PLAQUES, LO?
"DECEMBER 7, 1941, BECAME A DAY THAT THRUST THE UNITED STATES INTO A WAR THAT HAD BEEN RAGING ACROSS THE GLOBE FOR NEARLY A DECADE. THE JAPANESE ATTACK AGAINST THE U.S. NAVY'S PACIFIC FLEET AT PEARL HARBOR SHOCKED AND ENRAGED A NATION, PROMPTING A CONGRESSIONAL DECLARATION OF WAR.
"BATTLESHIPS THAT PREVIOUSLY DOMINATED THE SEA TOOK A BACK SEAT TO THE AIRCRAFT CARRIER DURING THE NAVAL WAR IN THE PACIFIC. CARRIERS HAD THE ABILITY TO DELIVER MASSIVE AMOUNTS OF FIREPOWER AT GREAT DISTANCES. THIS NEW STYLE OF NAVAL WARFARE PLAYED A DRAMATIC ROLE IN THE SUCCESS OF THE UNITED STATES' STRATEGY OF HOPPING FROM ONE ENEMY ISLAND TO ANOTHER.
"AFTER AMERICAN TROOPS LANDED ON ISLANDS IN THE PACIFIC, THEY FOUND THEMSELVES IN THE MIDDLE OF DENSE JUNGLES FIGHTING AGAINST A HOT, HUMID CLIMATE AND A WELL-FORTIFIED ENEMY."
"AFTER OVER TWO YEARS OF ATTACKING GERMAN-HELD POSITIONS IN FRANCE WITH BOMBER AIRCRAFT, THE ALLIES LAUNCHED THE D-DAY INVASION ON JUNE 6, 1944. THE JOINT OPERATION, CODE-NAMED 'OVERLORD,' SUCCESSFULLY LANDED ALLIED TROOPS ON THE SHORES OF NORMANDY THAT WERE HEAVILY LADEN WITH BEACH OBSTACLES AND EXPOSED TO A MOST HORRID PRE-SIGHTED GERMAN FIRE.

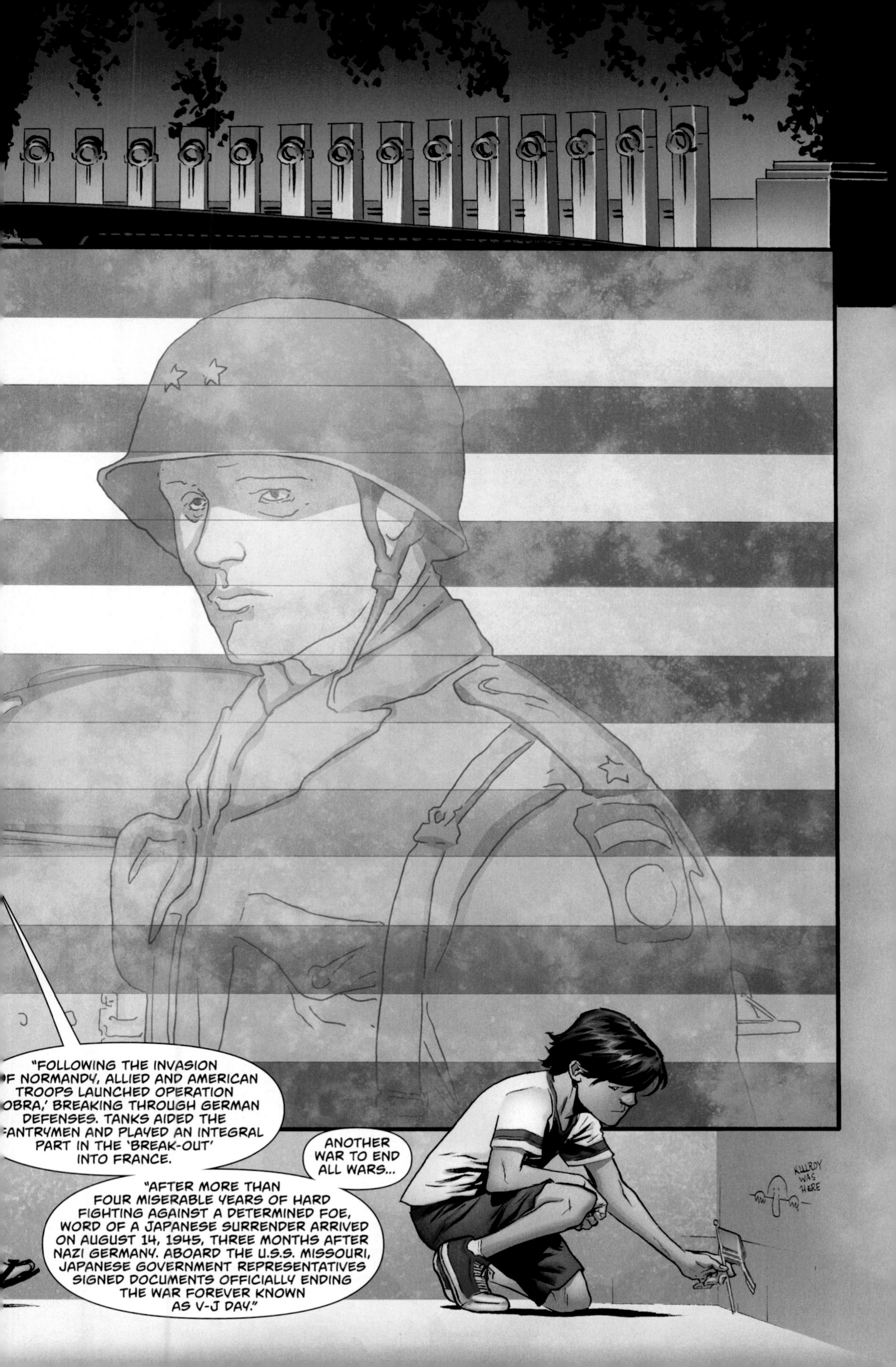

"FOLLOWING THE INVASION OF NORMANDY, ALLIED AND AMERICAN TROOPS LAUNCHED OPERATION 'COBRA,' BREAKING THROUGH GERMAN DEFENSES. TANKS AIDED THE INFANTRYMEN AND PLAYED AN INTEGRAL PART IN THE 'BREAK-OUT' INTO FRANCE.
ANOTHER WAR TO END ALL WARS...
"AFTER MORE THAN FOUR MISERABLE YEARS OF HARD FIGHTING AGAINST A DETERMINED FOE, WORD OF A JAPANESE SURRENDER ARRIVED ON AUGUST 14, 1945, THREE MONTHS AFTER NAZI GERMANY. ABOARD THE U.S.S. MISSOURI, JAPANESE GOVERNMENT REPRESENTATIVES SIGNED DOCUMENTS OFFICIALLY ENDING THE WAR FOREVER KNOWN AS V-J DAY."
KILROY WAS HERE

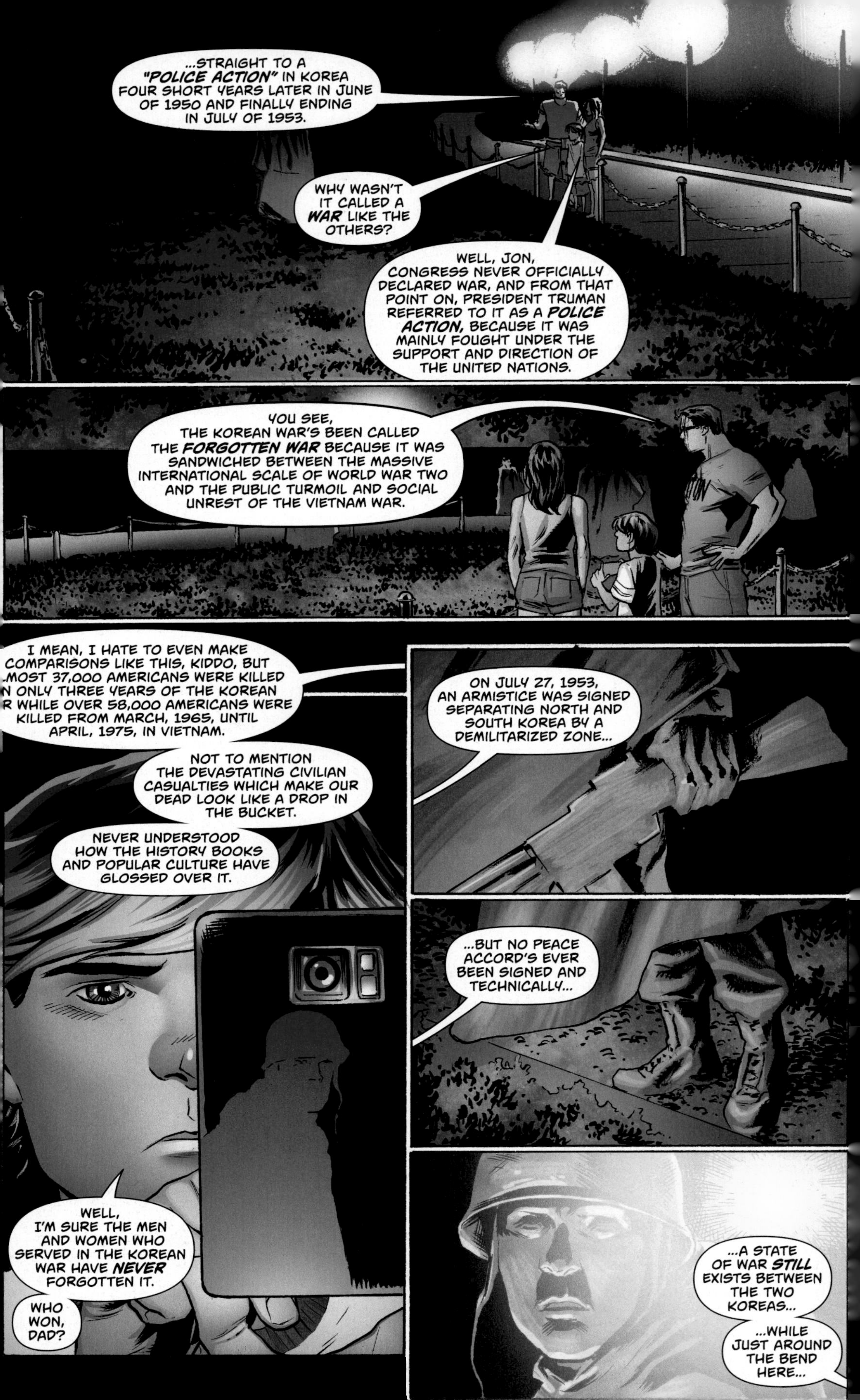
...STRAIGHT TO A "POLICE ACTION" IN KOREA FOUR SHORT YEARS LATER IN JUNE OF 1950 AND FINALLY ENDING IN JULY OF 1953.
WHY WASN'T IT CALLED A WAR LIKE THE OTHERS?
WELL, JON, CONGRESS NEVER OFFICIALLY DECLARED WAR, AND FROM THAT POINT ON, PRESIDENT TRUMAN REFERRED TO IT AS A POLICE ACTION, BECAUSE IT WAS MAINLY FOUGHT UNDER THE SUPPORT AND DIRECTION OF THE UNITED NATIONS.
YOU SEE, THE KOREAN WAR'S BEEN CALLED THE FORGOTTEN WAR BECAUSE IT WAS SANDWICHED BETWEEN THE MASSIVE INTERNATIONAL SCALE OF WORLD WAR TWO AND THE PUBLIC TURMOIL AND SOCIAL UNREST OF THE VIETNAM WAR.
I MEAN, I HATE TO EVEN MAKE COMPARISONS LIKE THIS, KIDDO, BUT LMOST 37,000 AMERICANS WERE KILLED N ONLY THREE YEARS OF THE KOREAN R WHILE OVER 58,000 AMERICANS WERE KILLED FROM MARCH, 1965, UNTIL APRIL, 1975, IN VIETNAM.
NOT TO MENTION THE DEVASTATING CIVILIAN CASUALTIES WHICH MAKE OUR DEAD LOOK LIKE A DROP IN THE BUCKET.
NEVER UNDERSTOOD HOW THE HISTORY BOOKS AND POPULAR CULTURE HAVE GLOSSED OVER IT.
WELL, I'M SURE THE MEN AND WOMEN WHO SERVED IN THE KOREAN WAR HAVE NEVER FORGOTTEN IT.
WHO WON, DAD?
ON JULY 27, 1953, AN ARMISTICE WAS SIGNED SEPARATING NORTH AND SOUTH KOREA BY A DEMILITARIZED ZONE...
...BUT NO PEACE ACCORD'S EVER BEEN SIGNED AND TECHNICALLY...
...A STATE OF WAR STILL EXISTS BETWEEN THE TWO KOREAS...
...WHILE JUST AROUND THE BEND HERE...

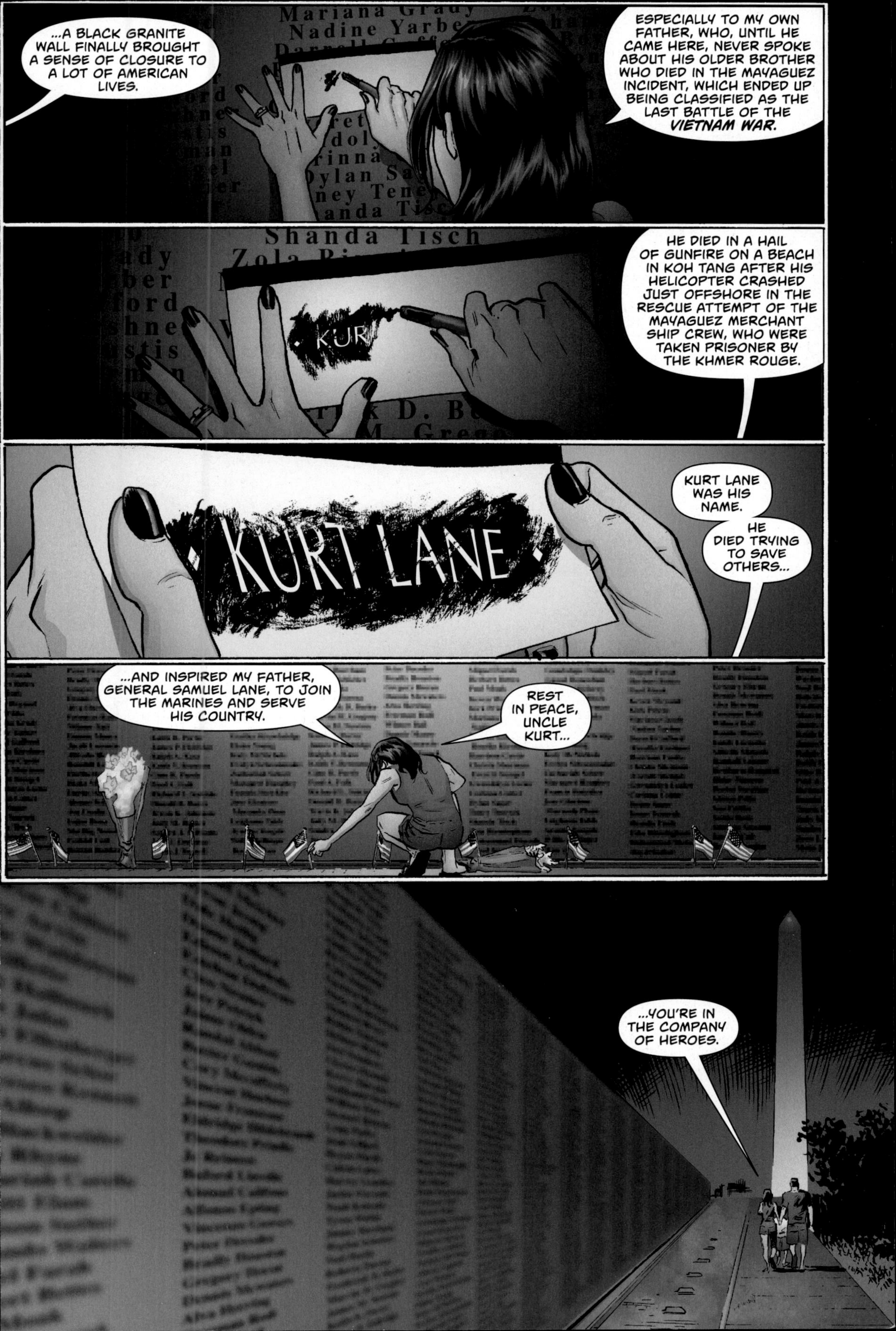
...A BLACK GRANITE WALL FINALLY BROUGHT A SENSE OF CLOSURE TO A LOT OF AMERICAN LIVES.
ESPECIALLY TO MY OWN FATHER, WHO, UNTIL HE CAME HERE, NEVER SPOKE ABOUT HIS OLDER BROTHER WHO DIED IN THE MAYAGUEZ INCIDENT, WHICH ENDED UP BEING CLASSIFIED AS THE LAST BATTLE OF THE VIETNAM WAR.
HE DIED IN A HAIL OF GUNFIRE ON A BEACH IN KOH TANG AFTER HIS HELICOPTER CRASHED JUST OFFSHORE IN THE RESCUE ATTEMPT OF THE MAYAGUEZ MERCHANT SHIP CREW, WHO WERE TAKEN PRISONER BY THE KHMER ROUGE.
KURT LANE
KURT LANE WAS HIS NAME.
HE DIED TRYING TO SAVE OTHERS...
...AND INSPIRED MY FATHER, GENERAL SAMUEL LANE, TO JOIN THE MARINES AND SERVE HIS COUNTRY.
REST IN PEACE, UNCLE KURT...
...YOU'RE IN THE COMPANY OF HEROES.

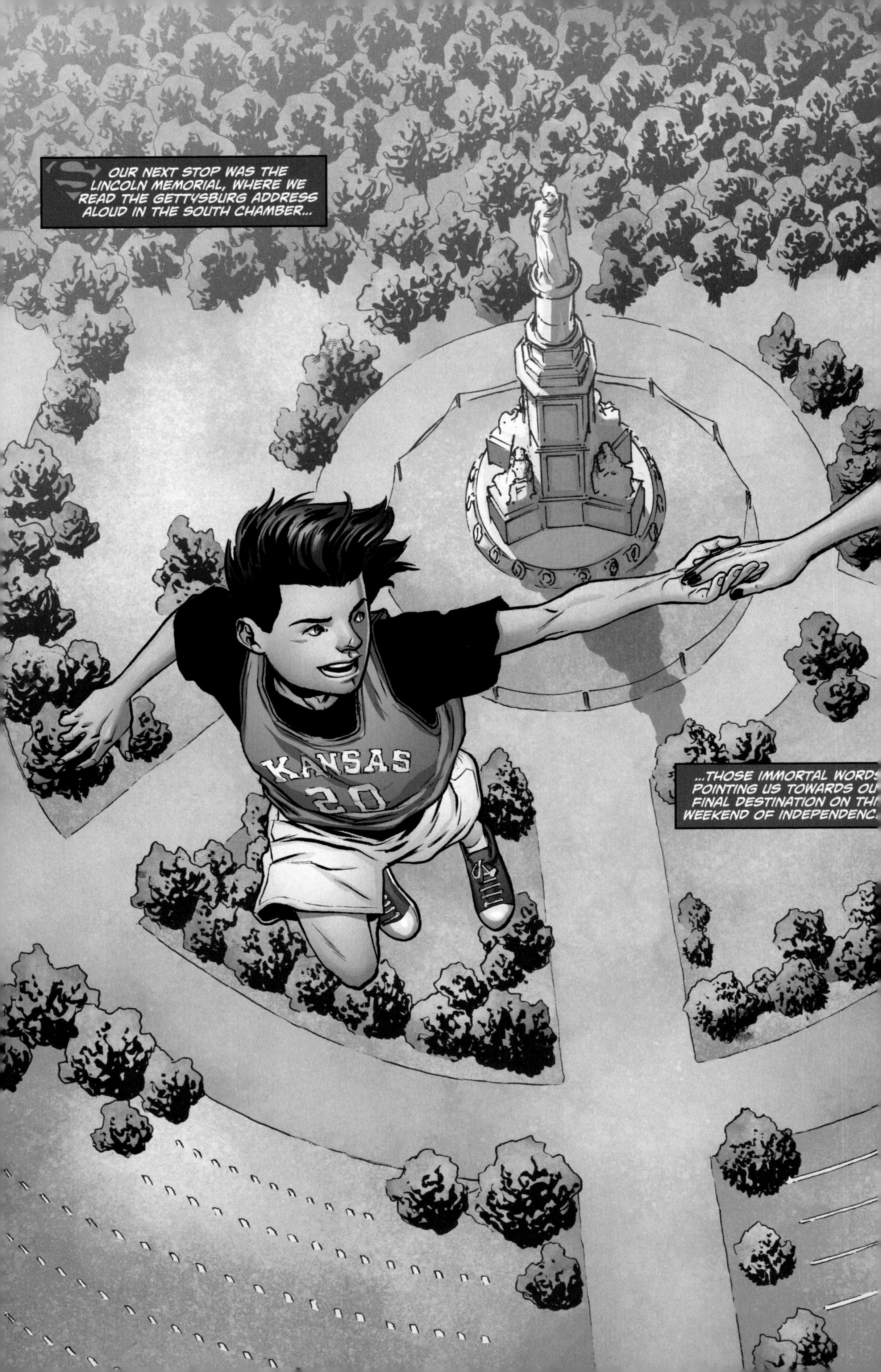
OUR NEXT STOP WAS THE LINCOLN MEMORIAL, WHERE WE READ THE GETTYSBURG ADDRESS ALOUD IN THE SOUTH CHAMBER...
...THOSE IMMORTAL WORDS POINTING US TOWARDS OU FINAL DESTINATION ON TH WEEKEND OF INDEPENDENC
KANSAS
20

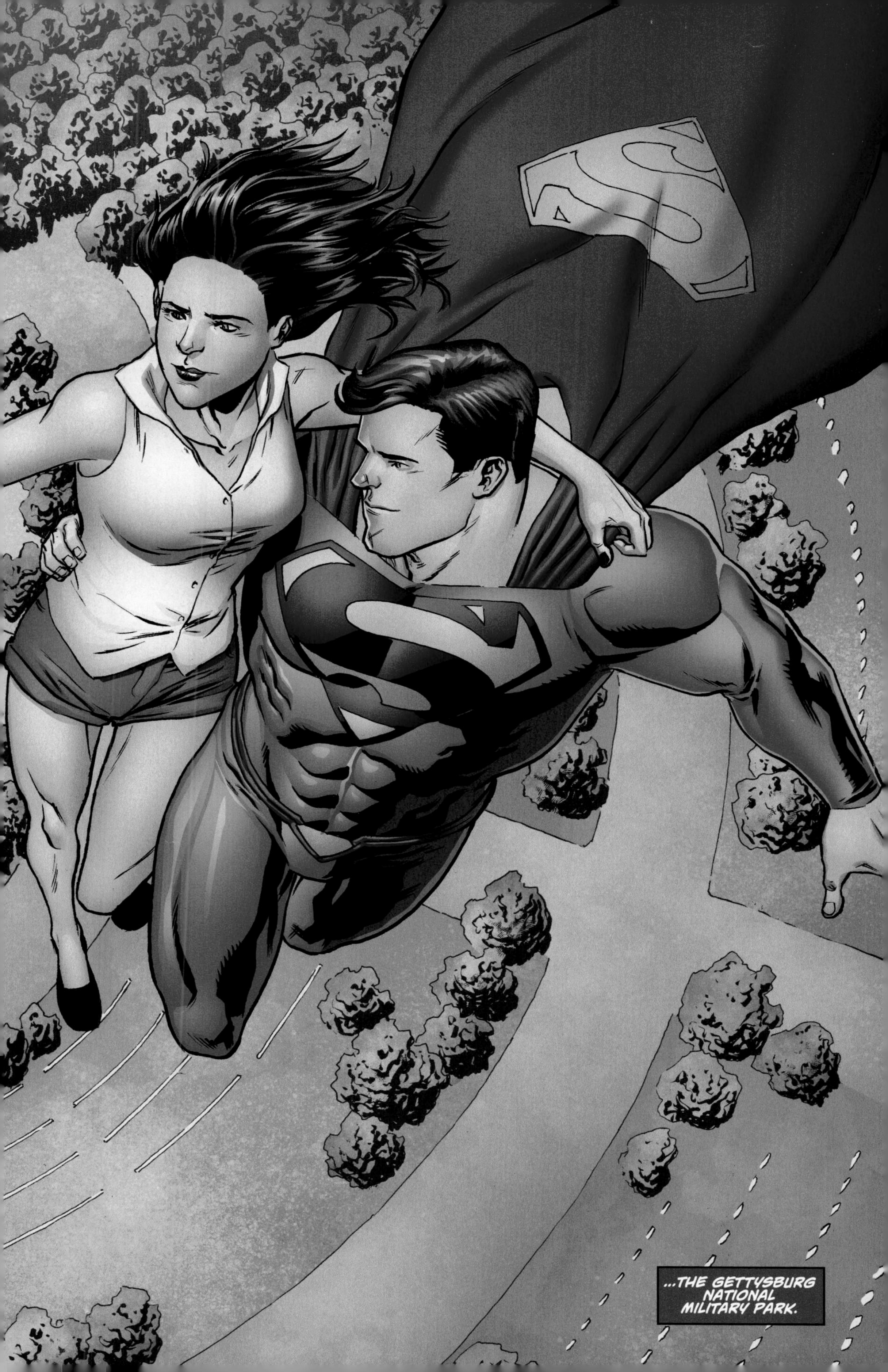
...THE GETTYSBURG NATIONAL MILITARY PARK.

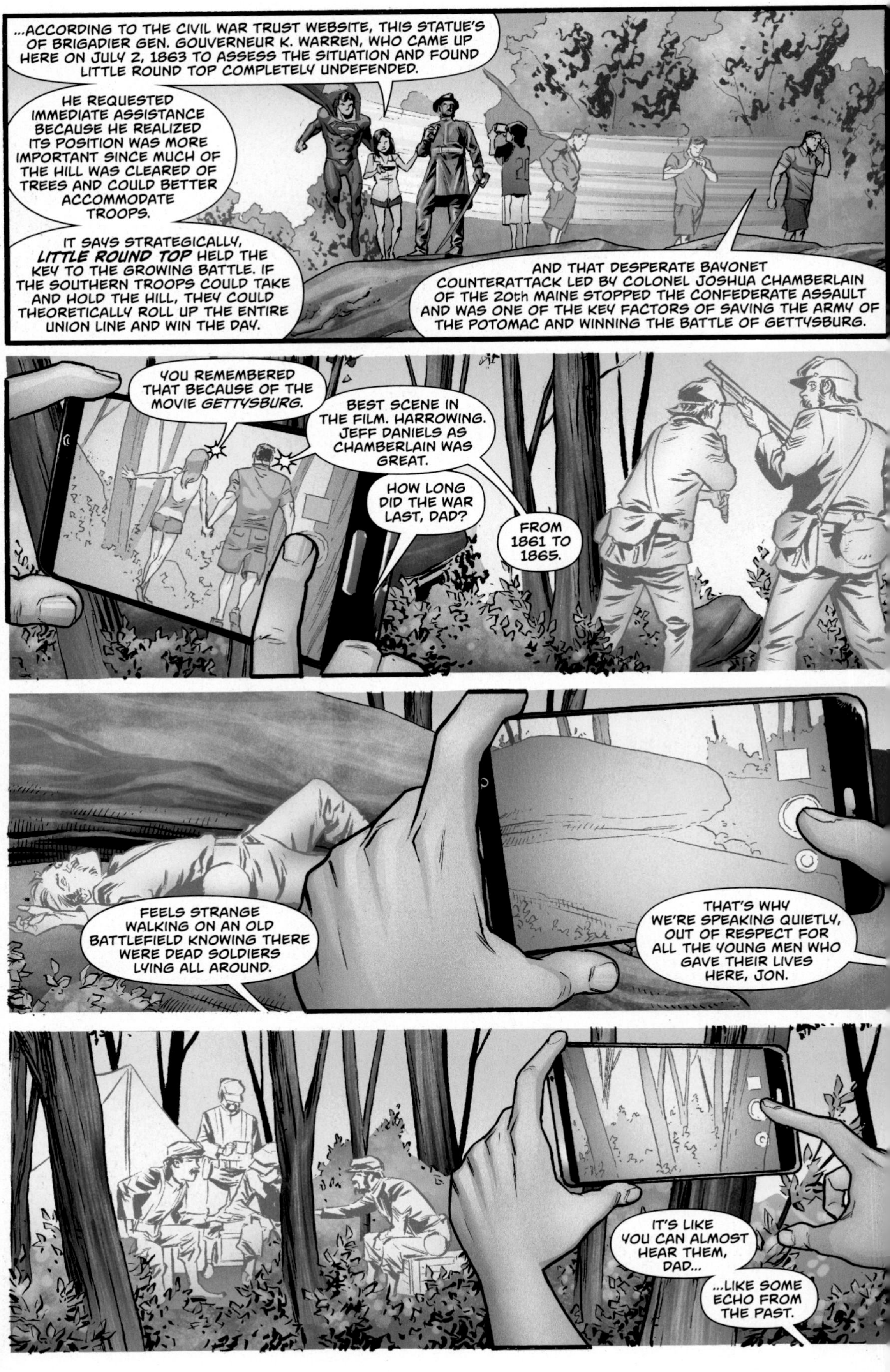
...ACCORDING TO THE CIVIL WAR TRUST WEBSITE, THIS STATUE'S OF BRIGADIER GEN. GOUVERNEUR K. WARREN, WHO CAME UP HERE ON JULY 2, 1863 TO ASSESS THE SITUATION AND FOUND LITTLE ROUND TOP COMPLETELY UNDEFENDED.
HE REQUESTED IMMEDIATE ASSISTANCE BECAUSE HE REALIZED ITS POSITION WAS MORE IMPORTANT SINCE MUCH OF THE HILL WAS CLEARED OF TREES AND COULD BETTER ACCOMMODATE TROOPS.
IT SAYS STRATEGICALLY, LITTLE ROUND TOP HELD THE KEY TO THE GROWING BATTLE. IF THE SOUTHERN TROOPS COULD TAKE AND HOLD THE HILL, THEY COULD THEORETICALLY ROLL UP THE ENTIRE UNION LINE AND WIN THE DAY.
AND THAT DESPERATE BAYONET COUNTERATTACK LED BY COLONEL JOSHUA CHAMBERLAIN OF THE 20th MAINE STOPPED THE CONFEDERATE ASSAULT AND WAS ONE OF THE KEY FACTORS OF SAVING THE ARMY OF THE POTOMAC AND WINNING THE BATTLE OF GETTYSBURG.
YOU REMEMBERED THAT BECAUSE OF THE MOVIE GETTYSBURG.
BEST SCENE IN THE FILM. HARROWING. JEFF DANIELS AS CHAMBERLAIN WAS GREAT.
HOW LONG DID THE WAR LAST, DAD?
FROM 1861 TO 1865.
FEELS STRANGE WALKING ON AN OLD BATTLEFIELD KNOWING THERE WERE DEAD SOLDIERS LYING ALL AROUND.
THAT'S WHY WE'RE SPEAKING QUIETLY, OUT OF RESPECT FOR ALL THE YOUNG MEN WHO GAVE THEIR LIVES HERE, JON.
IT'S LIKE YOU CAN ALMOST HEAR THEM, DAD...
...LIKE SOME ECHO FROM THE PAST.

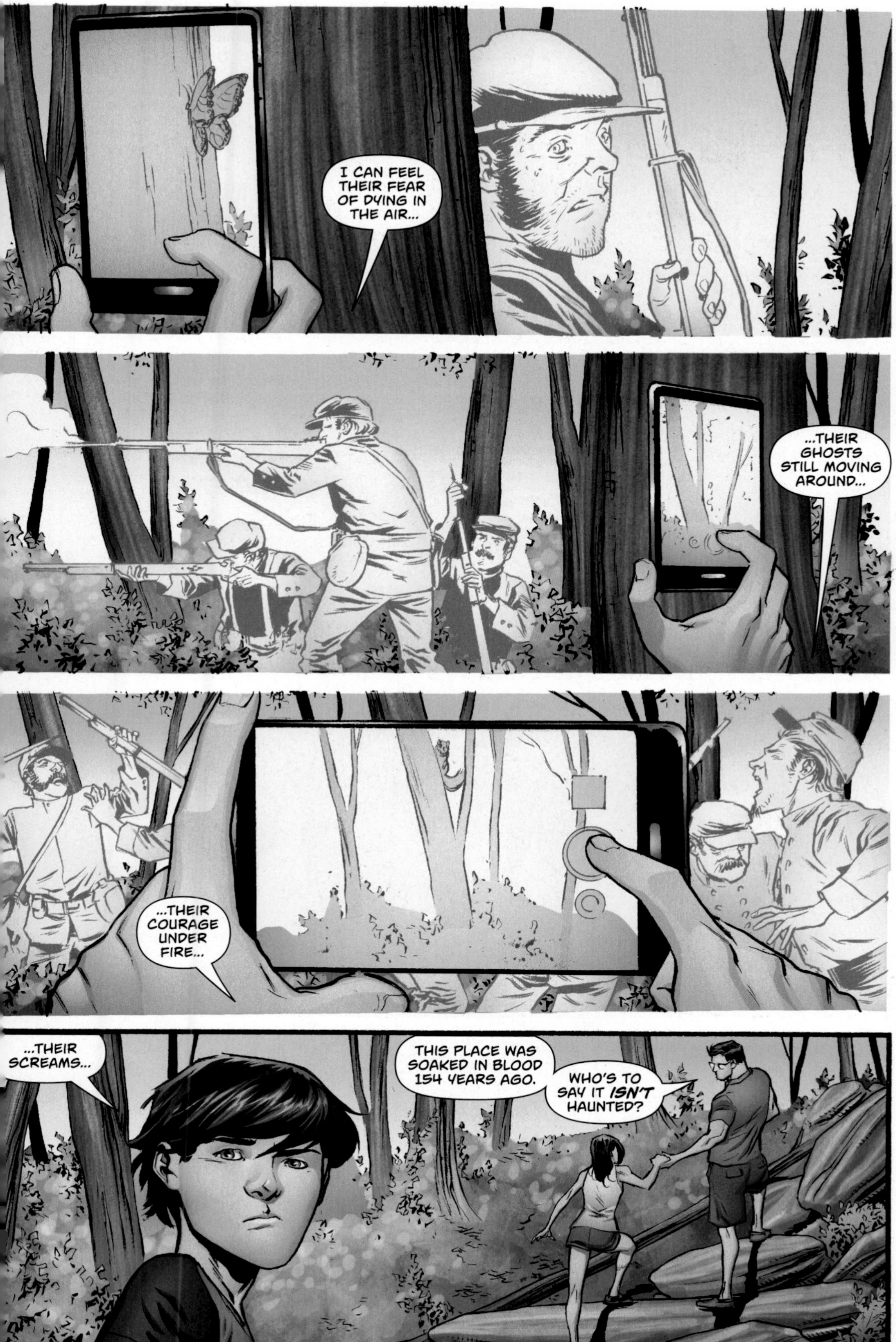
I CAN FEEL THEIR FEAR OF DYING IN THE AIR...
...THEIR GHOSTS STILL MOVING AROUND...
...THEIR COURAGE UNDER FIRE...
...THEIR SCREAMS...
THIS PLACE WAS SOAKED IN BLOOD 154 YEARS AGO.
WHO'S TO SAY IT *ISN'T* HAUNTED?

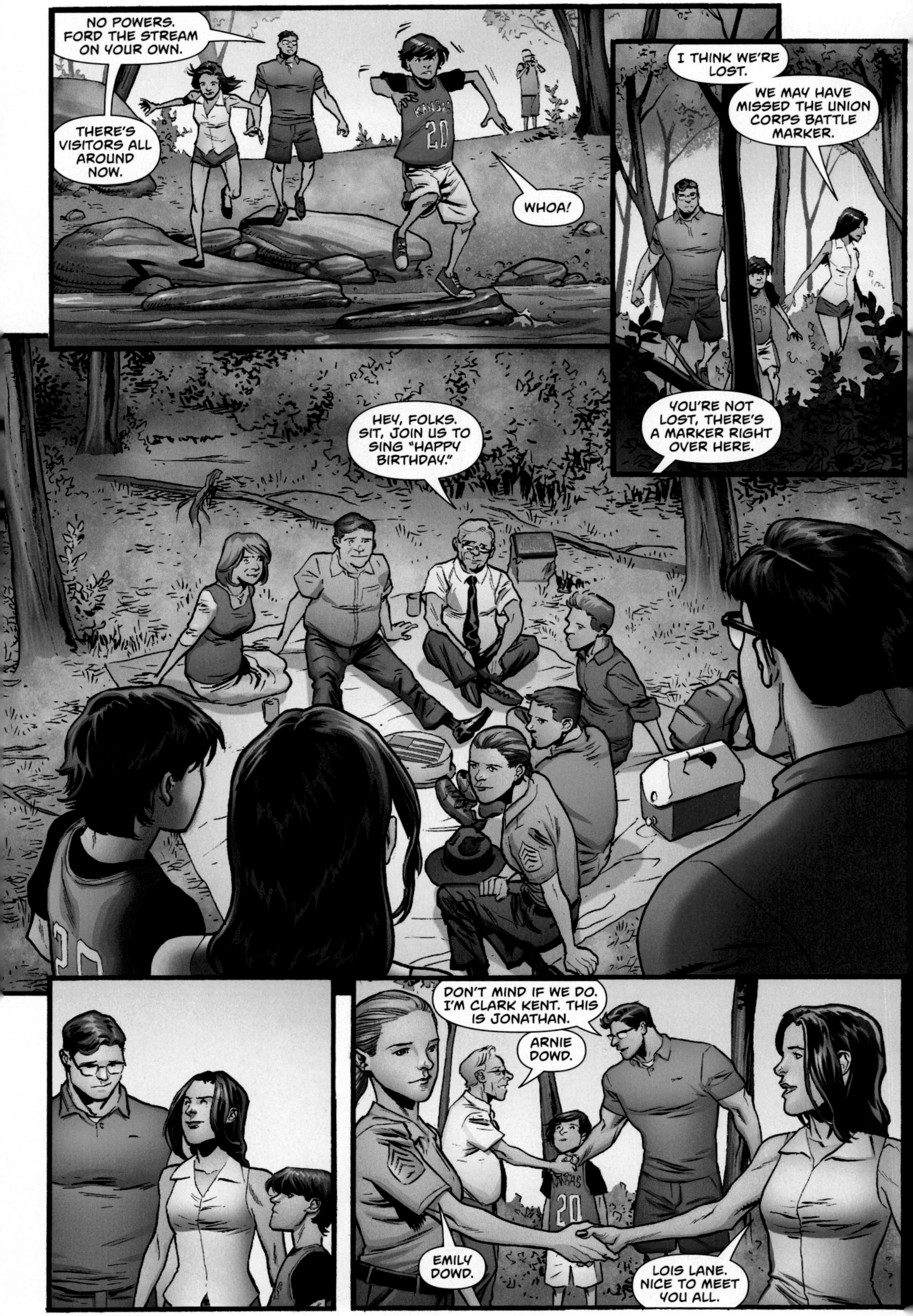
NO POWERS. FORD THE STREAM ON YOUR OWN.
THERE'S VISITORS ALL AROUND NOW.
WHOA!
I THINK WE'RE LOST.
WE MAY HAVE MISSED THE UNION CORPS BATTLE MARKER.
YOU'RE NOT LOST, THERE'S A MARKER RIGHT OVER HERE.
HEY, FOLKS. SIT, JOIN US TO SING "HAPPY BIRTHDAY."
DON'T MIND IF WE DO. I'M CLARK KENT. THIS IS JONATHAN.
ARNIE DOWD.
EMILY DOWD.
LOIS LANE. NICE TO MEET YOU ALL.

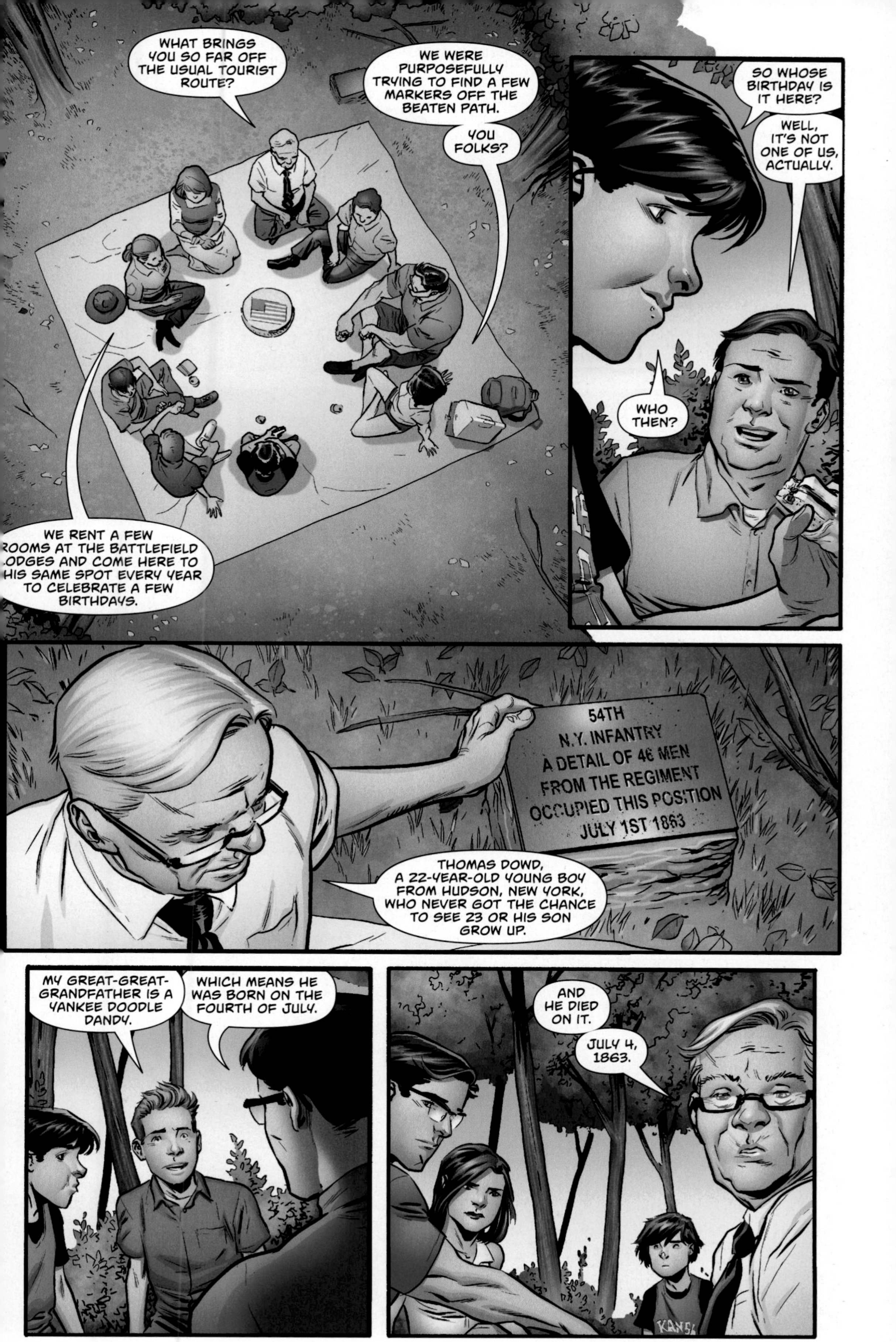
WHAT BRINGS YOU SO FAR OFF THE USUAL TOURIST ROUTE?
WE WERE PURPOSEFULLY TRYING TO FIND A FEW MARKERS OFF THE BEATEN PATH.
YOU FOLKS?
WE RENT A FEW ROOMS AT THE BATTLEFIELD LODGES AND COME HERE TO THIS SAME SPOT EVERY YEAR TO CELEBRATE A FEW BIRTHDAYS.
SO WHOSE BIRTHDAY IS IT HERE?
WELL, IT'S NOT ONE OF US, ACTUALLY.
WHO THEN?
54TH
N.Y. INFANTRY
A DETAIL OF 46 MEN
FROM THE REGIMENT
OCCUPIED THIS POSITION
JULY 1ST 1863
THOMAS DOWD, A 22-YEAR-OLD YOUNG BOY FROM HUDSON, NEW YORK, WHO NEVER GOT THE CHANCE TO SEE 23 OR HIS SON GROW UP.
MY GREAT-GREAT-GRANDFATHER IS A YANKEE DOODLE DANDY.
WHICH MEANS HE WAS BORN ON THE FOURTH OF JULY.
AND HE DIED ON IT.
JULY 4, 1863.

"TWO DAYS AFTER CONFEDERATE SHELLS RAINED DOWN ON FORT SUMTER IN CHARLESTON, SOUTH CAROLINA...

"...THOMAS AND A WHOLE GROUP OF HIS BRIGHT-EYED AND BUSHY-TAILED YOUNG TOWNSFOLK ENLISTED ON APRIL 14th, 1861, ALMOST 872 MILES AWAY.

"IT MIGHT AS WELL HAVE BEEN THE MOON, SINCE NO DOWD TILL THAT TIME HAD GONE MORE THAN FIVE MILES FROM HUDSON, NEW YORK...

"...SO ON THAT EASTER WEEKEND, THOMAS DIDN'T REALIZE HE WAS HUGGING HIS WIFE AND INFANT SON FOR THE LAST TIME.

"SOON ENOUGH HE WAS STANDING PICKET DUTY WHILE THE U.S. CAPITOL WAS BEING BUILT, ONE OF MANY DEFENSIVE POSITIONS HE'D TAKE WHILE WASHINGTON WAS UNDER THREAT OF ATTACK BY ROBERT E. LEE AND HIS CONFEDERATES.

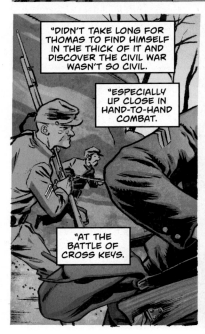

"DIDN'T TAKE LONG FOR THOMAS TO FIND HIMSELF IN THE THICK OF IT AND DISCOVER THE CIVIL WAR WASN'T SO CIVIL.

"ESPECIALLY UP CLOSE IN HAND-TO-HAND COMBAT.

"AT THE BATTLE OF CROSS KEYS.

"AND THE BATTLE OF BULL RUN.

"CHANCELLORSVILLE.

"AMERICANS AGAINST AMERICANS.

"NEIGHBOR VERSUS NEIGHBOR.

"SOMETIMES EVEN BROTHER VERSUS BROTHER."

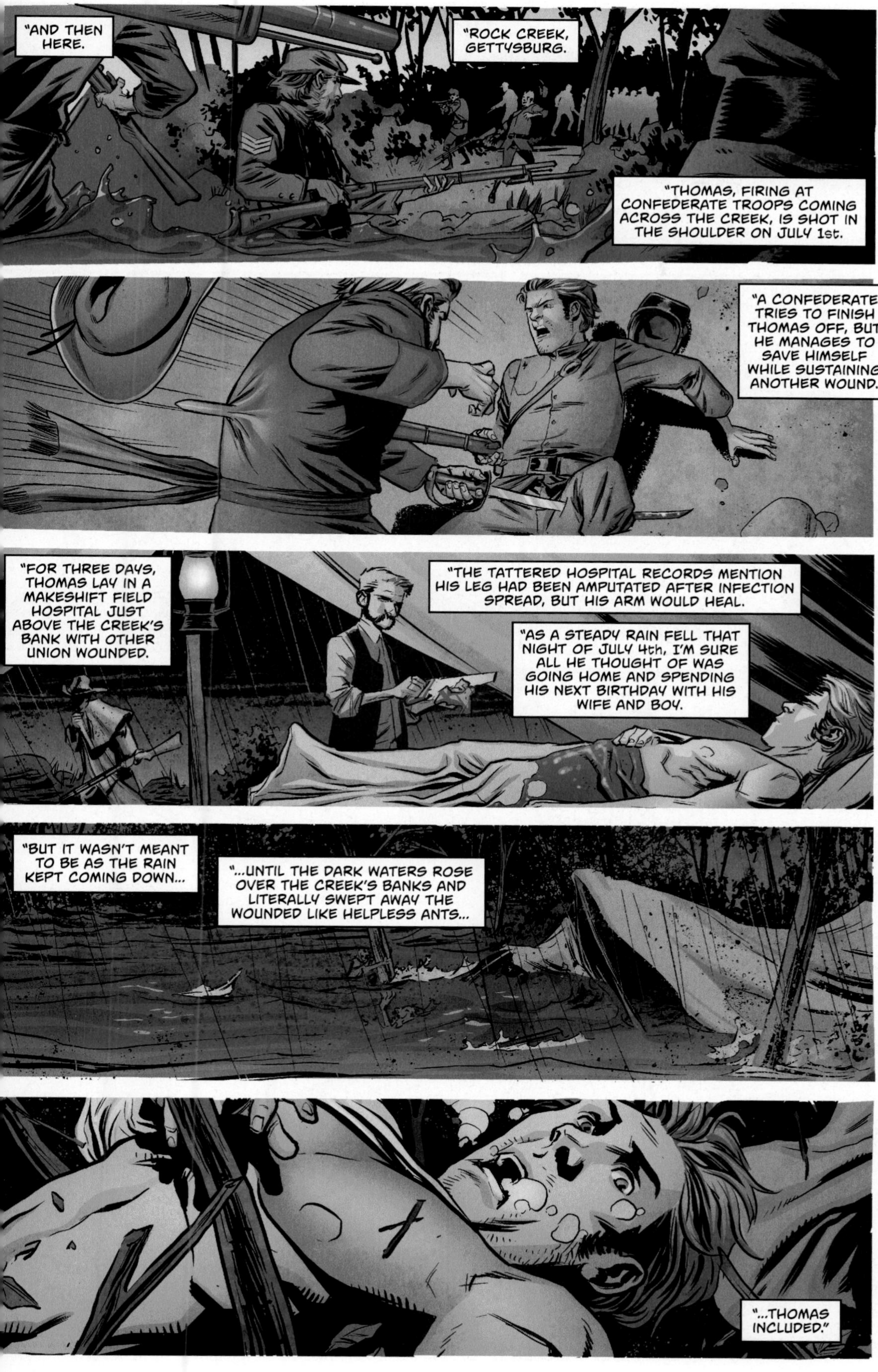
"AND THEN HERE.
"ROCK CREEK, GETTYSBURG.
"THOMAS, FIRING AT CONFEDERATE TROOPS COMING ACROSS THE CREEK, IS SHOT IN THE SHOULDER ON JULY 1st.
"A CONFEDERATE TRIES TO FINISH THOMAS OFF, BUT HE MANAGES TO SAVE HIMSELF WHILE SUSTAINING ANOTHER WOUND.
"FOR THREE DAYS, THOMAS LAY IN A MAKESHIFT FIELD HOSPITAL JUST ABOVE THE CREEK'S BANK WITH OTHER UNION WOUNDED.
"THE TATTERED HOSPITAL RECORDS MENTION HIS LEG HAD BEEN AMPUTATED AFTER INFECTION SPREAD, BUT HIS ARM WOULD HEAL.
"AS A STEADY RAIN FELL THAT NIGHT OF JULY 4th, I'M SURE ALL HE THOUGHT OF WAS GOING HOME AND SPENDING HIS NEXT BIRTHDAY WITH HIS WIFE AND BOY.
"BUT IT WASN'T MEANT TO BE AS THE RAIN KEPT COMING DOWN...
"...UNTIL THE DARK WATERS ROSE OVER THE CREEK'S BANKS AND LITERALLY SWEPT AWAY THE WOUNDED LIKE HELPLESS ANTS...
"...THOMAS INCLUDED."

UNION PATROLS SPENT TWO DAYS SEARCHING THE AREA AFTER THE FLASH FLOOD.

THEY FOUND ALL THE WOUNDED BODIES FROM THAT HORRIBLE NIGHT BUT ONE...

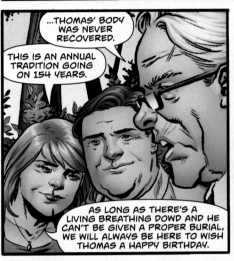

...THOMAS' BODY WAS NEVER RECOVERED.

THIS IS AN ANNUAL TRADITION GOING ON 154 YEARS.

AS LONG AS THERE'S A LIVING BREATHING DOWD AND HE CAN'T BE GIVEN A PROPER BURIAL, WE WILL ALWAYS BE HERE TO WISH THOMAS A HAPPY BIRTHDAY.

IT SEEMS ONLY APPROPRIATE THAT THE YOUNGEST ONE HERE LIGHTS THE CANDLE THIS YEAR.

Um, SURE, OKAY.

THANKS FOR SHARING THIS SPECIAL DAY WITH US.

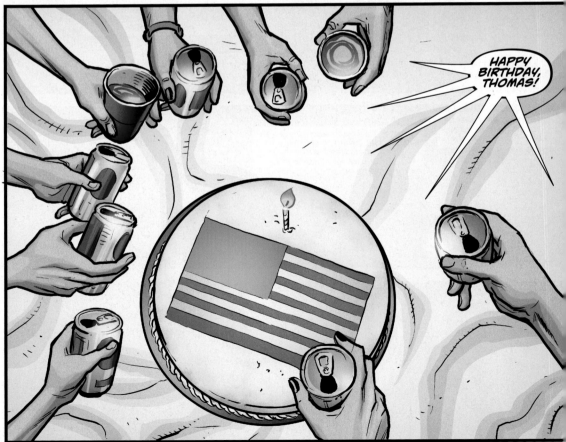

HAPPY BIRTHDAY, THOMAS!

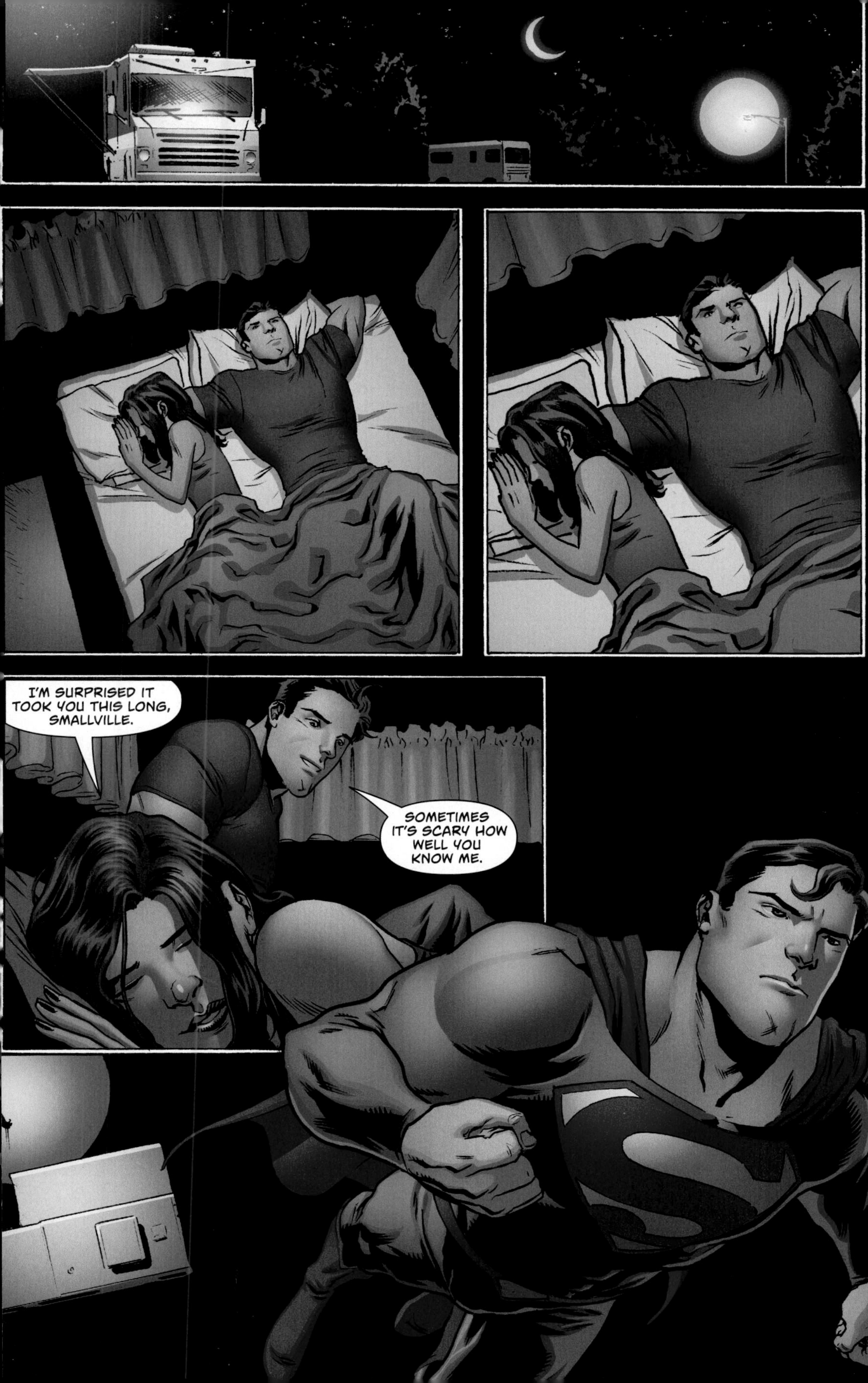
I'M SURPRISED IT TOOK YOU THIS LONG, SMALLVILLE.
SOMETIMES IT'S SCARY HOW WELL YOU KNOW ME.

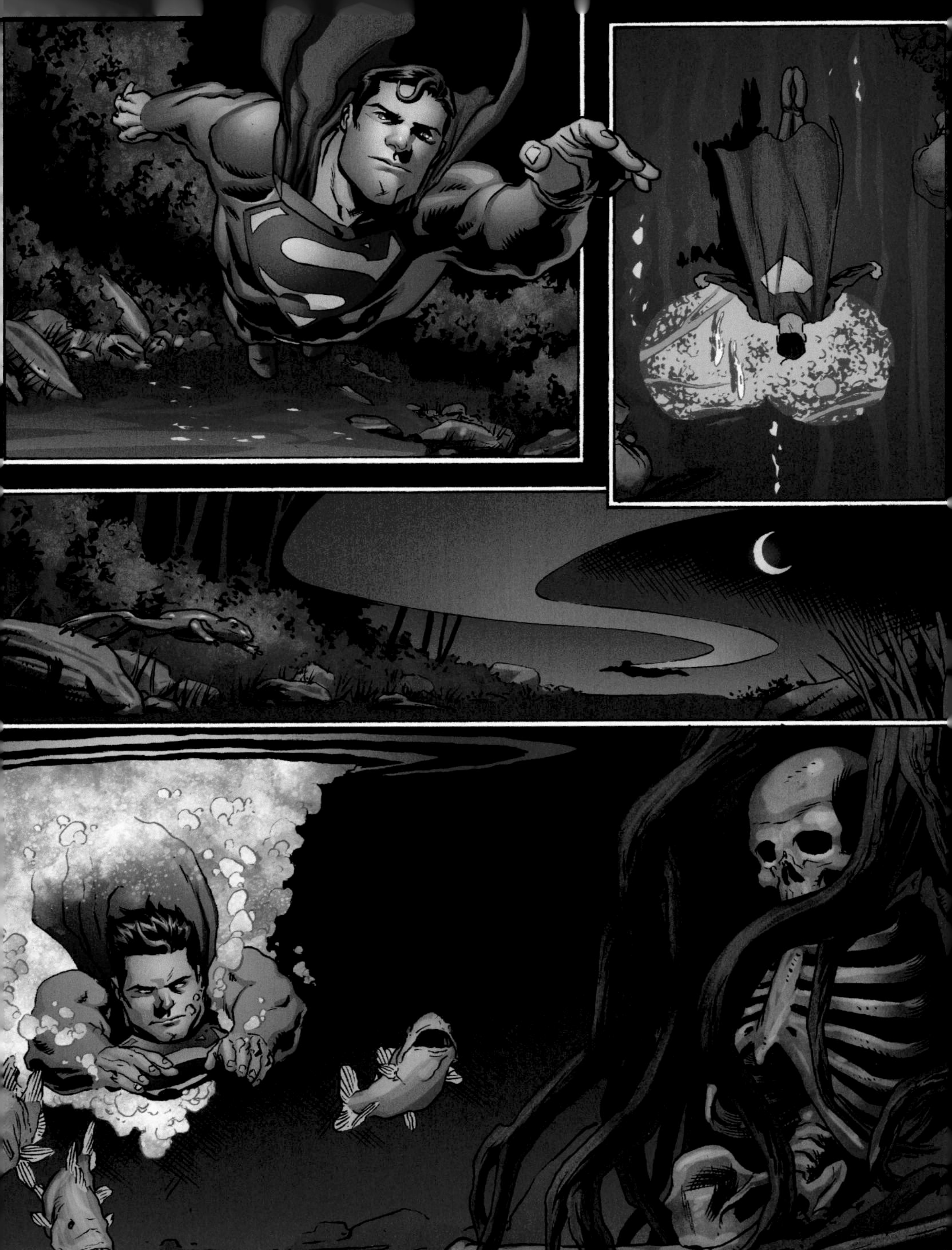

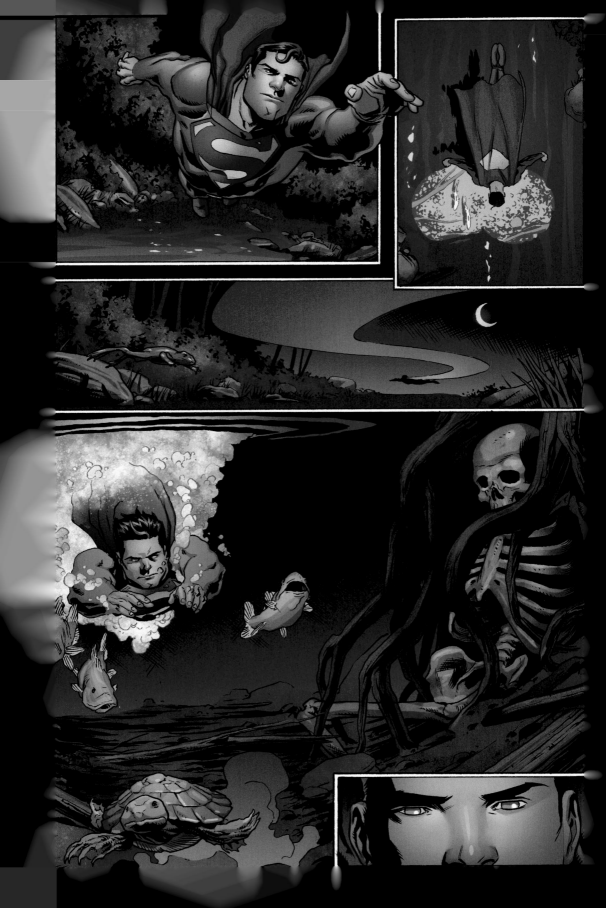

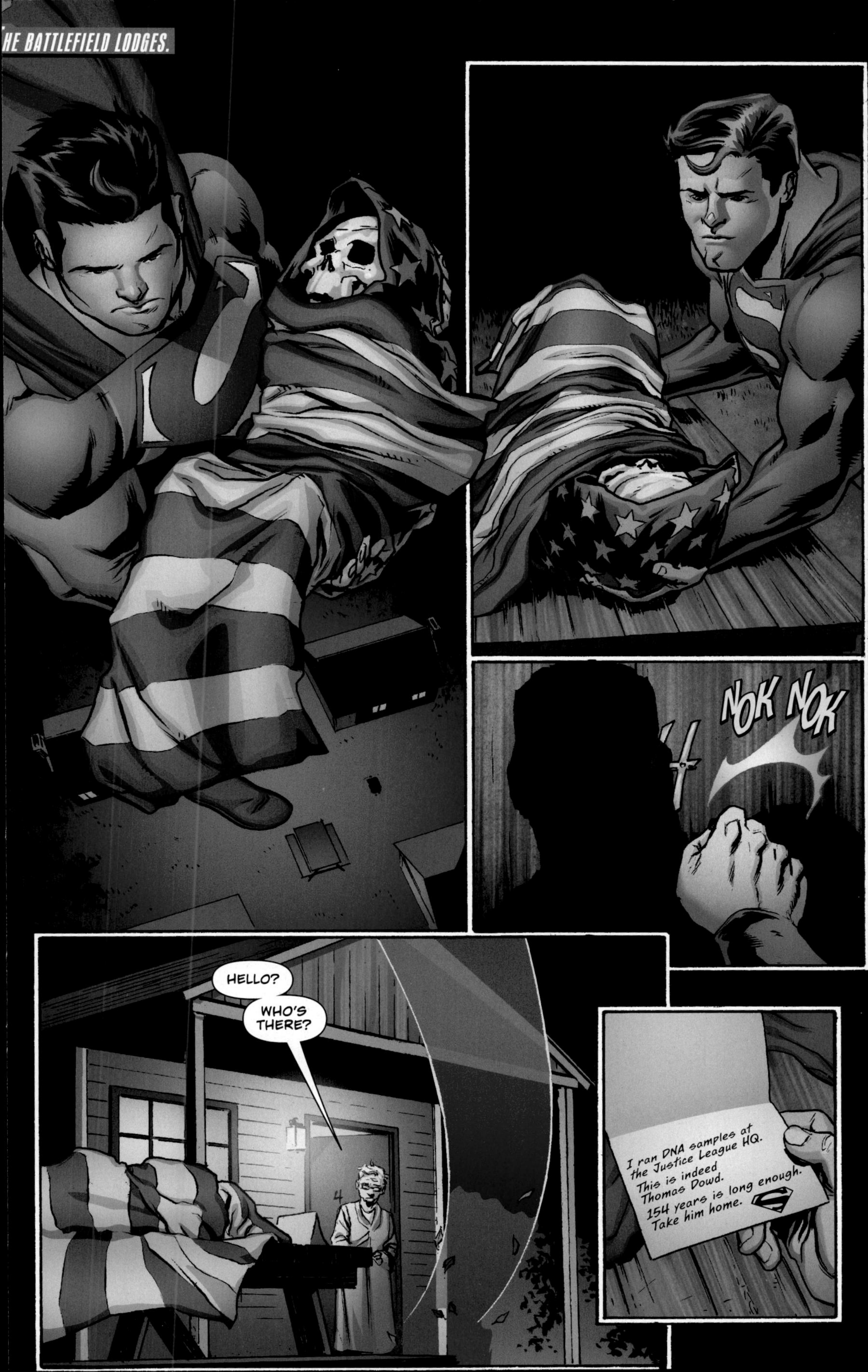
HE BATTLEFIELD LODGES.
NOK NOK
HELLO?
WHO'S THERE?
I ran DNA samples at the Justice League HQ. This is indeed Thomas Dowd. 154 years is long enough. Take him home.

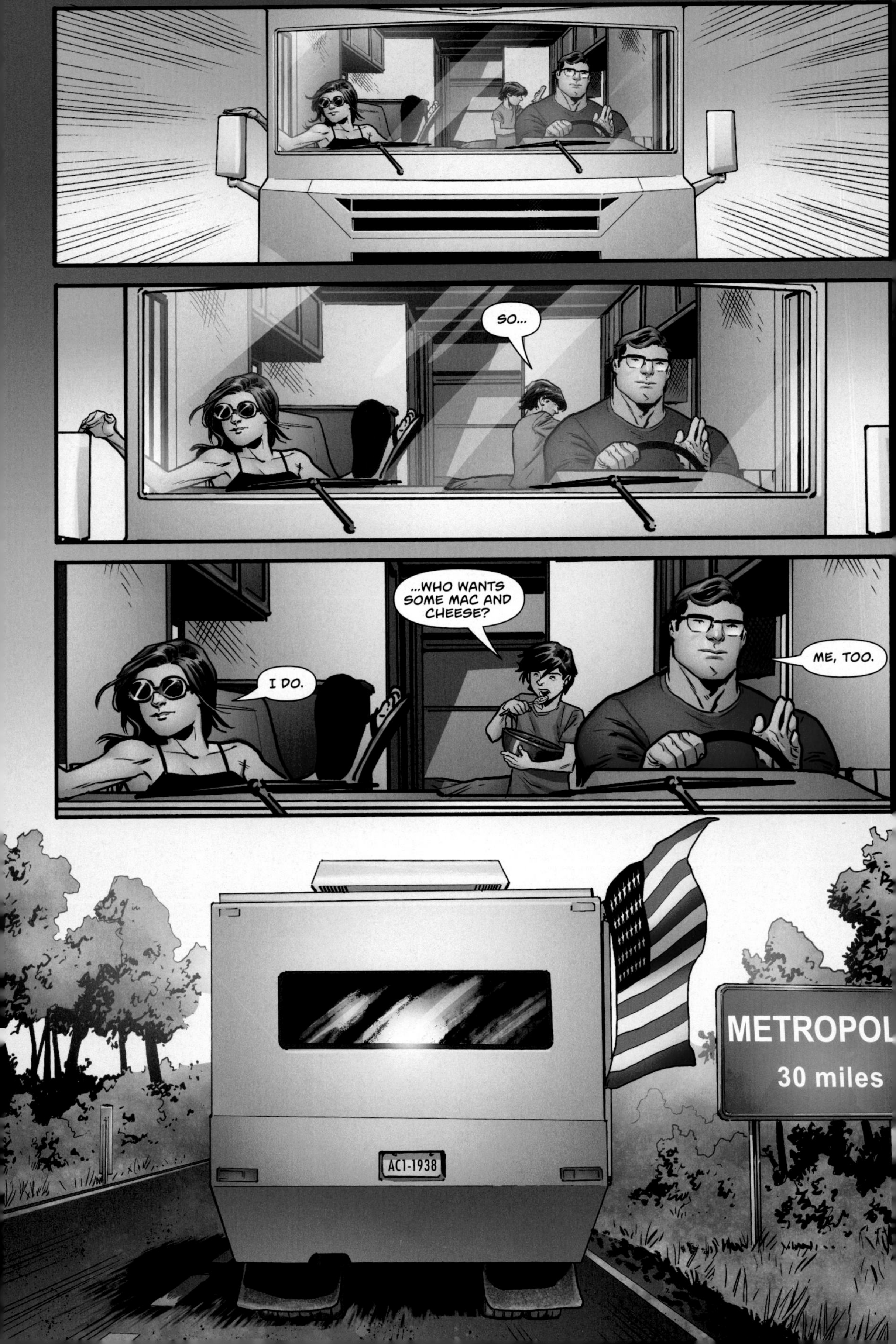
SO...
...WHO WANTS SOME MAC AND CHEESE?
I DO.
ME, TOO.
AC1-1938
METROPOL
30 miles

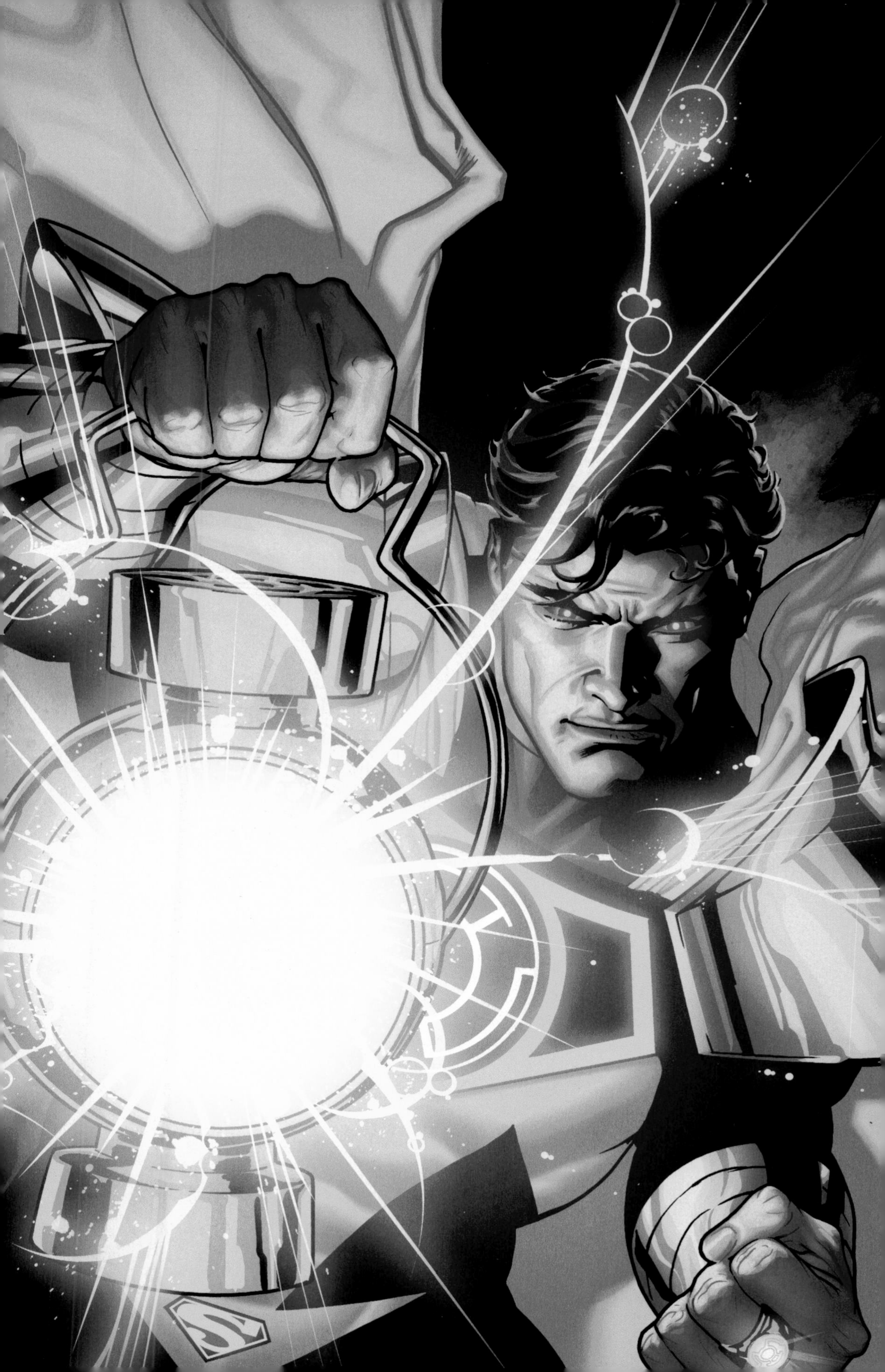

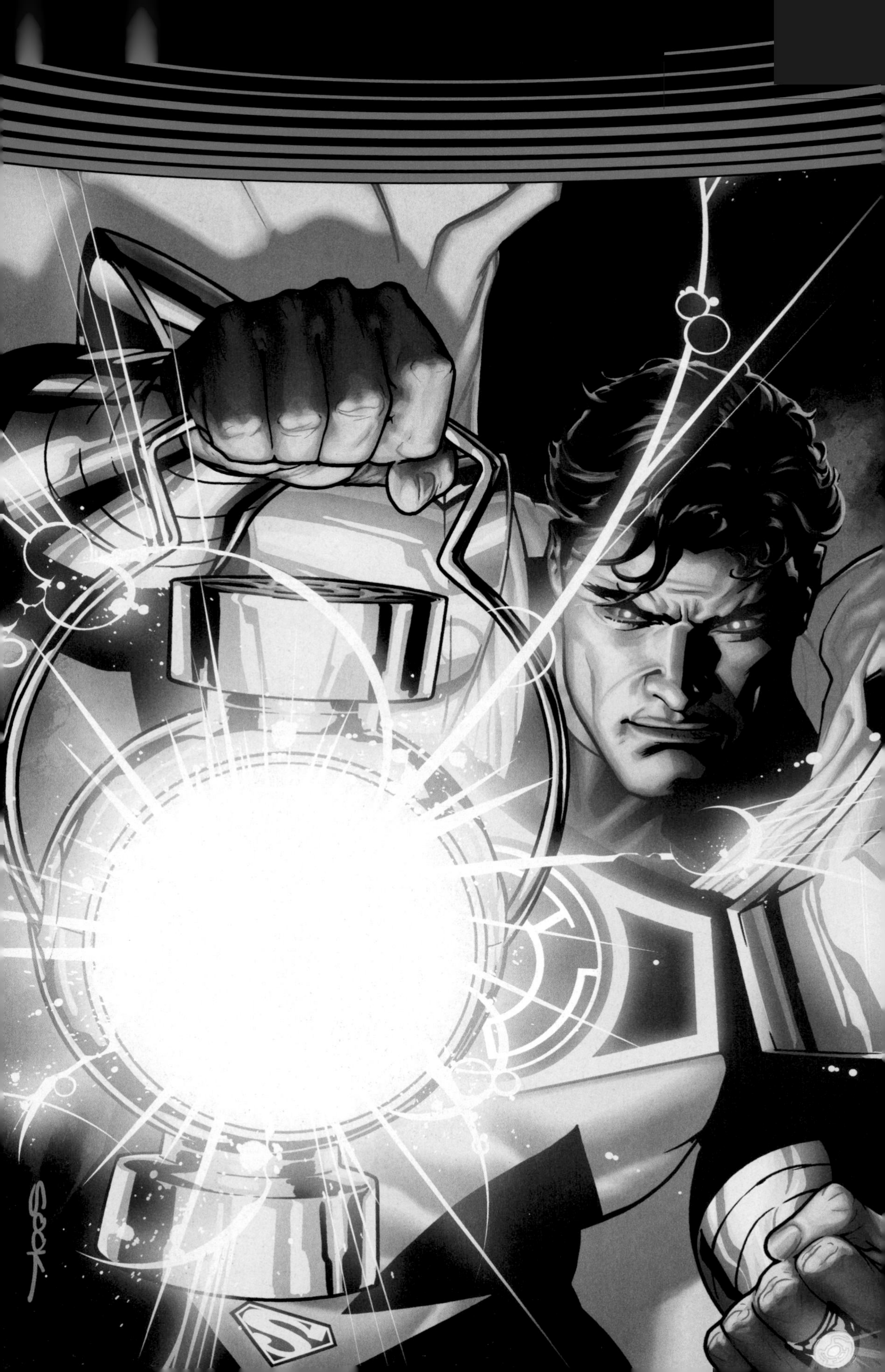

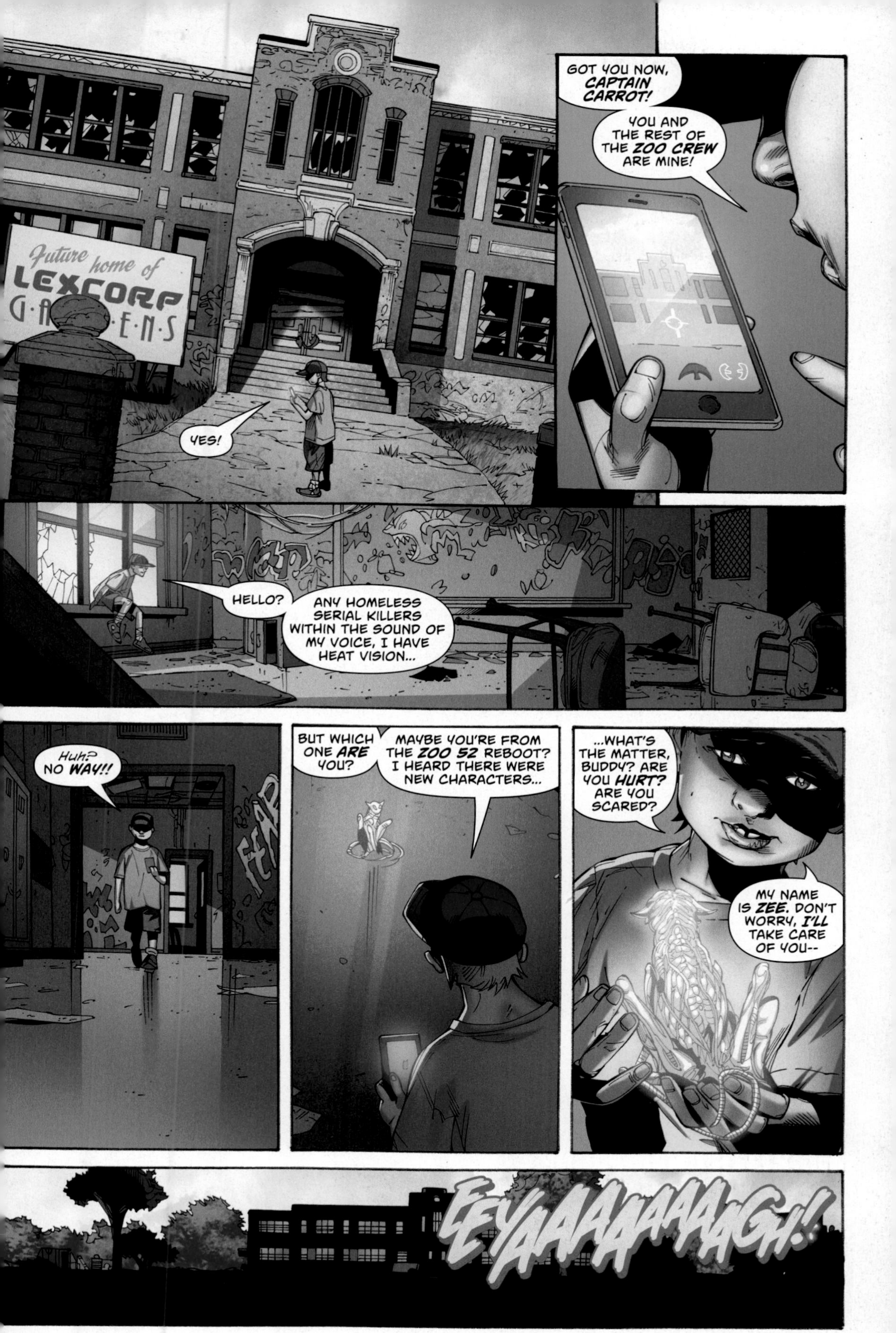
Future home of LEXCORP GA...ENS
YES!
GOT YOU NOW, CAPTAIN CARROT!
YOU AND THE REST OF THE ZOO CREW ARE MINE!
HELLO?
ANY HOMELESS SERIAL KILLERS WITHIN THE SOUND OF MY VOICE, I HAVE HEAT VISION...
Huh? NO WAY!!
BUT WHICH ONE ARE YOU?
MAYBE YOU'RE FROM THE ZOO 52 REBOOT? I HEARD THERE WERE NEW CHARACTERS...
...WHAT'S THE MATTER, BUDDY? ARE YOU HURT? ARE YOU SCARED?
MY NAME IS ZEE. DON'T WORRY, I'LL TAKE CARE OF YOU--
EEYAAAAAAAAAGH!

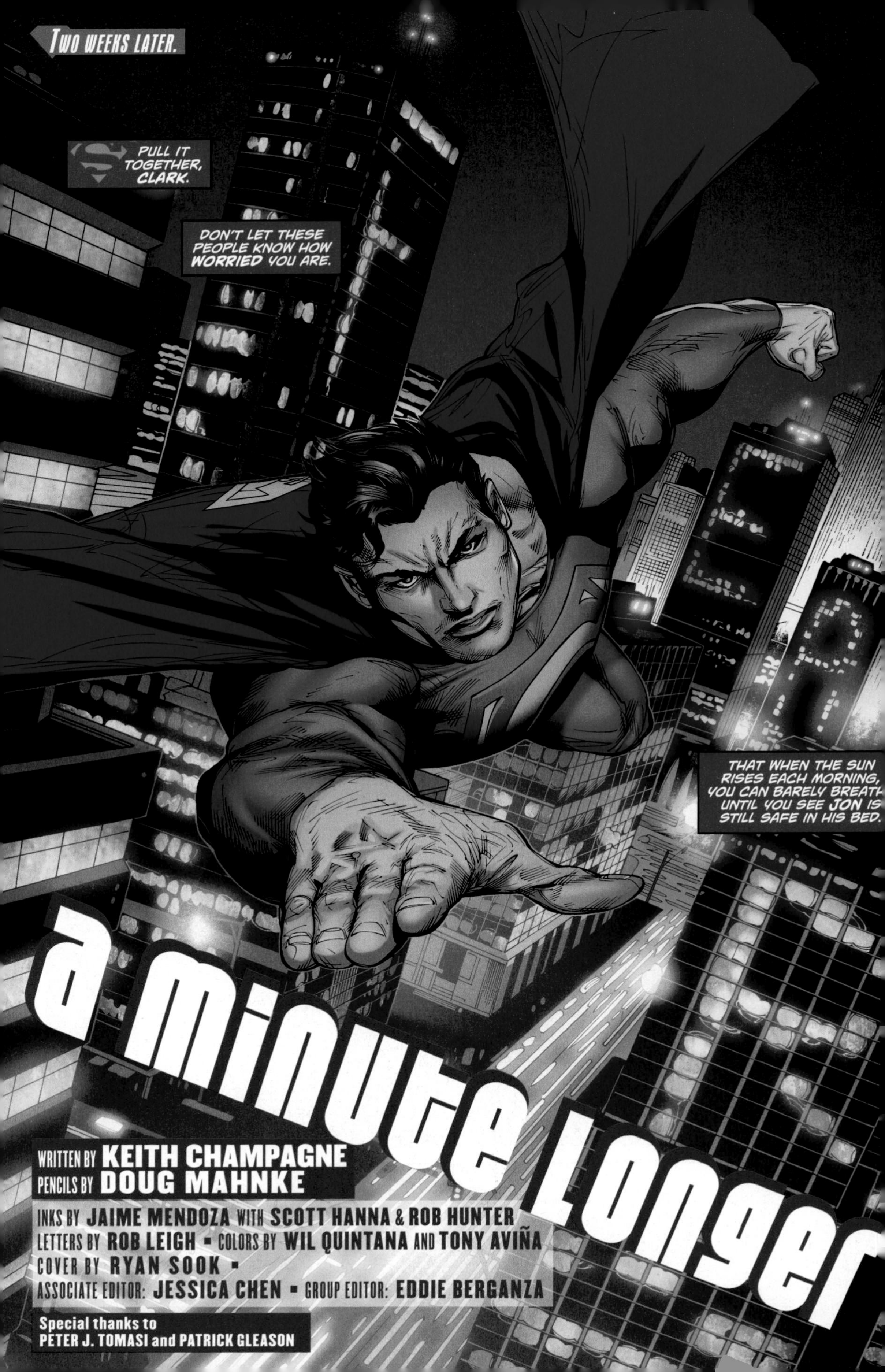
TWO WEEKS LATER.
PULL IT TOGETHER, CLARK.
DON'T LET THESE PEOPLE KNOW HOW WORRIED YOU ARE.
THAT WHEN THE SUN RISES EACH MORNING, YOU CAN BARELY BREATH UNTIL YOU SEE JON IS STILL SAFE IN HIS BED.
A MINUTE LONGER
WRITTEN BY KEITH CHAMPAGNE
PENCILS BY DOUG MAHNKE
INKS BY JAIME MENDOZA WITH SCOTT HANNA & ROB HUNTER
LETTERS BY ROB LEIGH ▪ COLORS BY WIL QUINTANA AND TONY AVIÑA
COVER BY RYAN SOOK ▪
ASSOCIATE EDITOR: JESSICA CHEN ▪ GROUP EDITOR: EDDIE BERGANZA
Special thanks to PETER J. TOMASI and PATRICK GLEASON

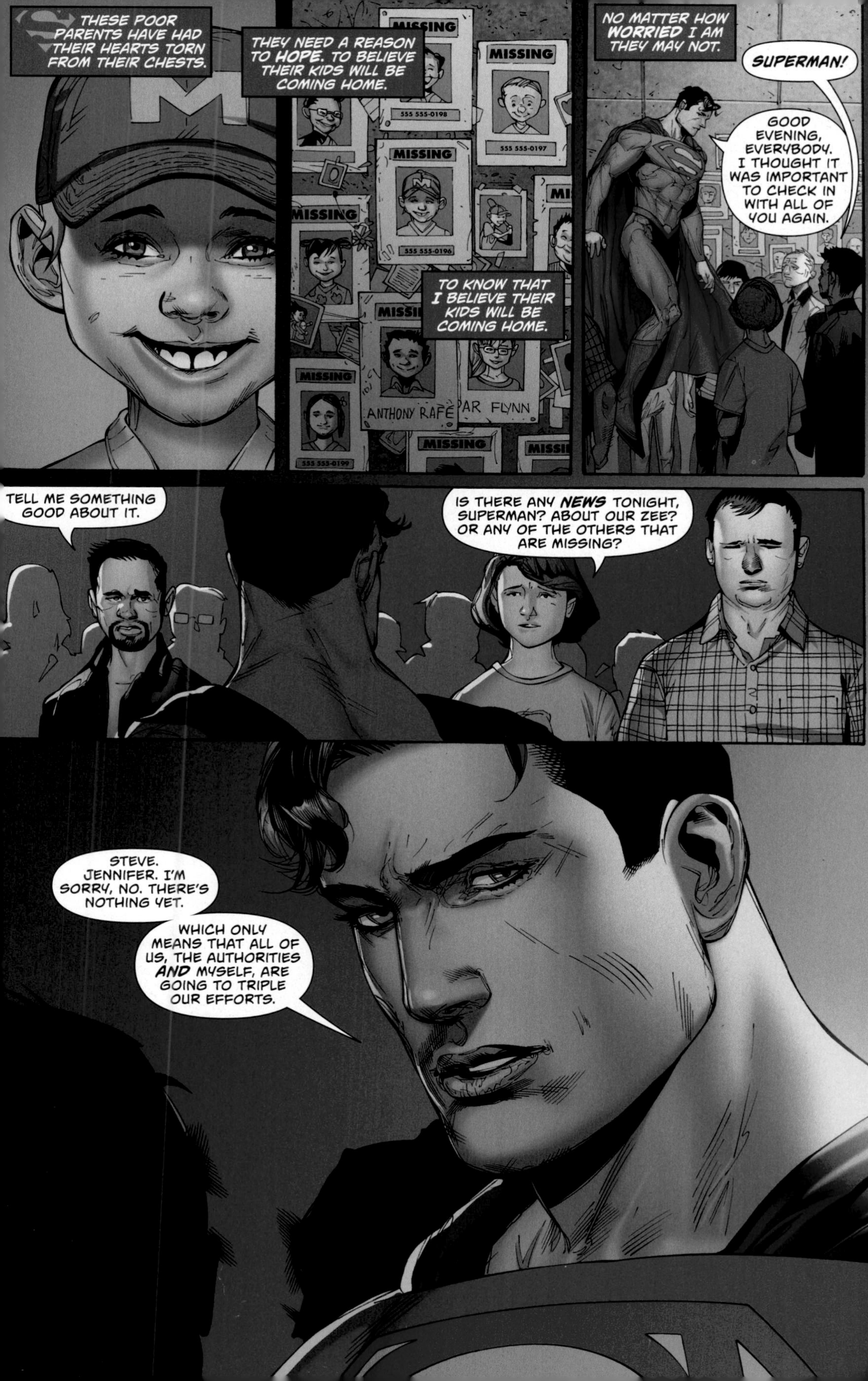
THESE POOR PARENTS HAVE HAD THEIR HEARTS TORN FROM THEIR CHESTS.
THEY NEED A REASON TO HOPE. TO BELIEVE THEIR KIDS WILL BE COMING HOME.
MISSING
555 555-0198
MISSING
555 555-0197
MISSING
555 555-0196
MISSING
MISSING
555 555-0199
ANTHONY RAFE
FLYNN
MISSING
TO KNOW THAT I BELIEVE THEIR KIDS WILL BE COMING HOME.
NO MATTER HOW WORRIED I AM THEY MAY NOT.
SUPERMAN!
GOOD EVENING, EVERYBODY. I THOUGHT IT WAS IMPORTANT TO CHECK IN WITH ALL OF YOU AGAIN.
TELL ME SOMETHING GOOD ABOUT IT.
IS THERE ANY NEWS TONIGHT, SUPERMAN? ABOUT OUR ZEE? OR ANY OF THE OTHERS THAT ARE MISSING?
STEVE. JENNIFER. I'M SORRY, NO. THERE'S NOTHING YET.
WHICH ONLY MEANS THAT ALL OF US, THE AUTHORITIES AND MYSELF, ARE GOING TO TRIPLE OUR EFFORTS.

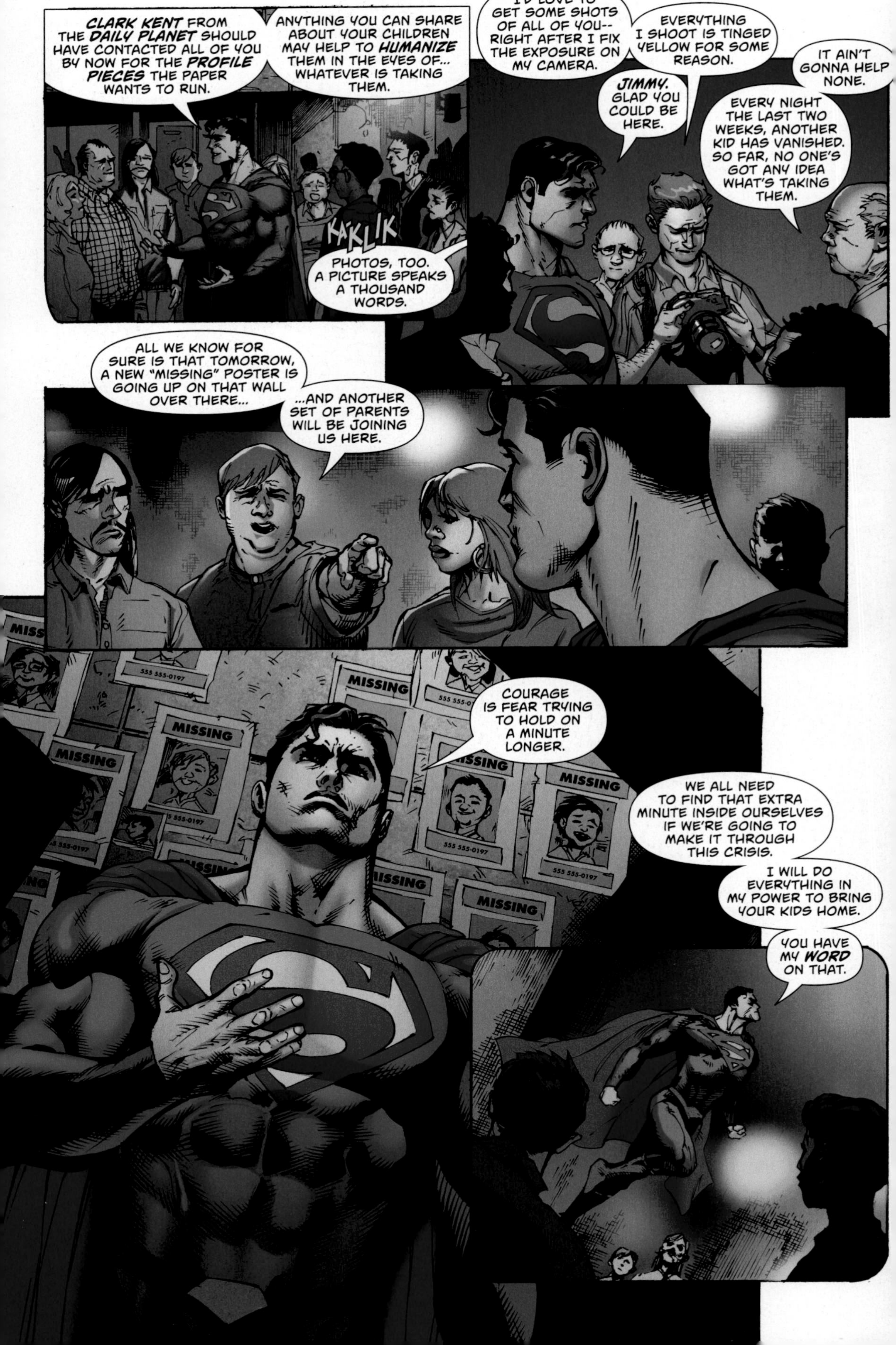
CLARK KENT FROM THE DAILY PLANET SHOULD HAVE CONTACTED ALL OF YOU BY NOW FOR THE PROFILE PIECES THE PAPER WANTS TO RUN.
ANYTHING YOU CAN SHARE ABOUT YOUR CHILDREN MAY HELP TO HUMANIZE THEM IN THE EYES OF... WHATEVER IS TAKING THEM.
KA-KLIK
PHOTOS, TOO. A PICTURE SPEAKS A THOUSAND WORDS.
I'D LOVE TO GET SOME SHOTS OF ALL OF YOU-- RIGHT AFTER I FIX THE EXPOSURE ON MY CAMERA.
EVERYTHING I SHOOT IS TINGED YELLOW FOR SOME REASON.
JIMMY. GLAD YOU COULD BE HERE.
IT AIN'T GONNA HELP NONE.
EVERY NIGHT THE LAST TWO WEEKS, ANOTHER KID HAS VANISHED. SO FAR, NO ONE'S GOT ANY IDEA WHAT'S TAKING THEM.
ALL WE KNOW FOR SURE IS THAT TOMORROW, A NEW "MISSING" POSTER IS GOING UP ON THAT WALL OVER THERE...
...AND ANOTHER SET OF PARENTS WILL BE JOINING US HERE.
MISSING
555 555-0197
COURAGE IS FEAR TRYING TO HOLD ON A MINUTE LONGER.
WE ALL NEED TO FIND THAT EXTRA MINUTE INSIDE OURSELVES IF WE'RE GOING TO MAKE IT THROUGH THIS CRISIS.
I WILL DO EVERYTHING IN MY POWER TO BRING YOUR KIDS HOME.
YOU HAVE MY WORD ON THAT.

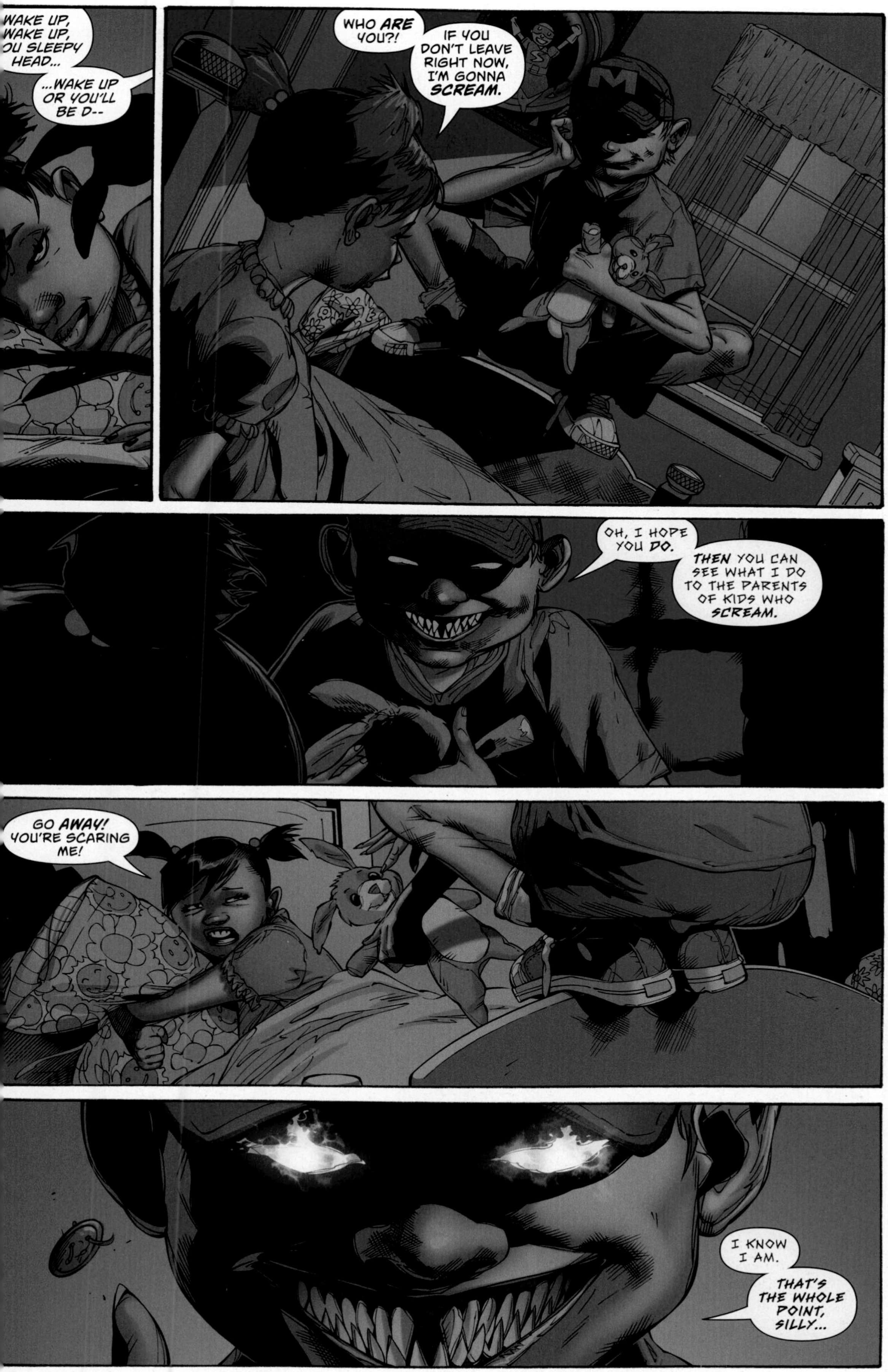

WAKE UP, WAKE UP, YOU SLEEPY HEAD...
...WAKE UP OR YOU'LL BE D--
WHO **ARE** YOU?!
IF YOU DON'T LEAVE RIGHT NOW, I'M GONNA **SCREAM**.
OH, I HOPE YOU **DO**.
THEN YOU CAN SEE WHAT I DO TO THE PARENTS OF KIDS WHO **SCREAM**.
GO **AWAY**! YOU'RE SCARING ME!
I KNOW I AM.
THAT'S THE WHOLE POINT, SILLY...

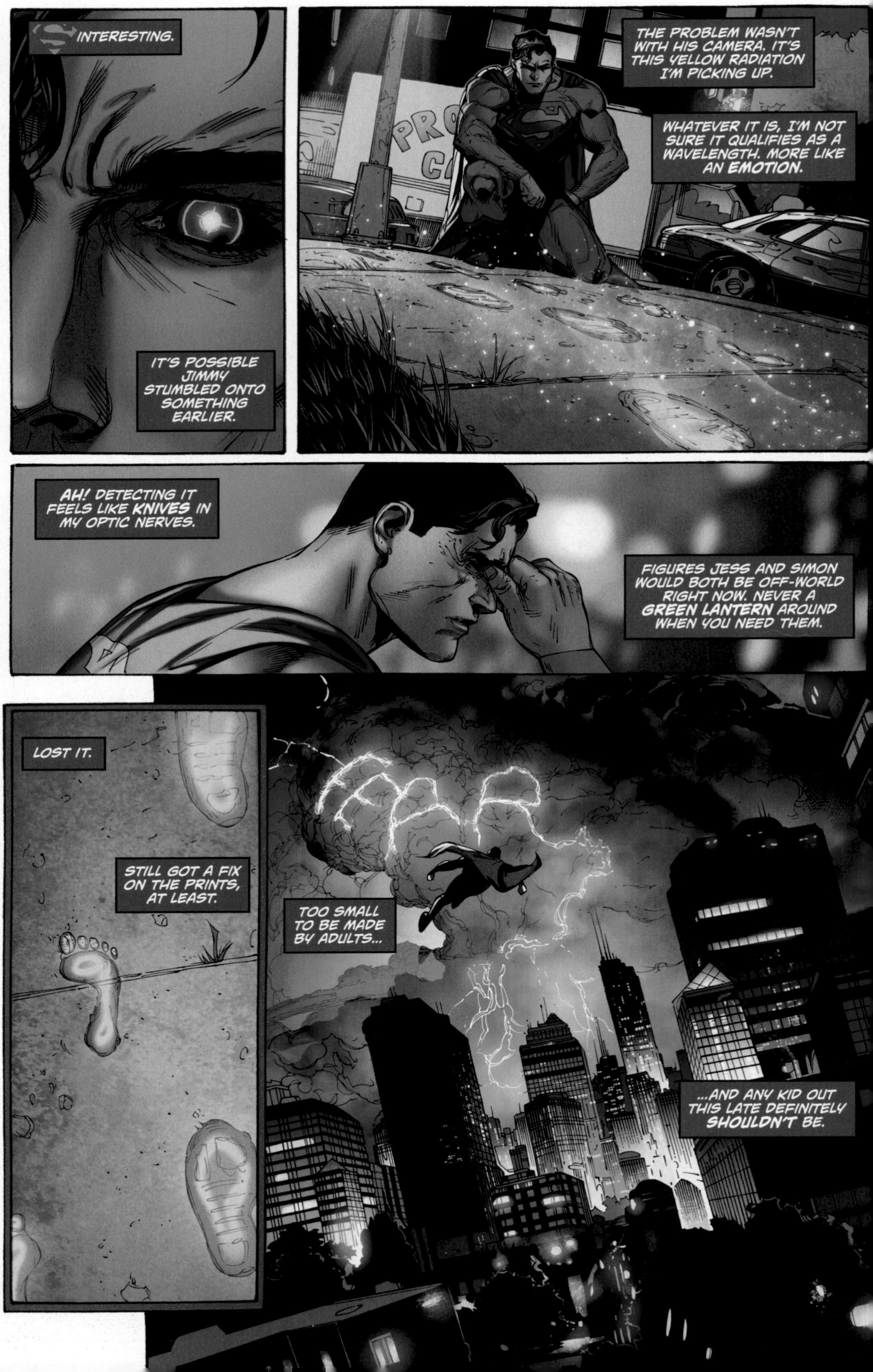
INTERESTING.
IT'S POSSIBLE JIMMY STUMBLED ONTO SOMETHING EARLIER.
THE PROBLEM WASN'T WITH HIS CAMERA. IT'S THIS YELLOW RADIATION I'M PICKING UP.
WHATEVER IT IS, I'M NOT SURE IT QUALIFIES AS A WAVELENGTH. MORE LIKE AN EMOTION.
AH! DETECTING IT FEELS LIKE KNIVES IN MY OPTIC NERVES.
FIGURES JESS AND SIMON WOULD BOTH BE OFF-WORLD RIGHT NOW. NEVER A GREEN LANTERN AROUND WHEN YOU NEED THEM.
LOST IT.
STILL GOT A FIX ON THE PRINTS, AT LEAST.
TOO SMALL TO BE MADE BY ADULTS...
FEAR
...AND ANY KID OUT THIS LATE DEFINITELY SHOULDN'T BE.

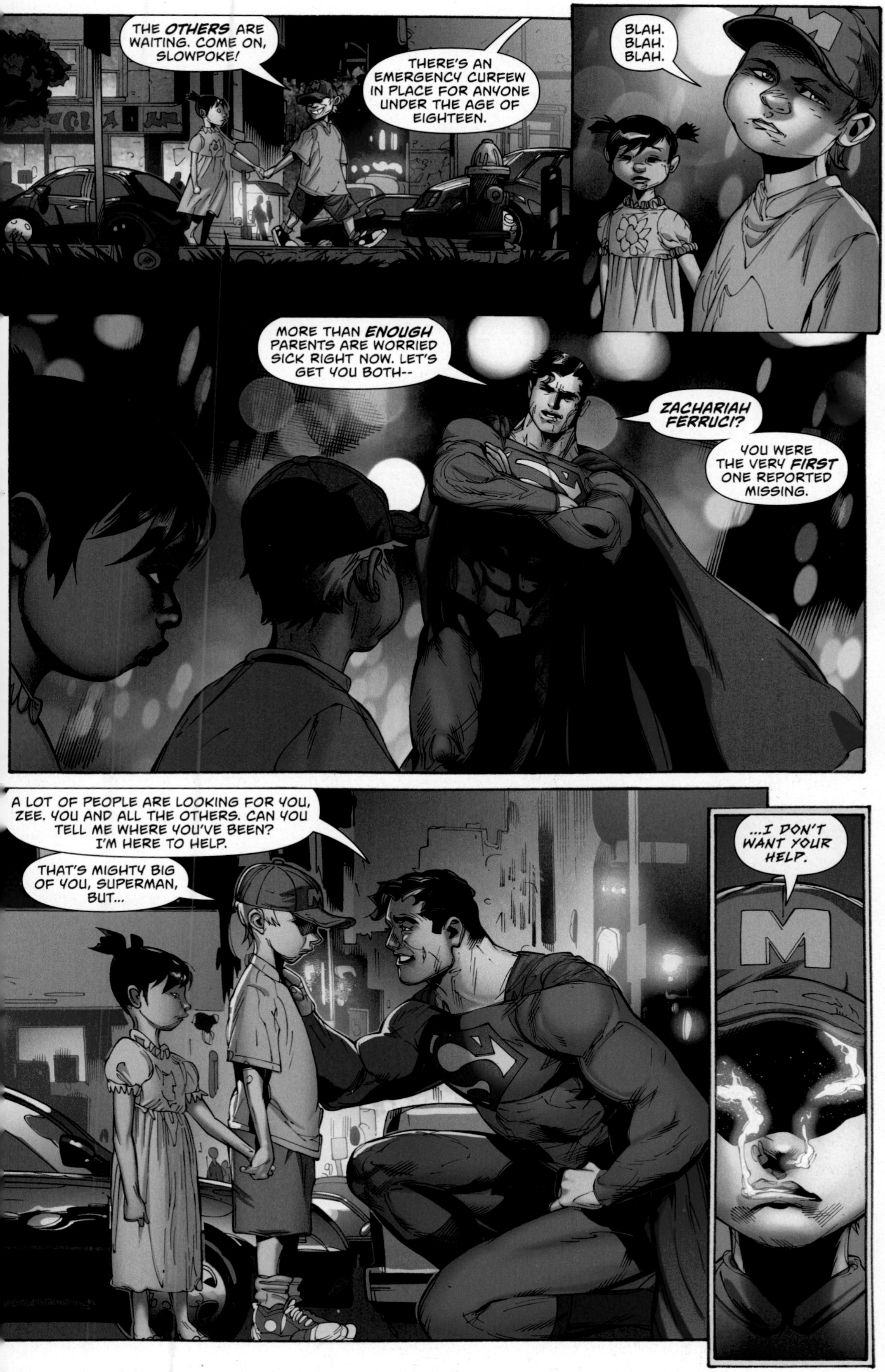
THE OTHERS ARE WAITING. COME ON, SLOWPOKE!
THERE'S AN EMERGENCY CURFEW IN PLACE FOR ANYONE UNDER THE AGE OF EIGHTEEN.
BLAH. BLAH. BLAH.
MORE THAN ENOUGH PARENTS ARE WORRIED SICK RIGHT NOW. LET'S GET YOU BOTH--
ZACHARIAH FERRUCI?
YOU WERE THE VERY FIRST ONE REPORTED MISSING.
A LOT OF PEOPLE ARE LOOKING FOR YOU, ZEE. YOU AND ALL THE OTHERS. CAN YOU TELL ME WHERE YOU'VE BEEN? I'M HERE TO HELP.
THAT'S MIGHTY BIG OF YOU, SUPERMAN, BUT...
...I DON'T WANT YOUR HELP.

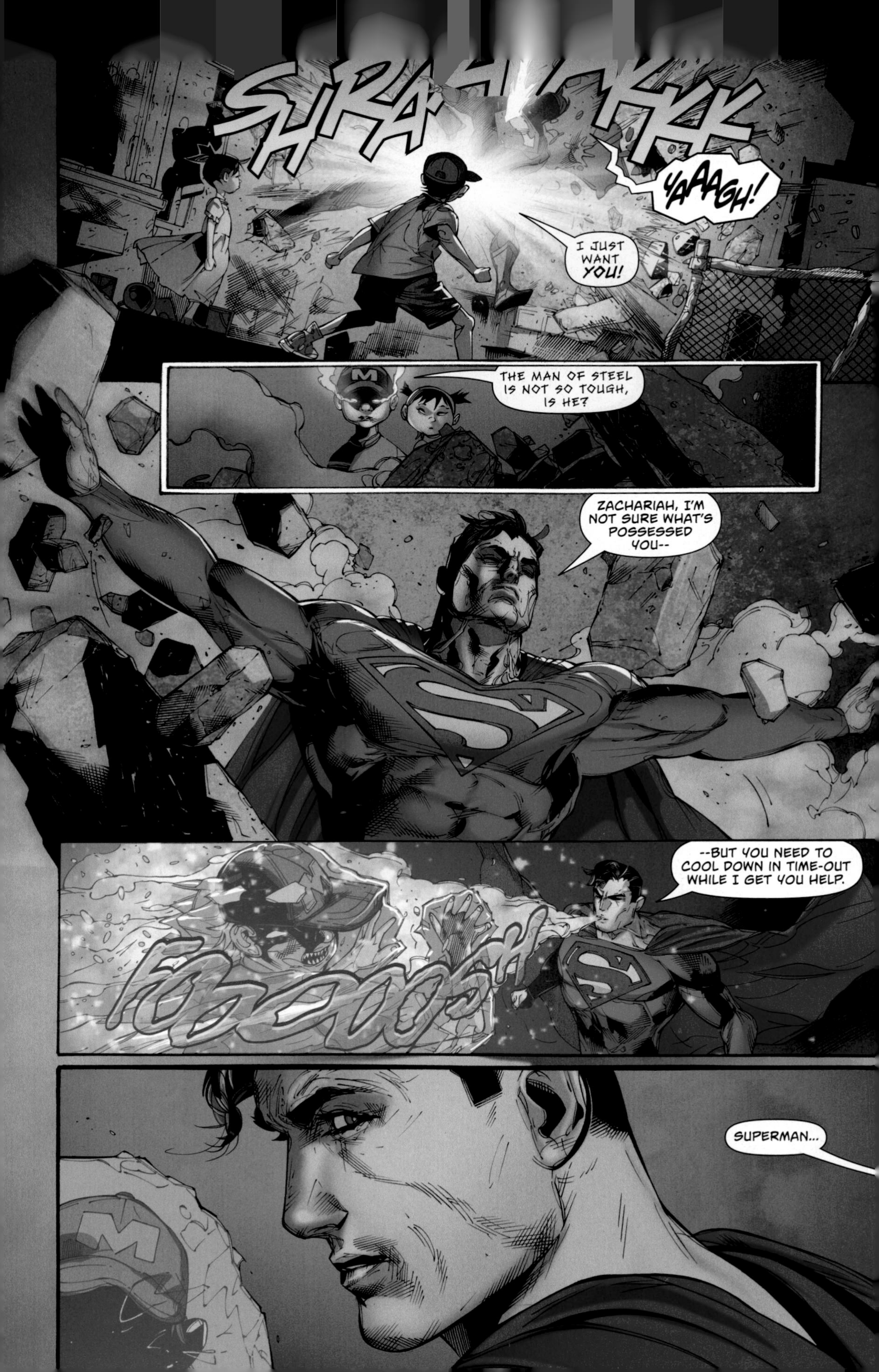

YAAAGH!
I JUST WANT YOU!
THE MAN OF STEEL IS NOT SO TOUGH, IS HE?
ZACHARIAH, I'M NOT SURE WHAT'S POSSESSED YOU--
--BUT YOU NEED TO COOL DOWN IN TIME-OUT WHILE I GET YOU HELP.
SUPERMAN...

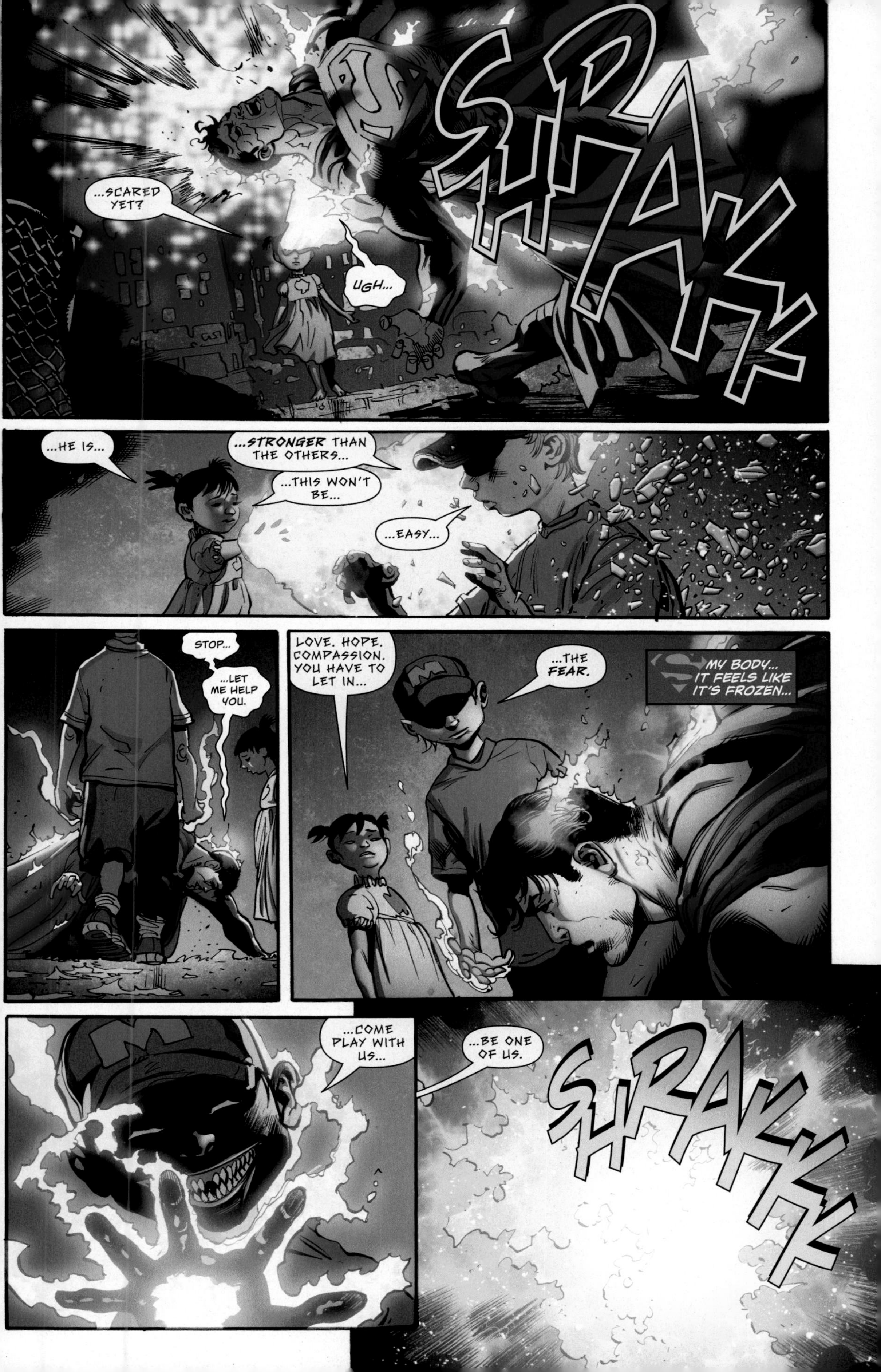
SHRAKK
...SCARED YET?
UGH...
...HE IS...
...STRONGER THAN THE OTHERS...
...THIS WON'T BE...
...EASY...
STOP...
...LET ME HELP YOU.
LOVE. HOPE. COMPASSION. YOU HAVE TO LET IN...
...THE FEAR.
MY BODY... IT FEELS LIKE IT'S FROZEN...
...COME PLAY WITH US...
...BE ONE OF US.
SHRAKK

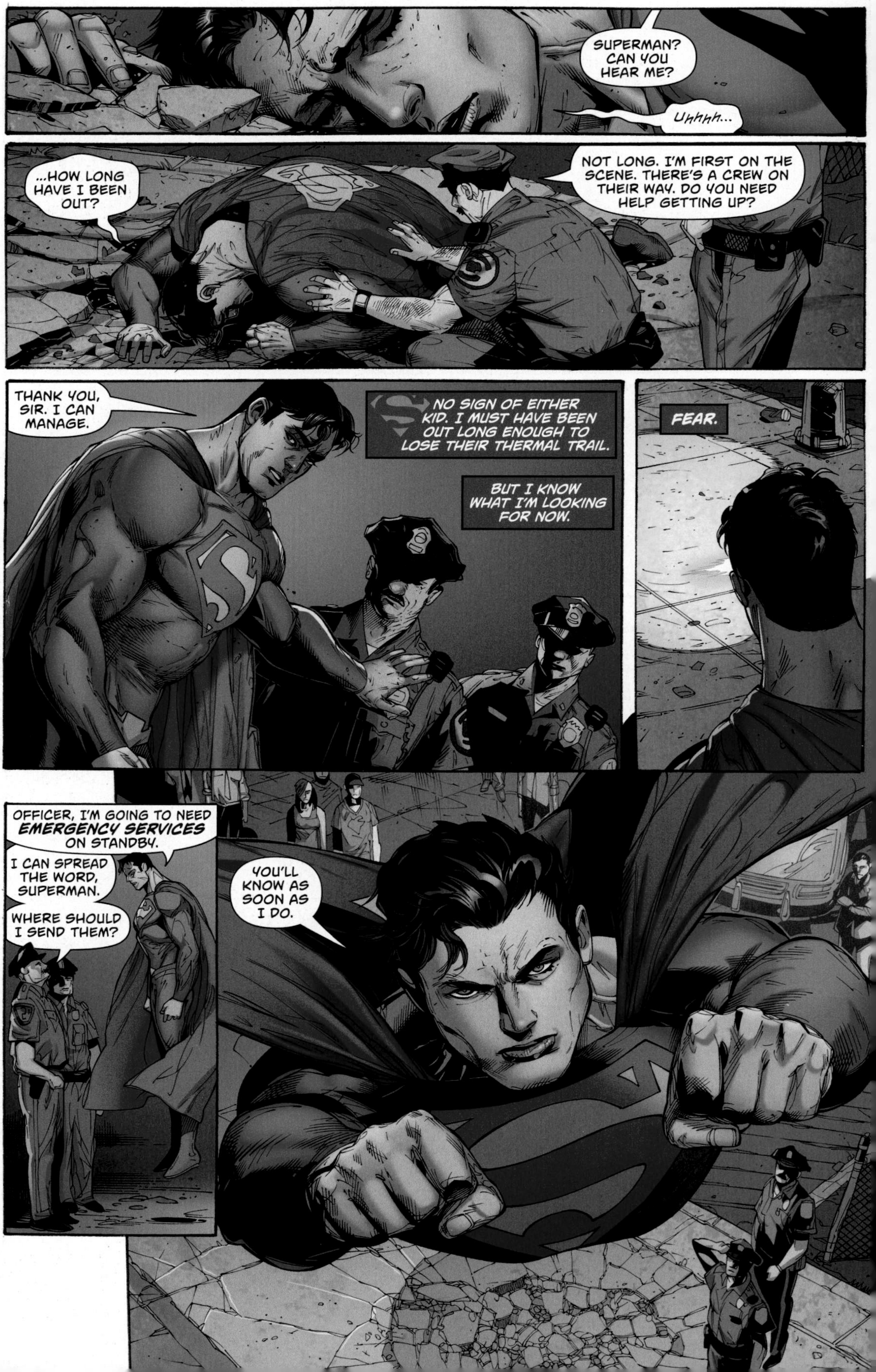
SUPERMAN? CAN YOU HEAR ME?
Uhhhh...
...HOW LONG HAVE I BEEN OUT?
NOT LONG. I'M FIRST ON THE SCENE. THERE'S A CREW ON THEIR WAY. DO YOU NEED HELP GETTING UP?
THANK YOU, SIR. I CAN MANAGE.
NO SIGN OF EITHER KID. I MUST HAVE BEEN OUT LONG ENOUGH TO LOSE THEIR THERMAL TRAIL.
BUT I KNOW WHAT I'M LOOKING FOR NOW.
FEAR.
OFFICER, I'M GOING TO NEED EMERGENCY SERVICES ON STANDBY.
I CAN SPREAD THE WORD, SUPERMAN.
WHERE SHOULD I SEND THEM?
YOU'LL KNOW AS SOON AS I DO.

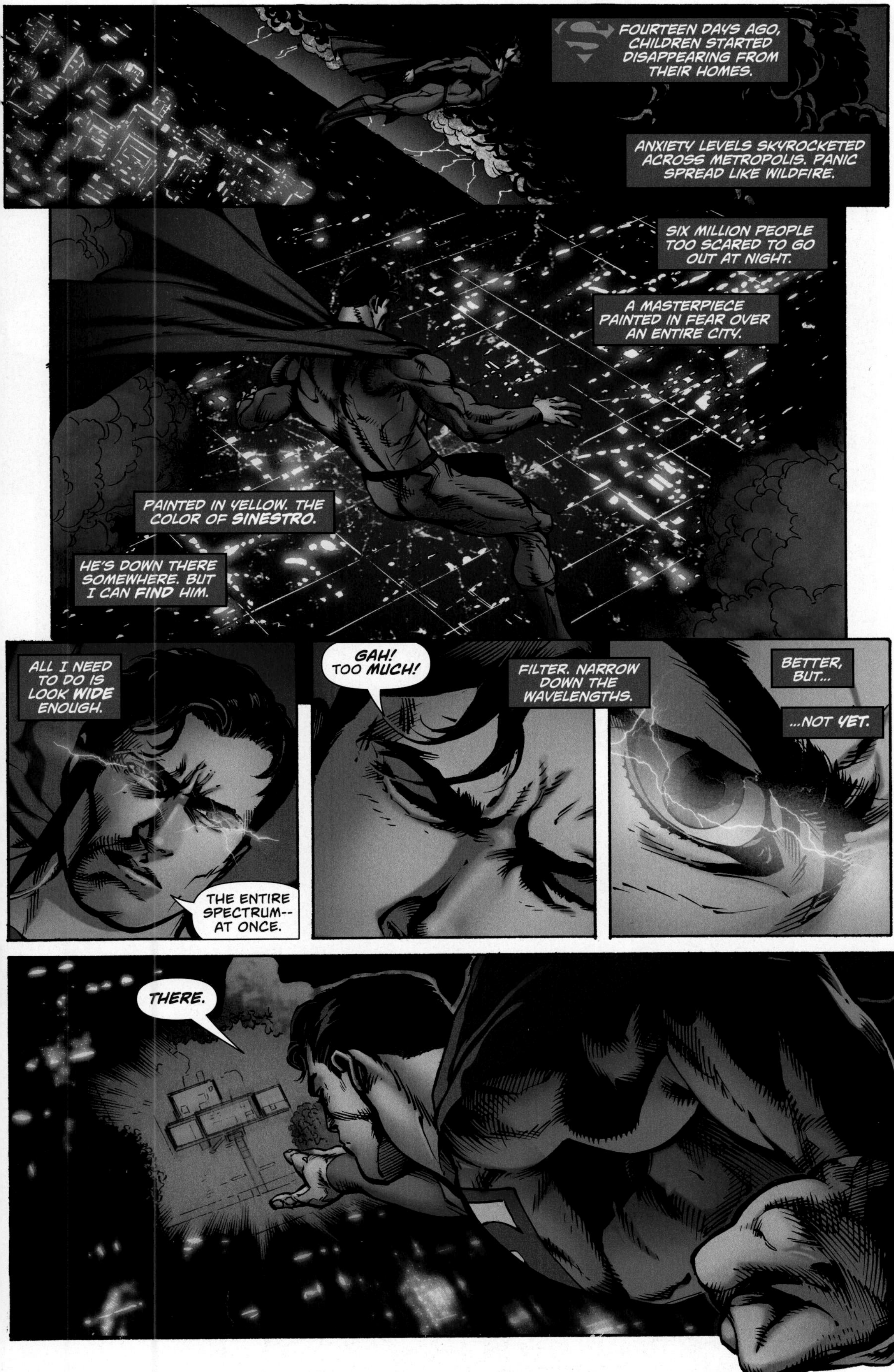
FOURTEEN DAYS AGO, CHILDREN STARTED DISAPPEARING FROM THEIR HOMES.
ANXIETY LEVELS SKYROCKETED ACROSS METROPOLIS. PANIC SPREAD LIKE WILDFIRE.
SIX MILLION PEOPLE TOO SCARED TO GO OUT AT NIGHT.
A MASTERPIECE PAINTED IN FEAR OVER AN ENTIRE CITY.
PAINTED IN YELLOW. THE COLOR OF SINESTRO.
HE'S DOWN THERE SOMEWHERE. BUT I CAN FIND HIM.
ALL I NEED TO DO IS LOOK WIDE ENOUGH.
THE ENTIRE SPECTRUM-- AT ONCE.
GAH! TOO MUCH!
FILTER. NARROW DOWN THE WAVELENGTHS.
BETTER, BUT...
...NOT YET.
THERE.

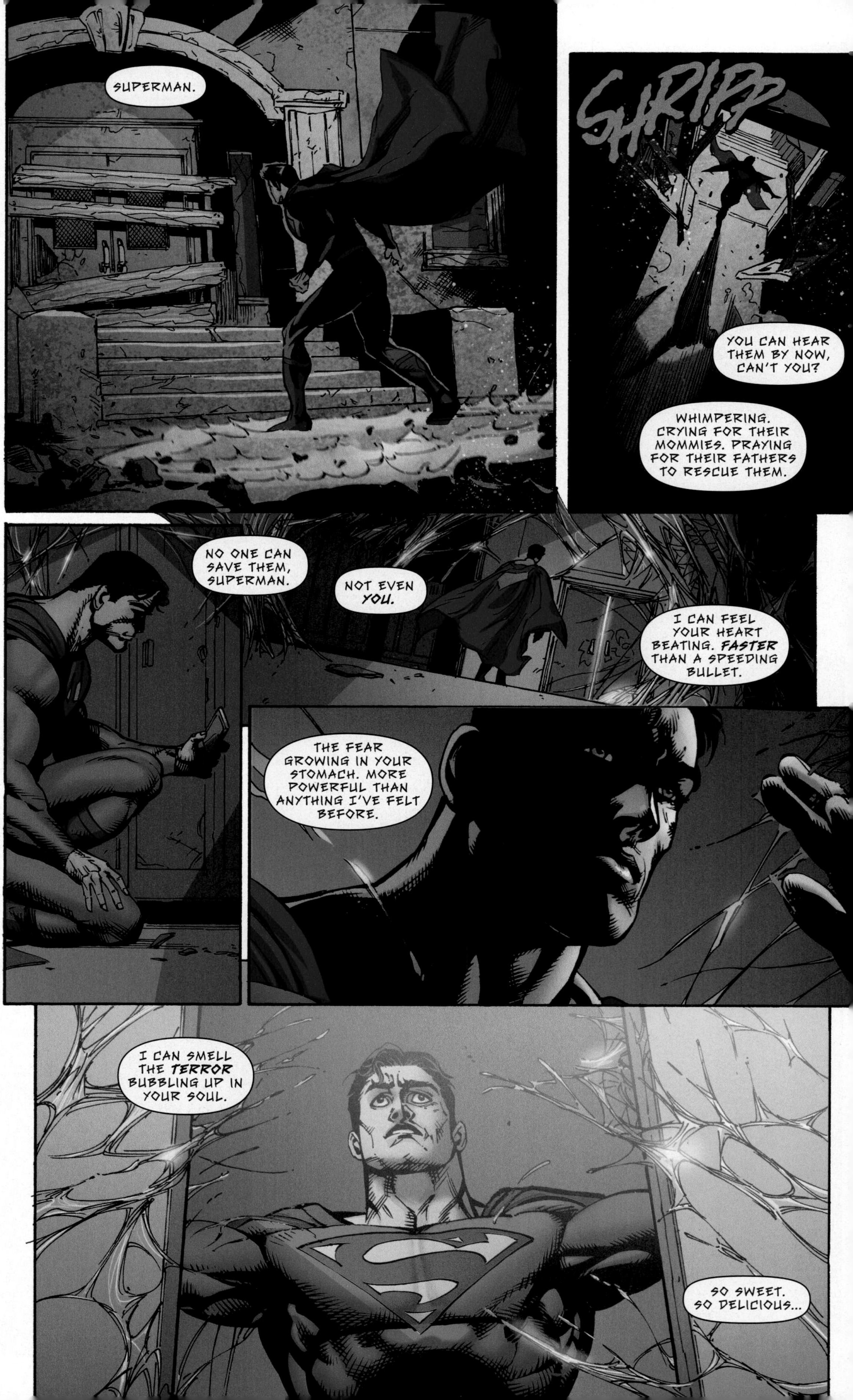
SUPERMAN.
SHRIPP
YOU CAN HEAR THEM BY NOW, CAN'T YOU?
WHIMPERING. CRYING FOR THEIR MOMMIES. PRAYING FOR THEIR FATHERS TO RESCUE THEM.
NO ONE CAN SAVE THEM, SUPERMAN.
NOT EVEN *YOU.*
I CAN FEEL YOUR HEART BEATING. *FASTER* THAN A SPEEDING BULLET.
THE FEAR GROWING IN YOUR STOMACH. MORE POWERFUL THAN ANYTHING I'VE FELT BEFORE.
I CAN SMELL THE *TERROR* BUBBLING UP IN YOUR SOUL.
SO SWEET. SO DELICIOUS...

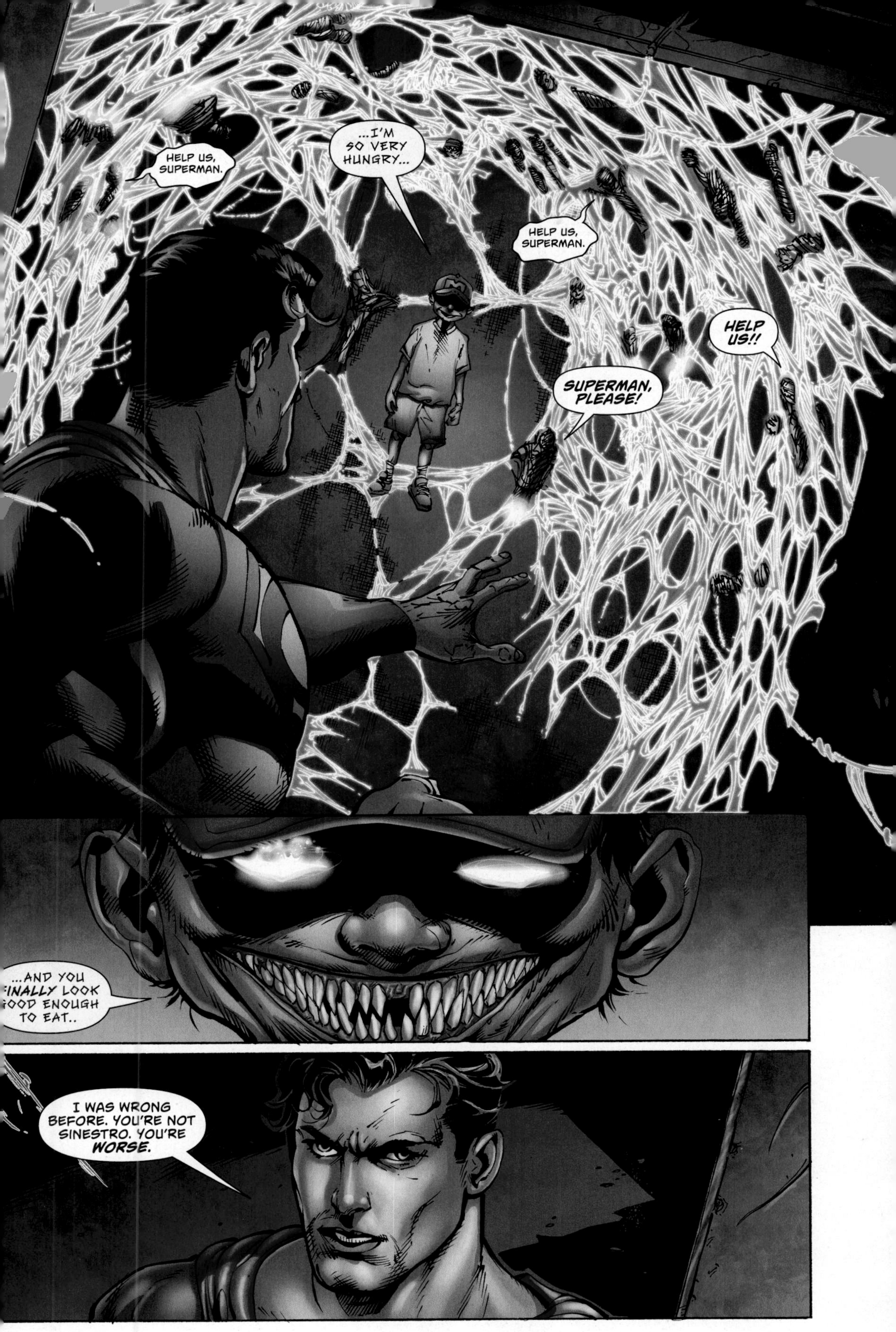
HELP US, SUPERMAN.
...I'M SO VERY HUNGRY...
HELP US, SUPERMAN.
HELP US!!
SUPERMAN, PLEASE!
...AND YOU FINALLY LOOK GOOD ENOUGH TO EAT..
I WAS WRONG BEFORE. YOU'RE NOT SINESTRO. YOU'RE WORSE.

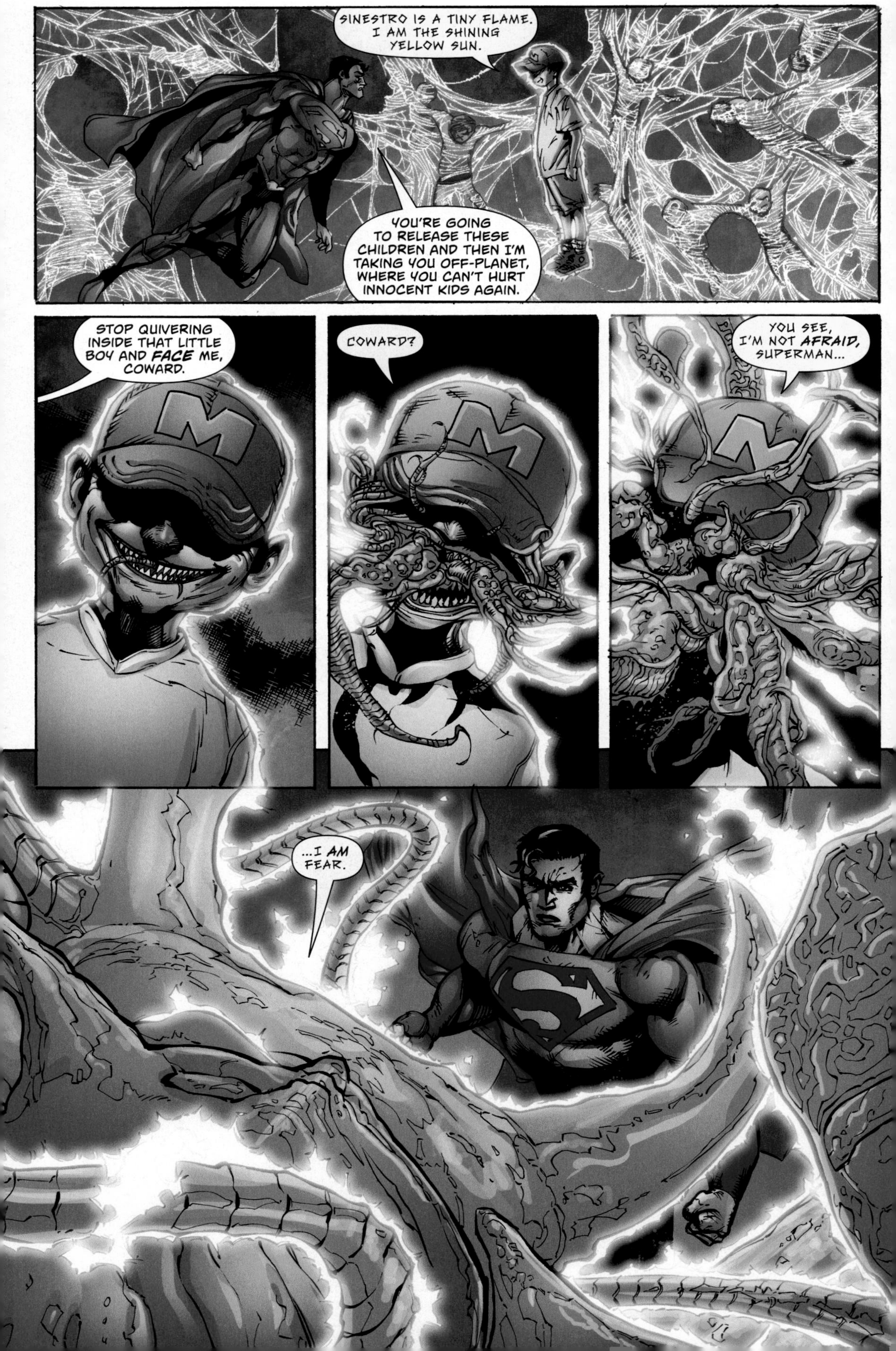
SINESTRO IS A TINY FLAME. I AM THE SHINING YELLOW SUN.
YOU'RE GOING TO RELEASE THESE CHILDREN AND THEN I'M TAKING YOU OFF-PLANET, WHERE YOU CAN'T HURT INNOCENT KIDS AGAIN.
STOP QUIVERING INSIDE THAT LITTLE BOY AND FACE ME, COWARD.
COWARD?
YOU SEE, I'M NOT AFRAID, SUPERMAN...
...I AM FEAR.

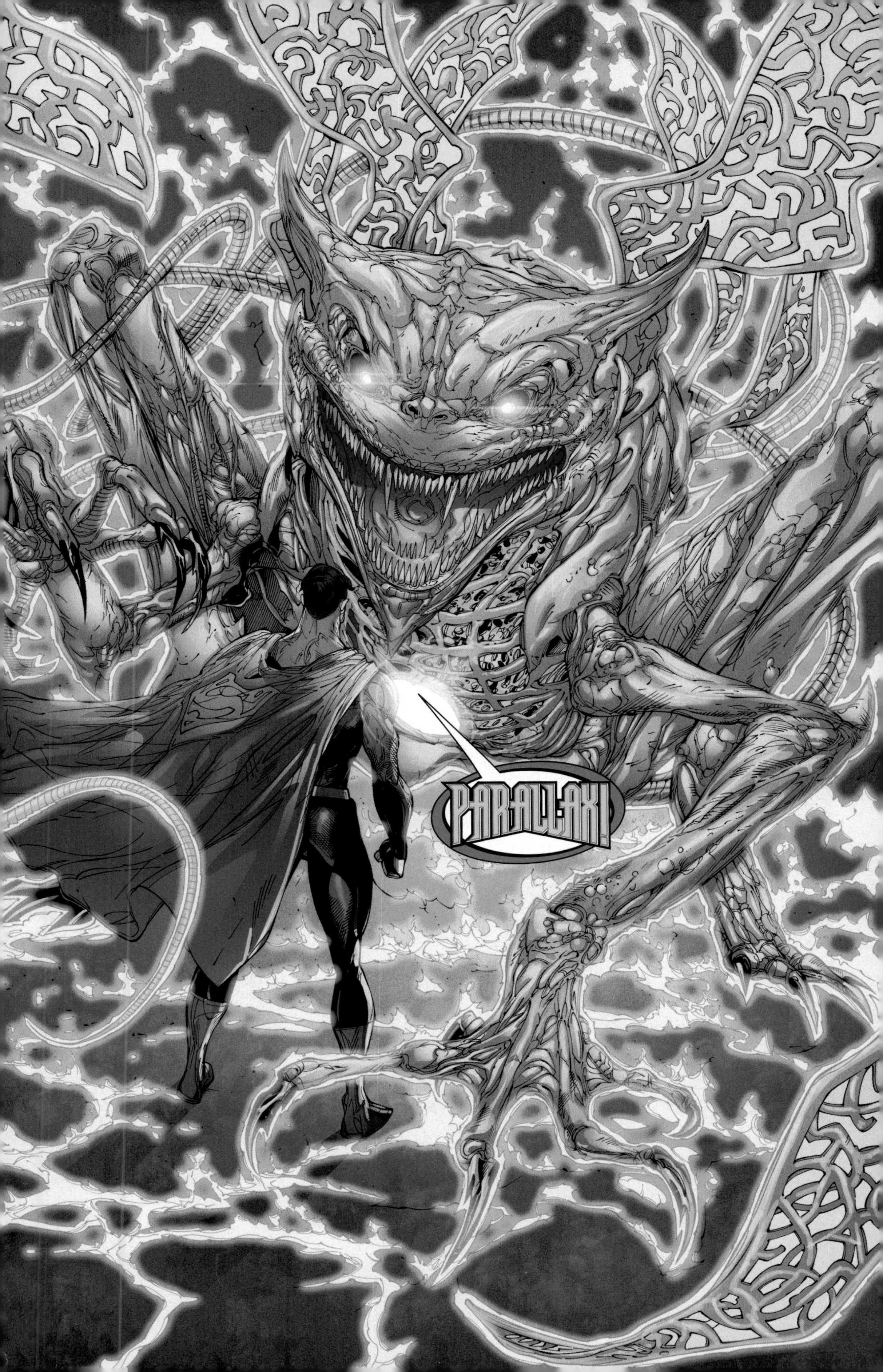
PARALLAX!

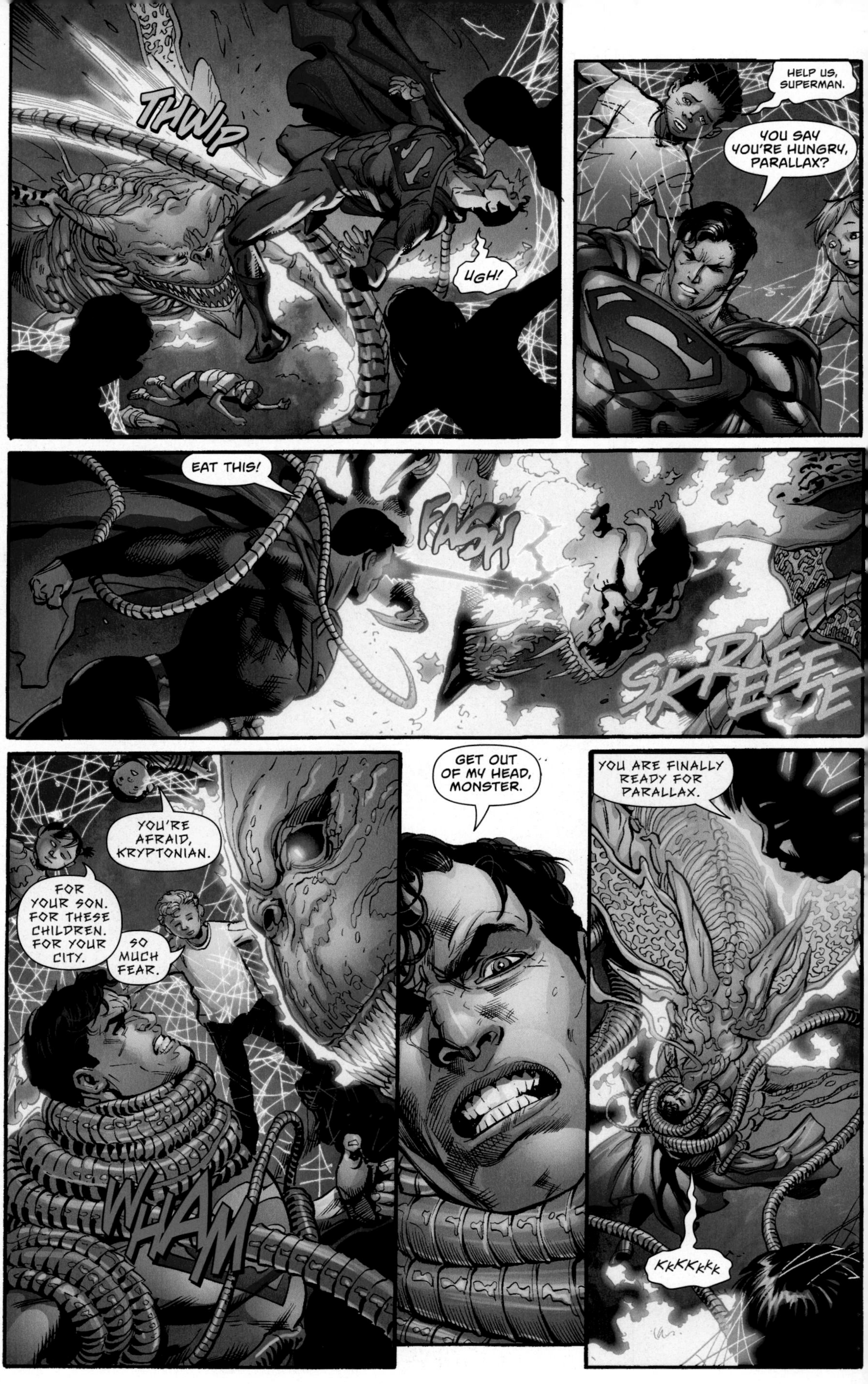
THWIP
UGH!
HELP US, SUPERMAN.
YOU SAY YOU'RE HUNGRY, PARALLAX?
EAT THIS!
FASH
SKREEEE
YOU'RE AFRAID, KRYPTONIAN.
FOR YOUR SON. FOR THESE CHILDREN. FOR YOUR CITY.
SO MUCH FEAR.
WHAM
GET OUT OF MY HEAD, MONSTER.
YOU ARE FINALLY READY FOR PARALLAX.
KKKKKKK

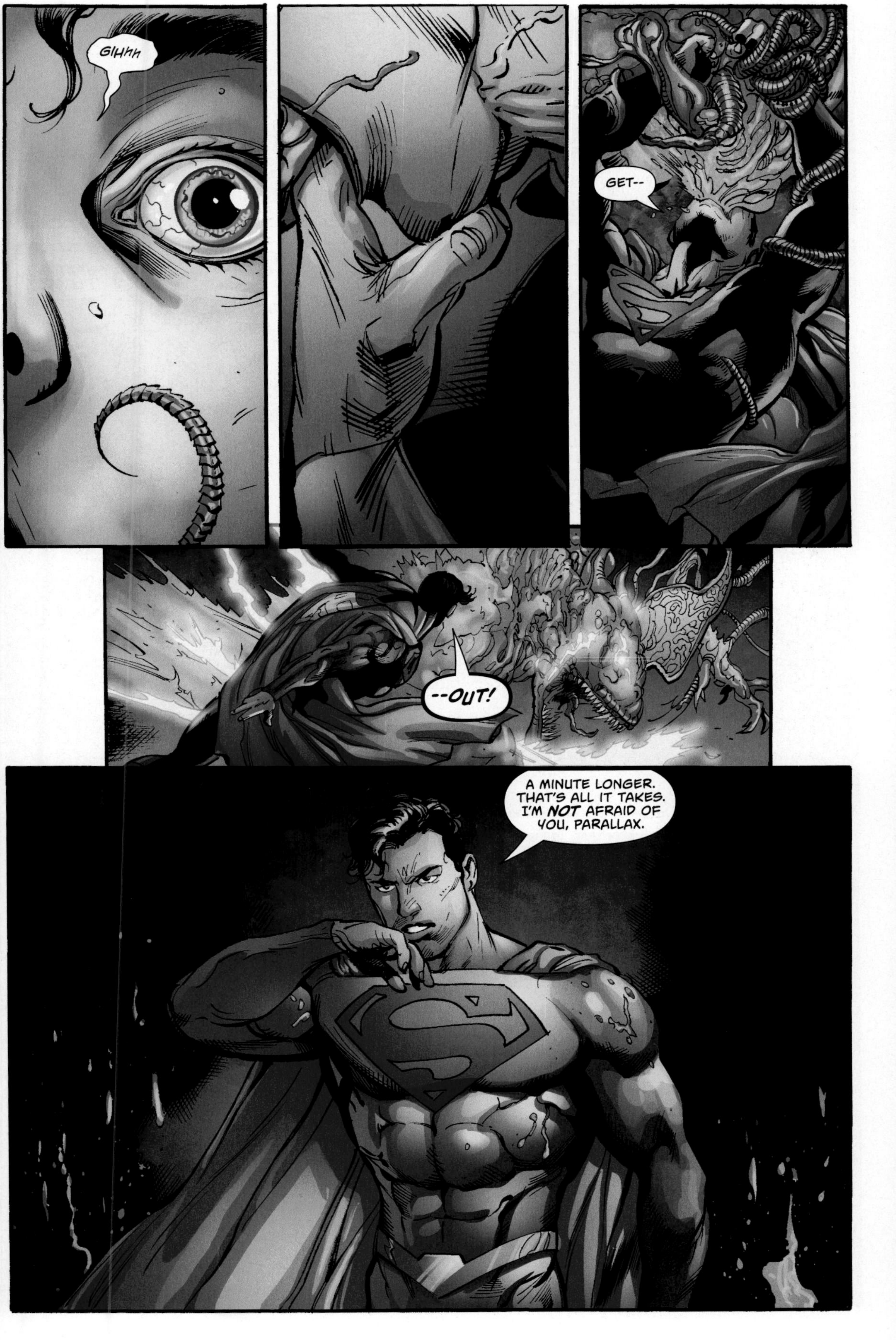
GIHHH
GET--
--OUT!
A MINUTE LONGER. THAT'S ALL IT TAKES. I'M NOT AFRAID OF YOU, PARALLAX.

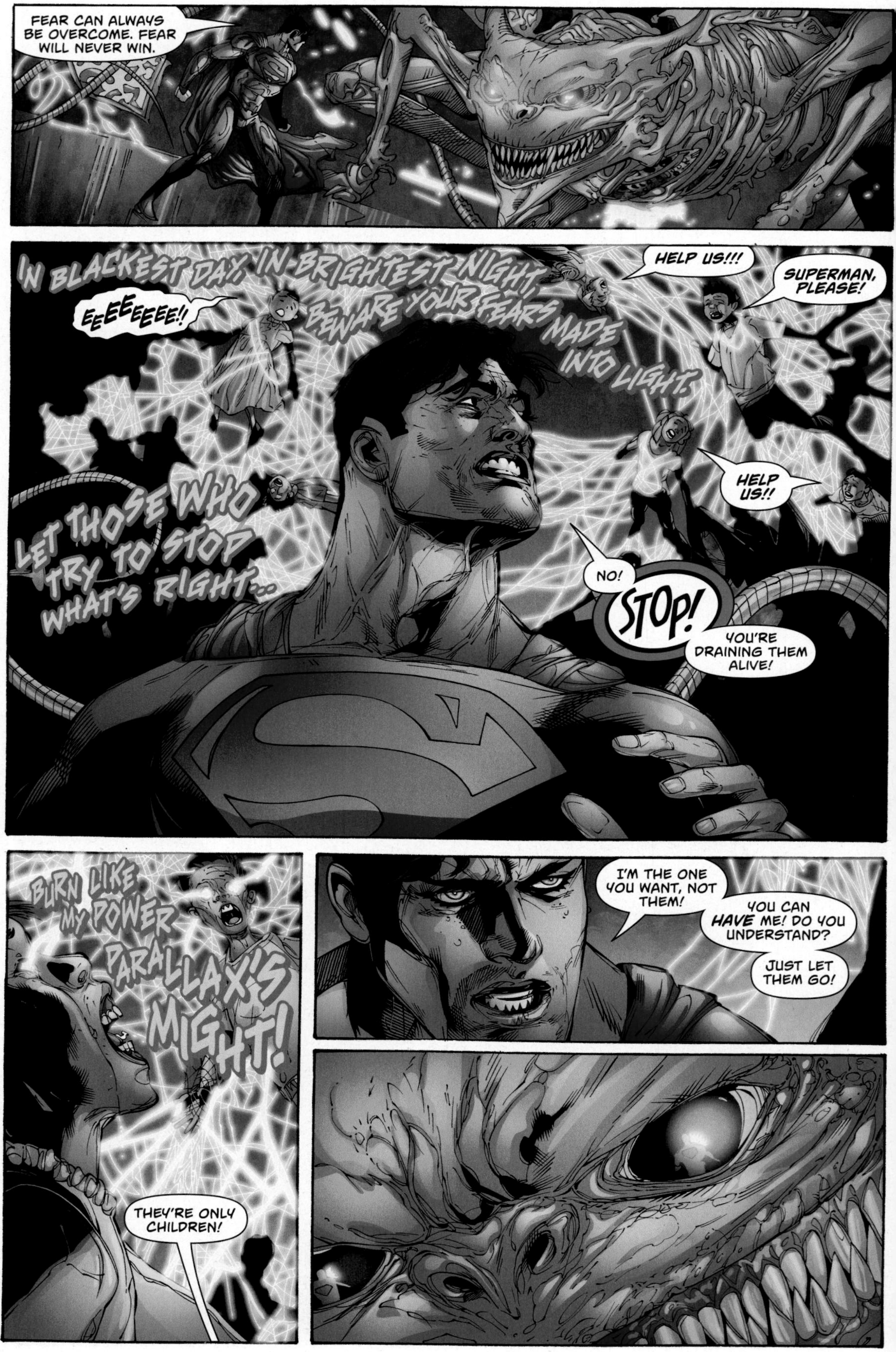
FEAR CAN ALWAYS BE OVERCOME. FEAR WILL NEVER WIN.
IN BLACKEST DAY, IN BRIGHTEST NIGHT,
EEEEEEEE!!
BEWARE YOUR FEARS MADE INTO LIGHT.
HELP US!!!
SUPERMAN, PLEASE!
LET THOSE WHO TRY TO STOP WHAT'S RIGHT...
HELP US!!
NO!
STOP!
YOU'RE DRAINING THEM ALIVE!
BURN LIKE MY POWER PARALLAX'S MIGHT!
THEY'RE ONLY CHILDREN!
I'M THE ONE YOU WANT, NOT THEM!
YOU CAN HAVE ME! DO YOU UNDERSTAND?
JUST LET THEM GO!

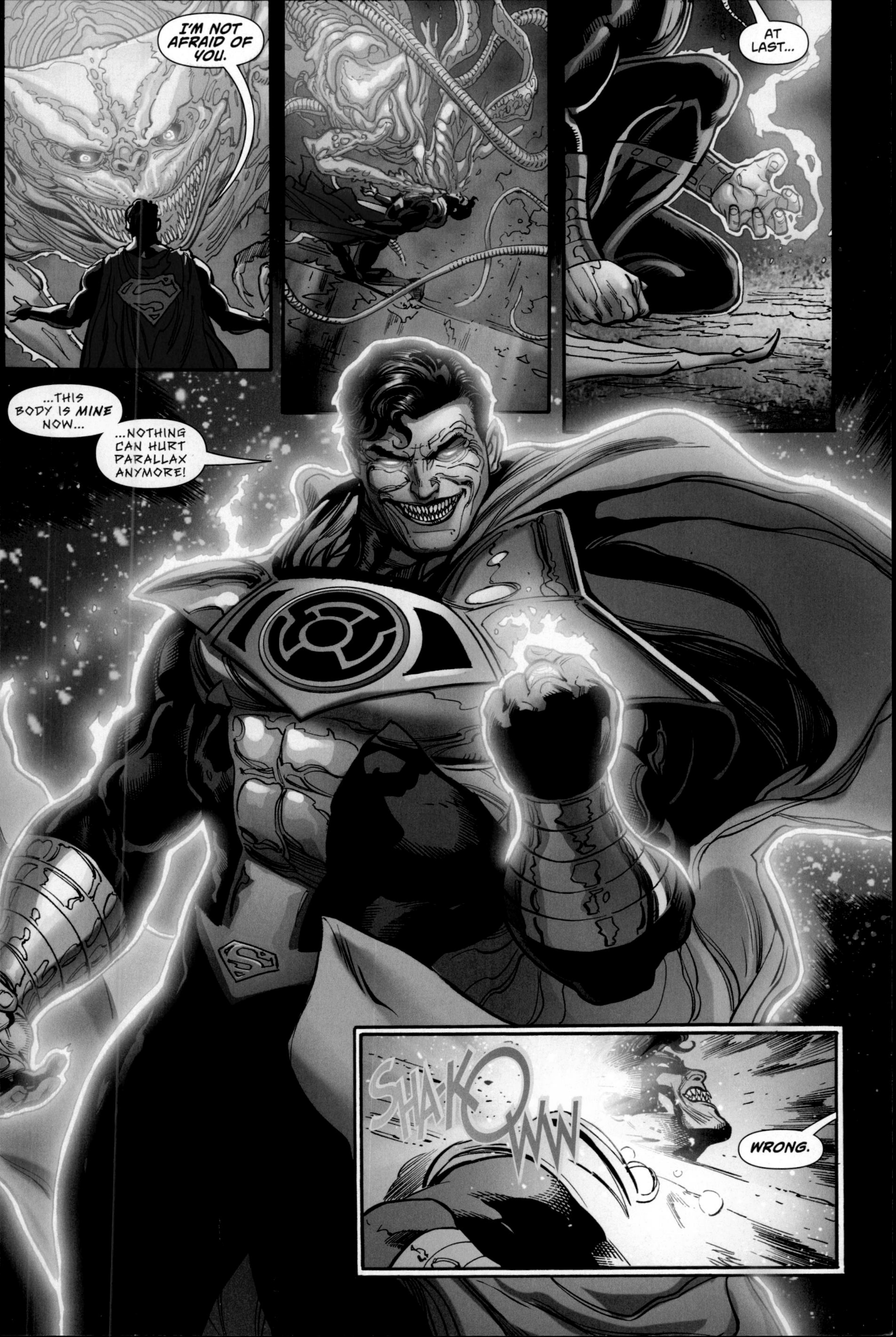
I'M NOT AFRAID OF YOU.
AT LAST...
...THIS BODY IS MINE NOW...
...NOTHING CAN HURT PARALLAX ANYMORE!
SHA-KOWWW
WRONG.

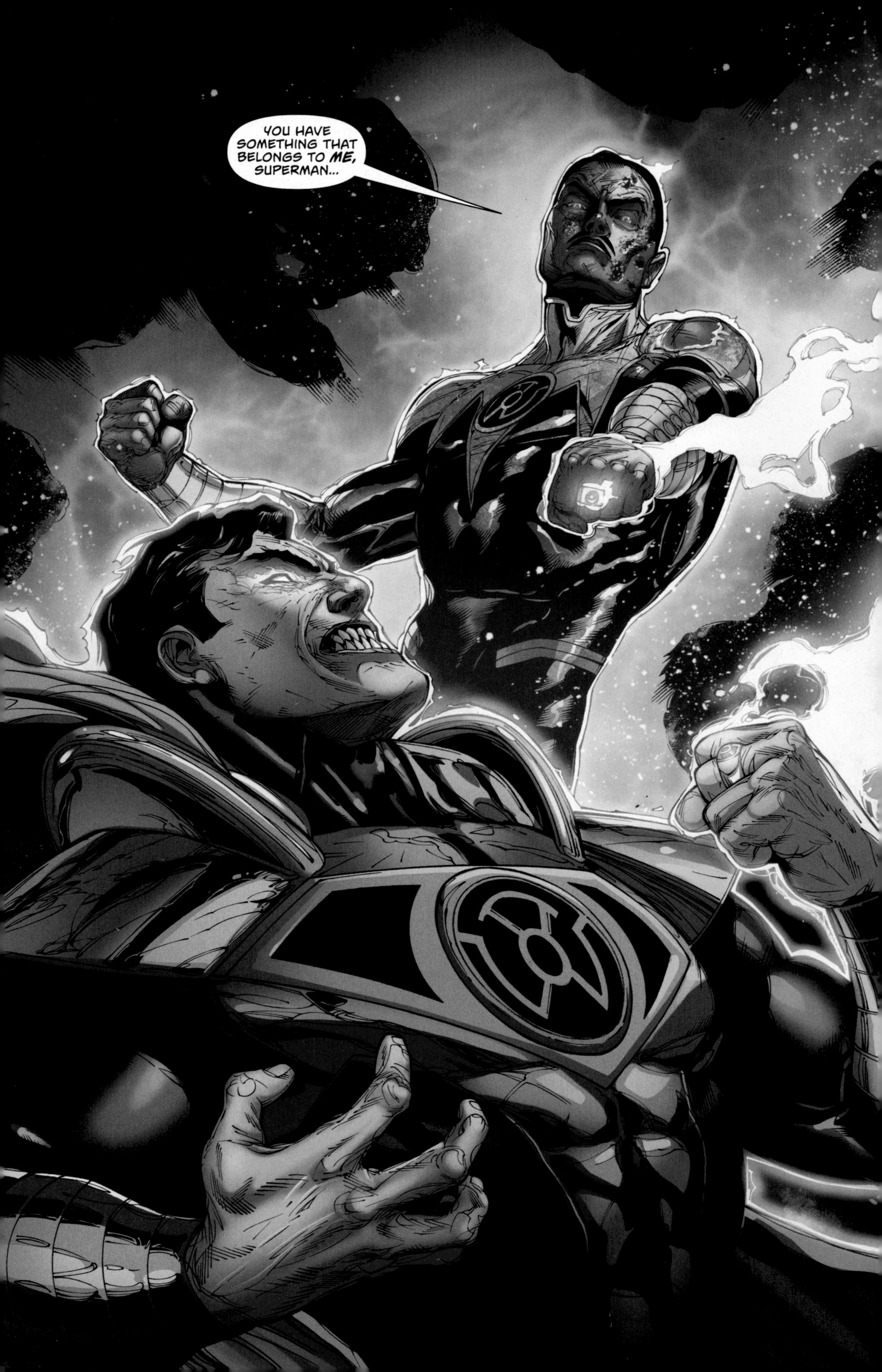
YOU HAVE SOMETHING THAT BELONGS TO ME, SUPERMAN...

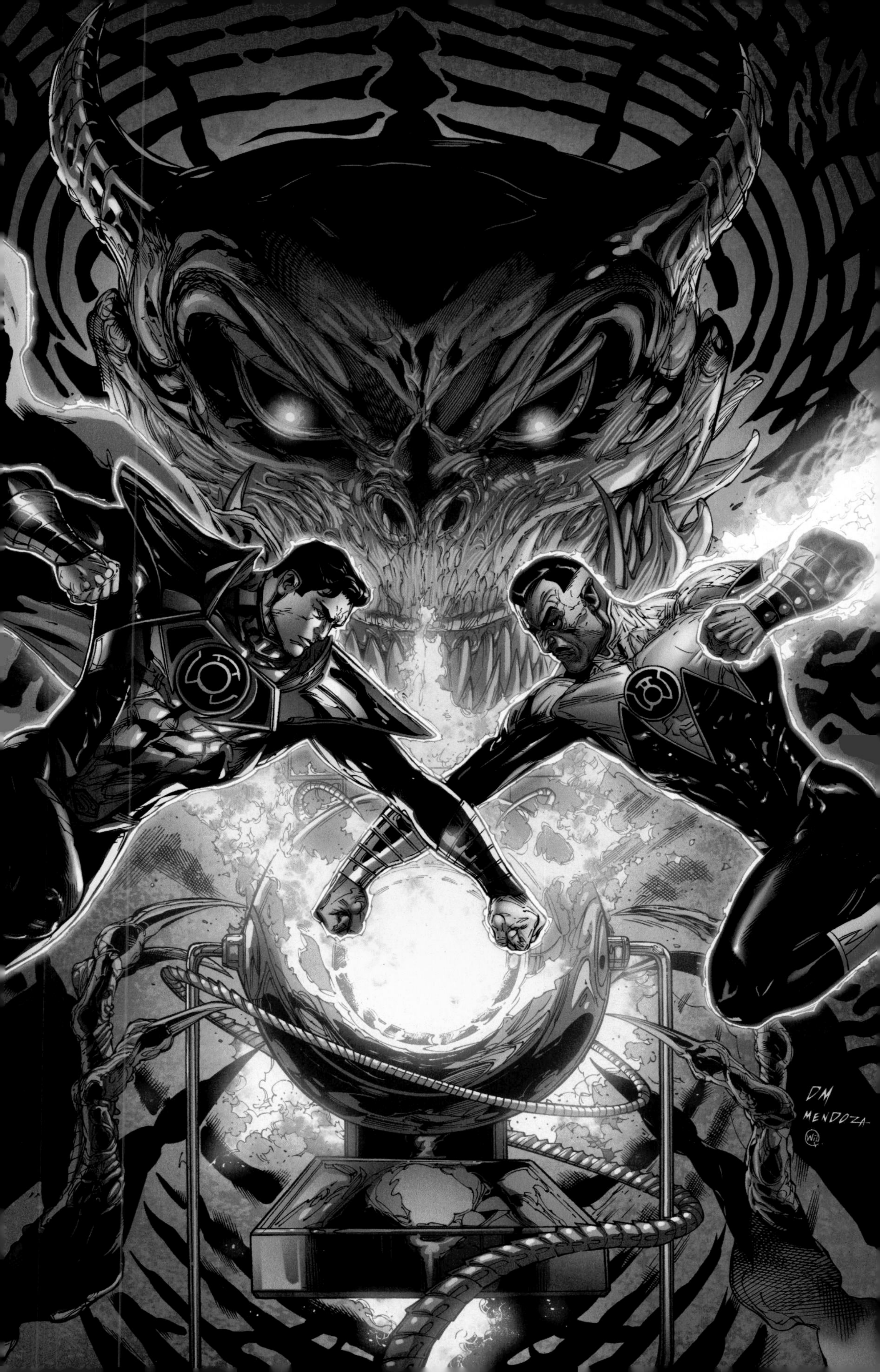
DM
MENDOZA

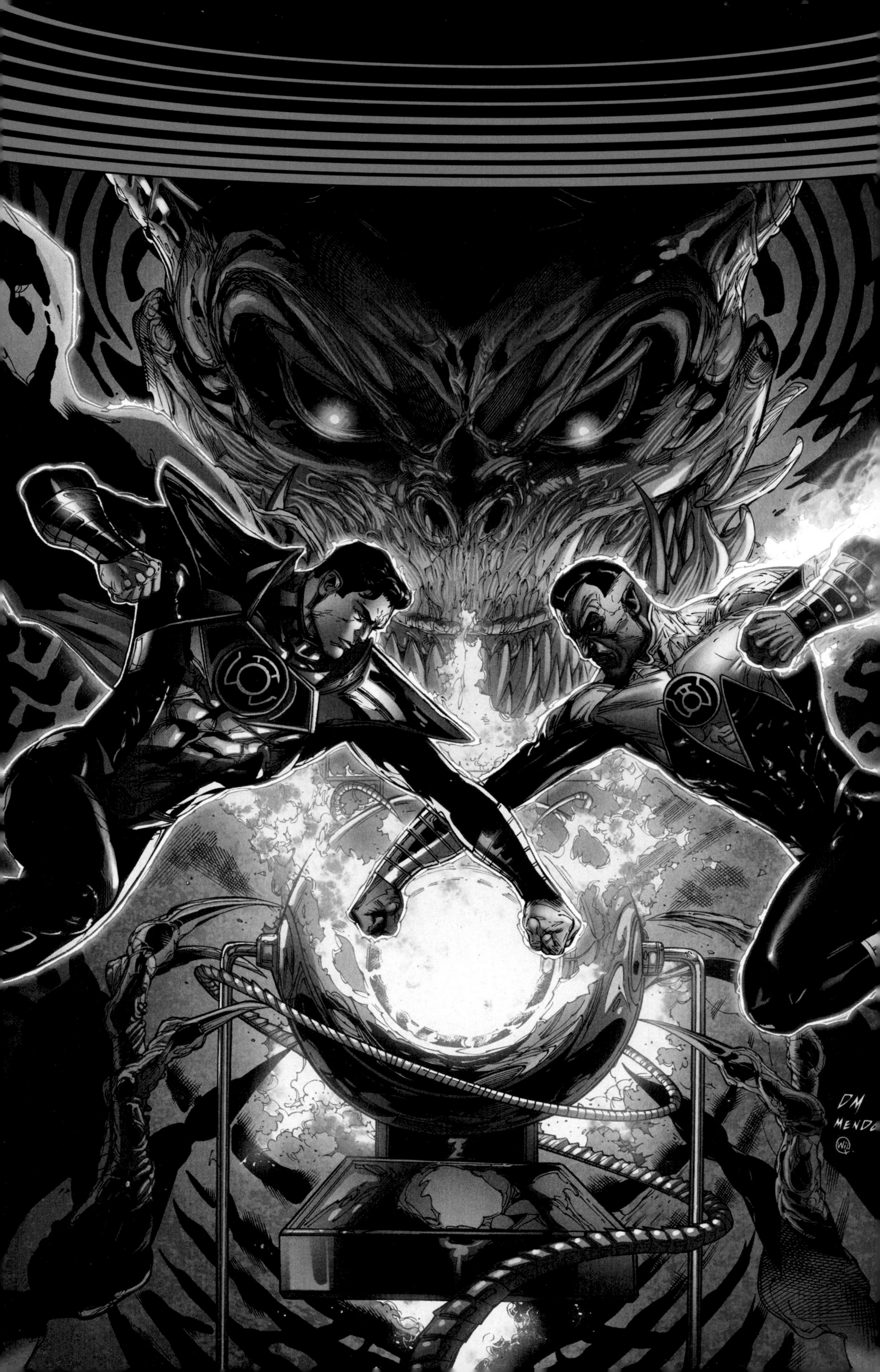

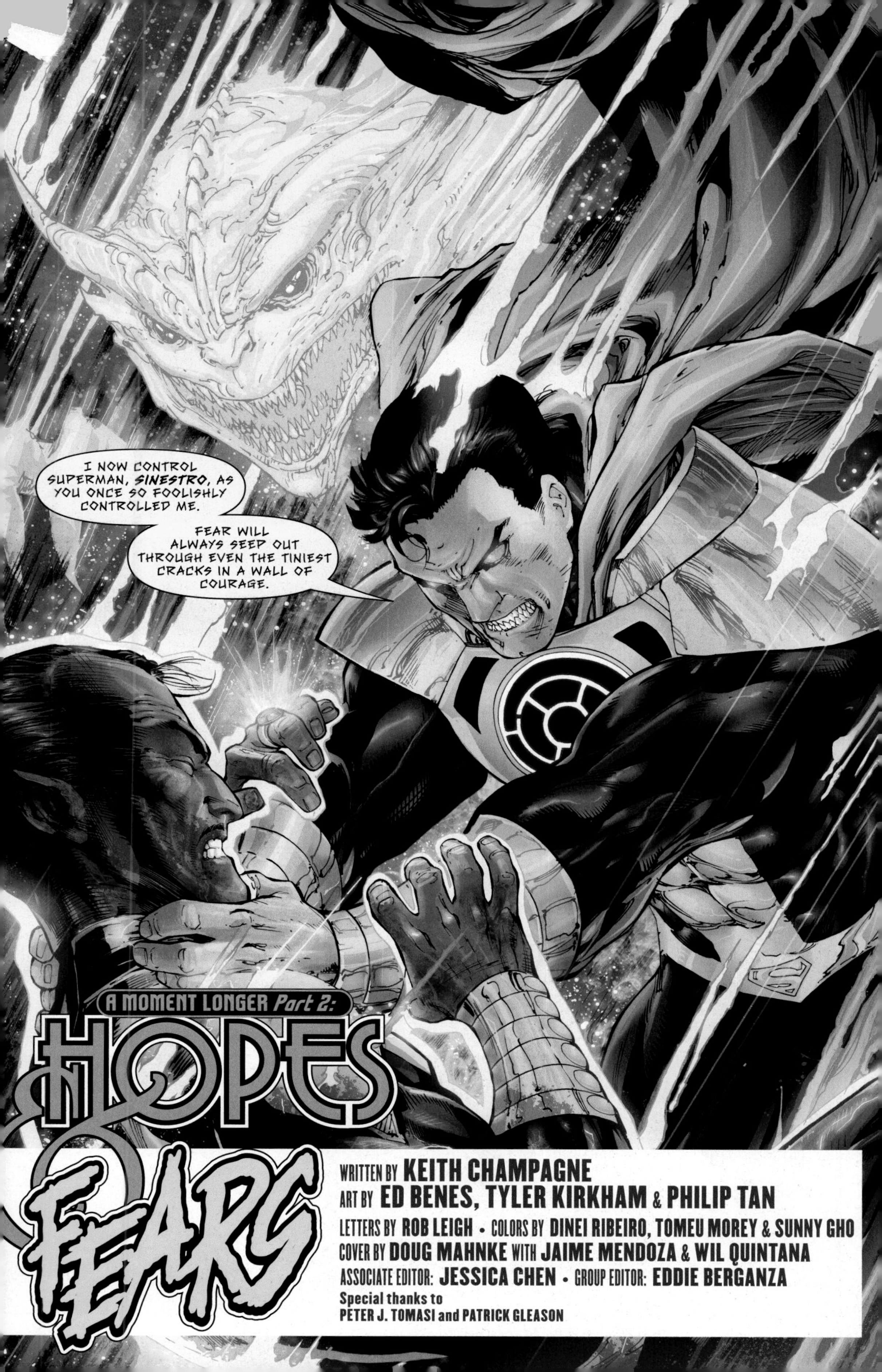
I NOW CONTROL SUPERMAN, SINESTRO, AS YOU ONCE SO FOOLISHLY CONTROLLED ME.
FEAR WILL ALWAYS SEEP OUT THROUGH EVEN THE TINIEST CRACKS IN A WALL OF COURAGE.
A MOMENT LONGER Part 2:
HOPES & FEARS
WRITTEN BY KEITH CHAMPAGNE
ART BY ED BENES, TYLER KIRKHAM & PHILIP TAN
LETTERS BY ROB LEIGH • COLORS BY DINEI RIBEIRO, TOMEU MOREY & SUNNY GHO
COVER BY DOUG MAHNKE WITH JAIME MENDOZA & WIL QUINTANA
ASSOCIATE EDITOR: JESSICA CHEN • GROUP EDITOR: EDDIE BERGANZA
Special thanks to
PETER J. TOMASI and PATRICK GLEASON

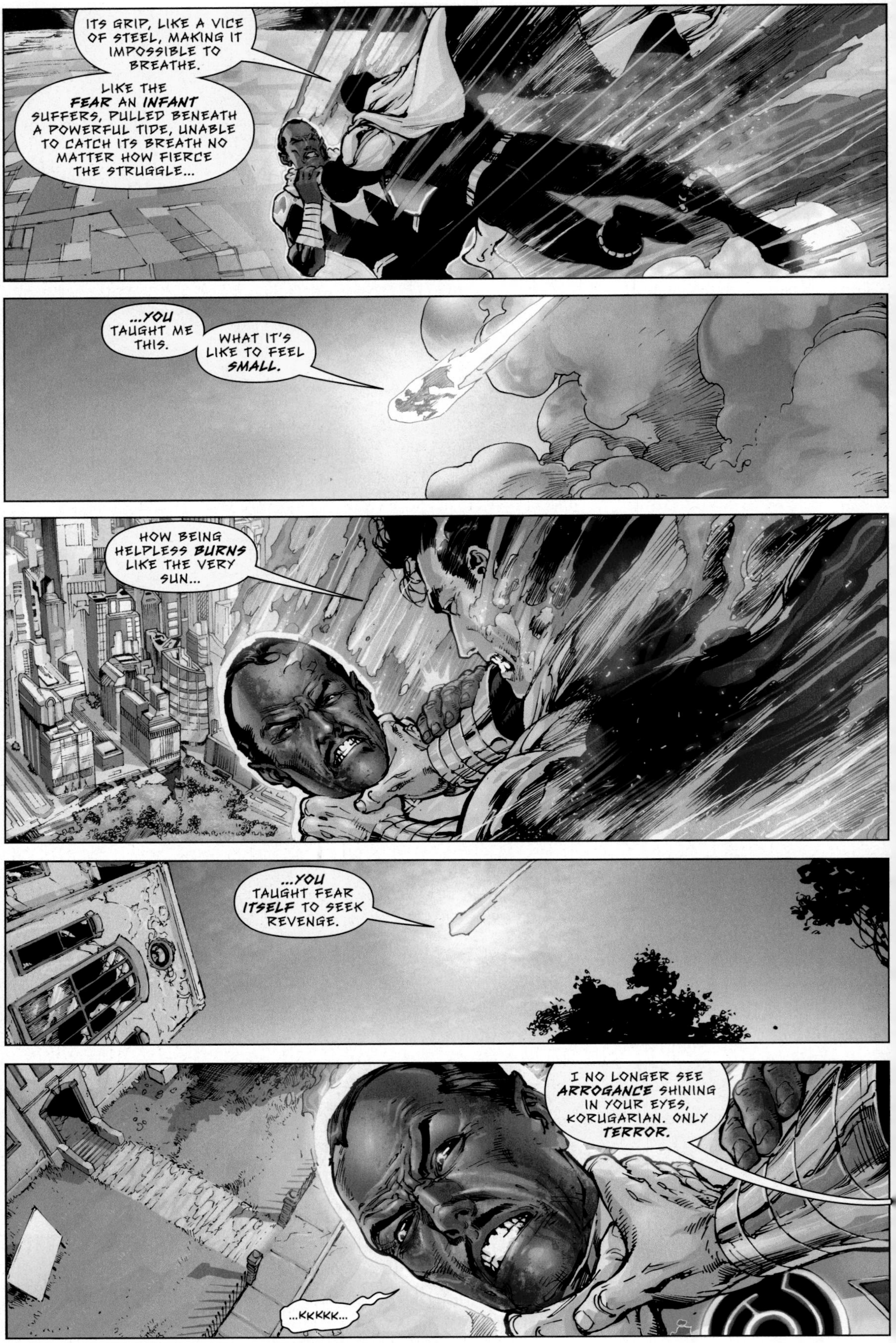

ITS GRIP, LIKE A VICE OF STEEL, MAKING IT IMPOSSIBLE TO BREATHE.
LIKE THE **FEAR** AN **INFANT** SUFFERS, PULLED BENEATH A POWERFUL TIDE, UNABLE TO CATCH ITS BREATH NO MATTER HOW FIERCE THE STRUGGLE...
...**YOU** TAUGHT ME THIS.
WHAT IT'S LIKE TO FEEL **SMALL.**
HOW BEING HELPLESS **BURNS** LIKE THE VERY SUN...
...**YOU** TAUGHT FEAR **ITSELF** TO SEEK REVENGE.
I NO LONGER SEE **ARROGANCE** SHINING IN YOUR EYES, KORUGARIAN. ONLY **TERROR.**
...KKKKK...

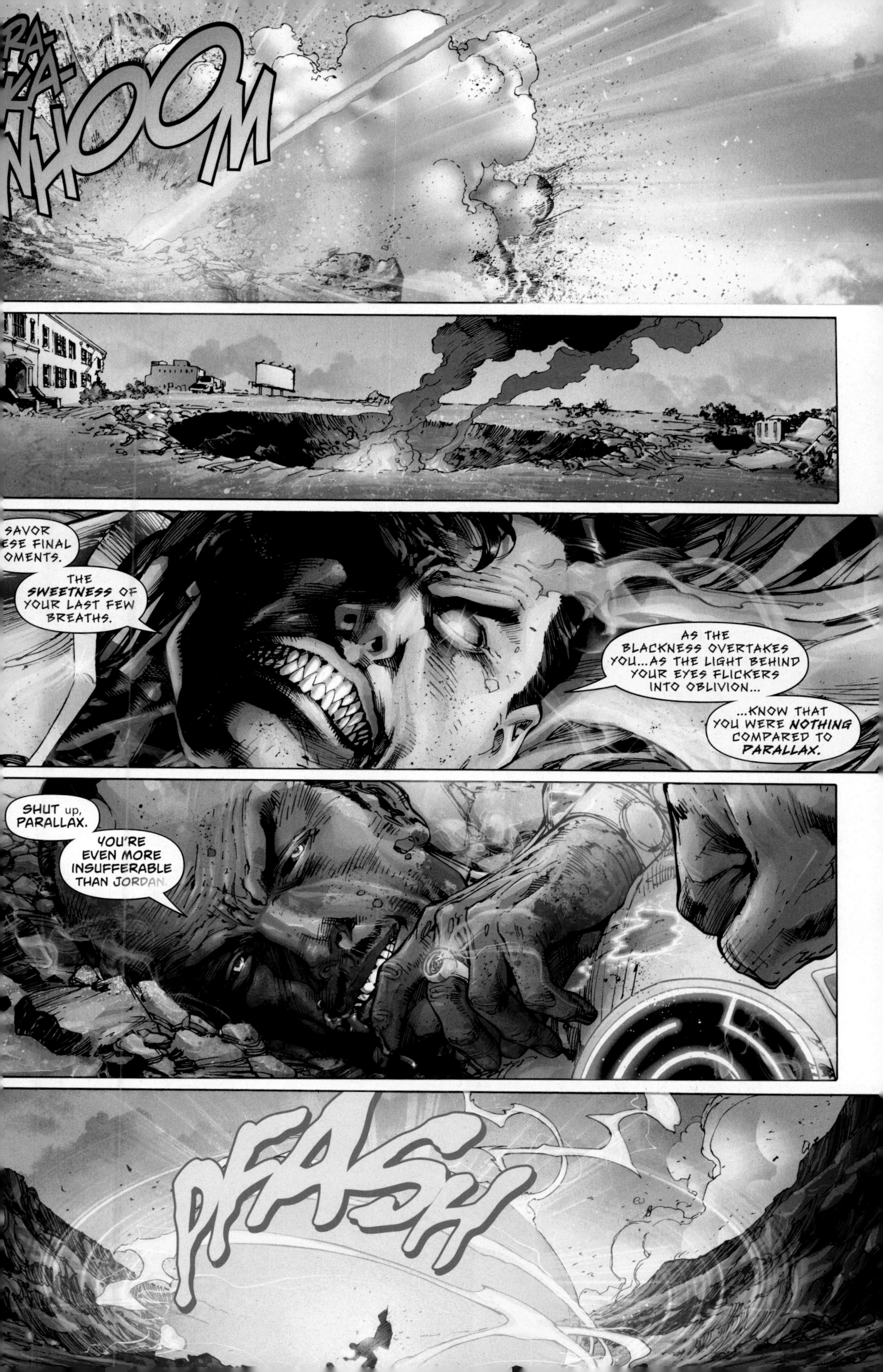

RA-KA-NHOOM
SAVOR ESE FINAL OMENTS.
THE SWEETNESS OF YOUR LAST FEW BREATHS.
AS THE BLACKNESS OVERTAKES YOU...AS THE LIGHT BEHIND YOUR EYES FLICKERS INTO OBLIVION...
...KNOW THAT YOU WERE NOTHING COMPARED TO PARALLAX.
SHUT up, PARALLAX.
YOU'RE EVEN MORE INSUFFERABLE THAN JORDAN.

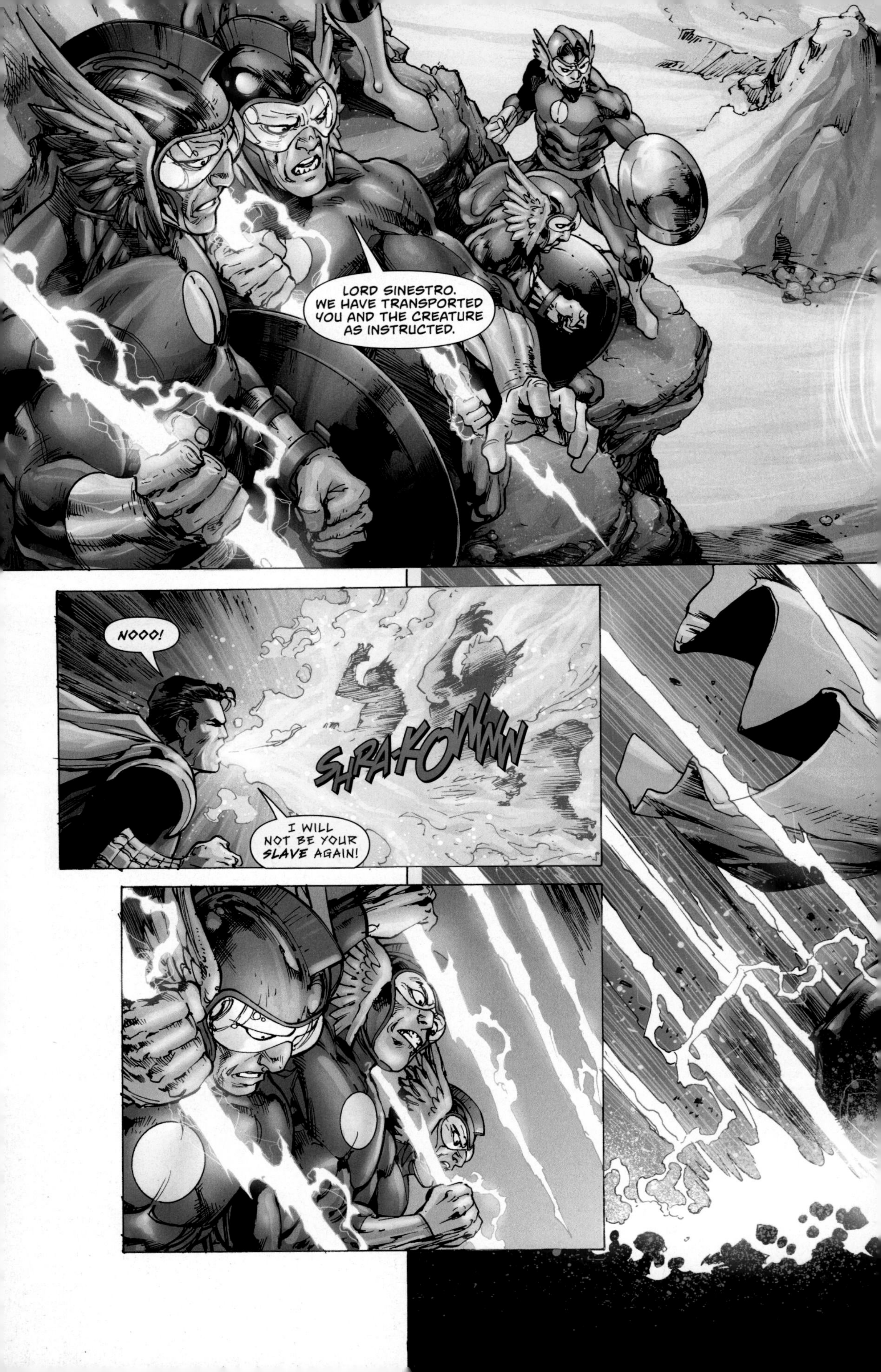
LORD SINESTRO. WE HAVE TRANSPORTED YOU AND THE CREATURE AS INSTRUCTED.
NOOO!
SHRAKOWWW
I WILL NOT BE YOUR SLAVE AGAIN!

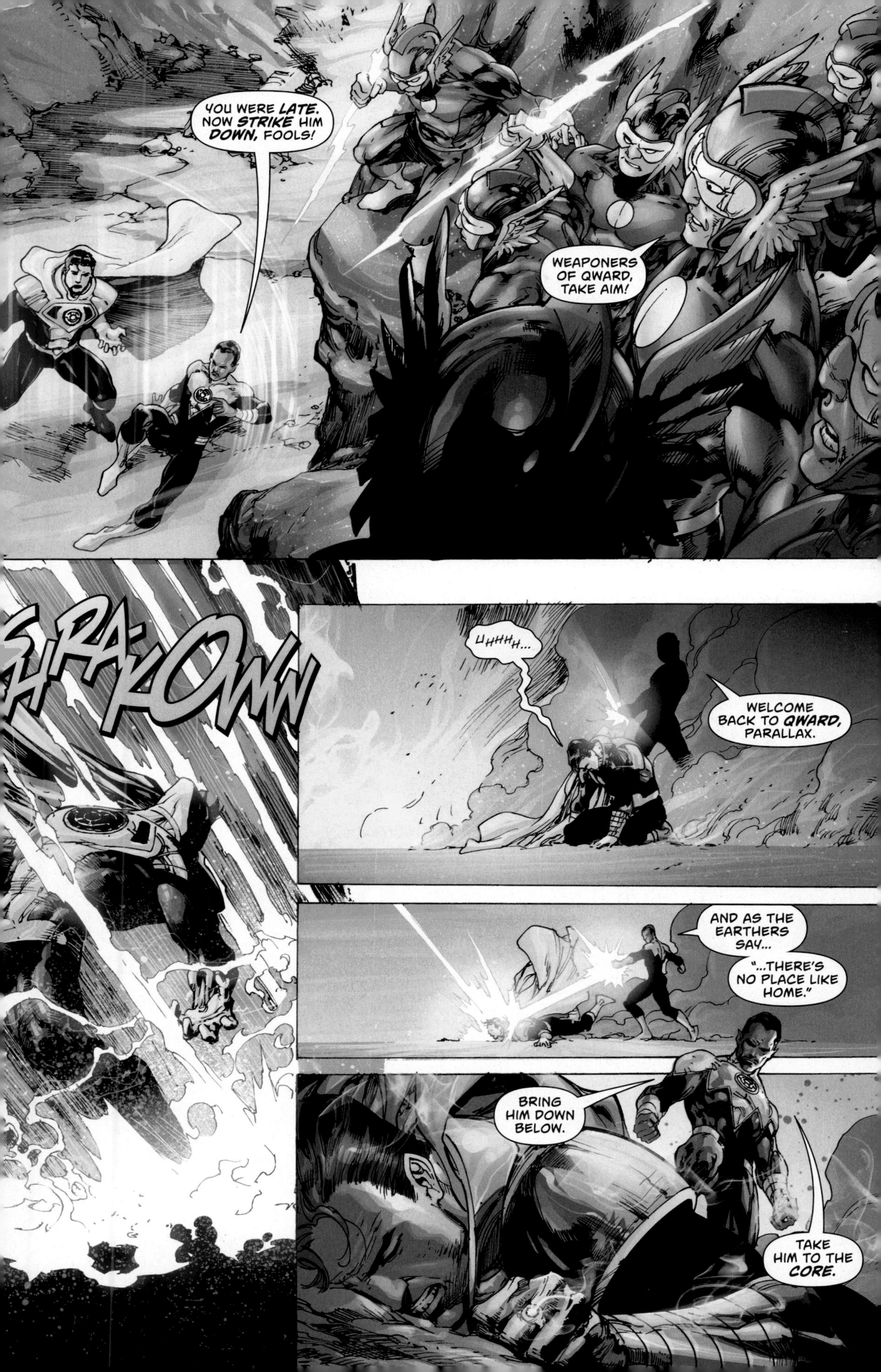
YOU WERE LATE. NOW STRIKE HIM DOWN, FOOLS!
WEAPONERS OF QWARD, TAKE AIM!
SHRA-KOWN
UHHHH...
WELCOME BACK TO QWARD, PARALLAX.
AND AS THE EARTHERS SAY...
"...THERE'S NO PLACE LIKE HOME."
BRING HIM DOWN BELOW.
TAKE HIM TO THE CORE.

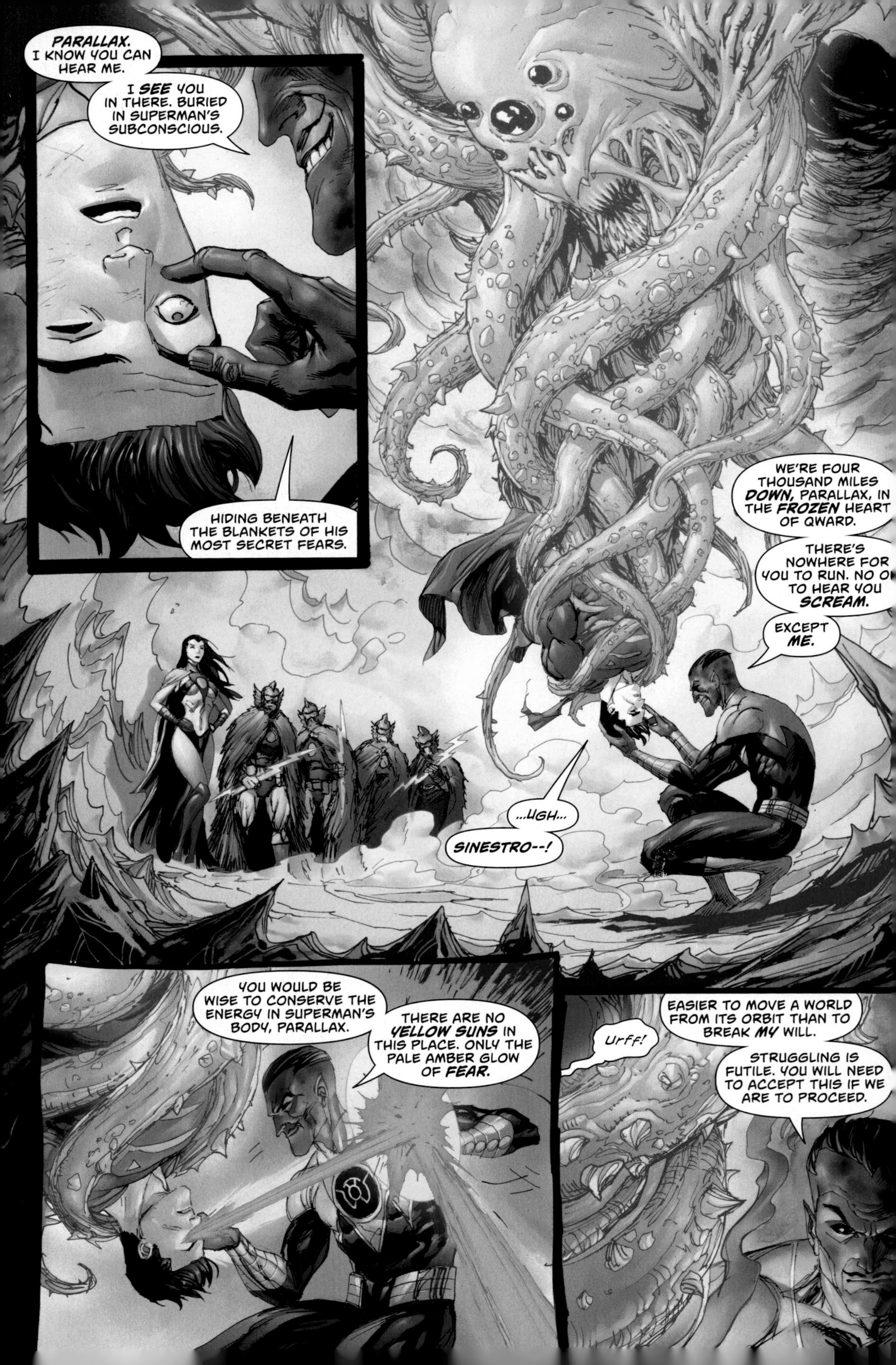
PARALLAX. I KNOW YOU CAN HEAR ME.
I SEE YOU IN THERE. BURIED IN SUPERMAN'S SUBCONSCIOUS.
HIDING BENEATH THE BLANKETS OF HIS MOST SECRET FEARS.
WE'RE FOUR THOUSAND MILES DOWN, PARALLAX, IN THE FROZEN HEART OF QWARD.
THERE'S NOWHERE FOR YOU TO RUN. NO O
TO HEAR YOU SCREAM.
EXCEPT ME.
...UGH...
SINESTRO--!
YOU WOULD BE WISE TO CONSERVE THE ENERGY IN SUPERMAN'S BODY, PARALLAX.
THERE ARE NO YELLOW SUNS IN THIS PLACE. ONLY THE PALE AMBER GLOW OF FEAR.
Urff!
EASIER TO MOVE A WORLD FROM ITS ORBIT THAN TO BREAK MY WILL.
STRUGGLING IS FUTILE. YOU WILL NEED TO ACCEPT THIS IF WE ARE TO PROCEED.

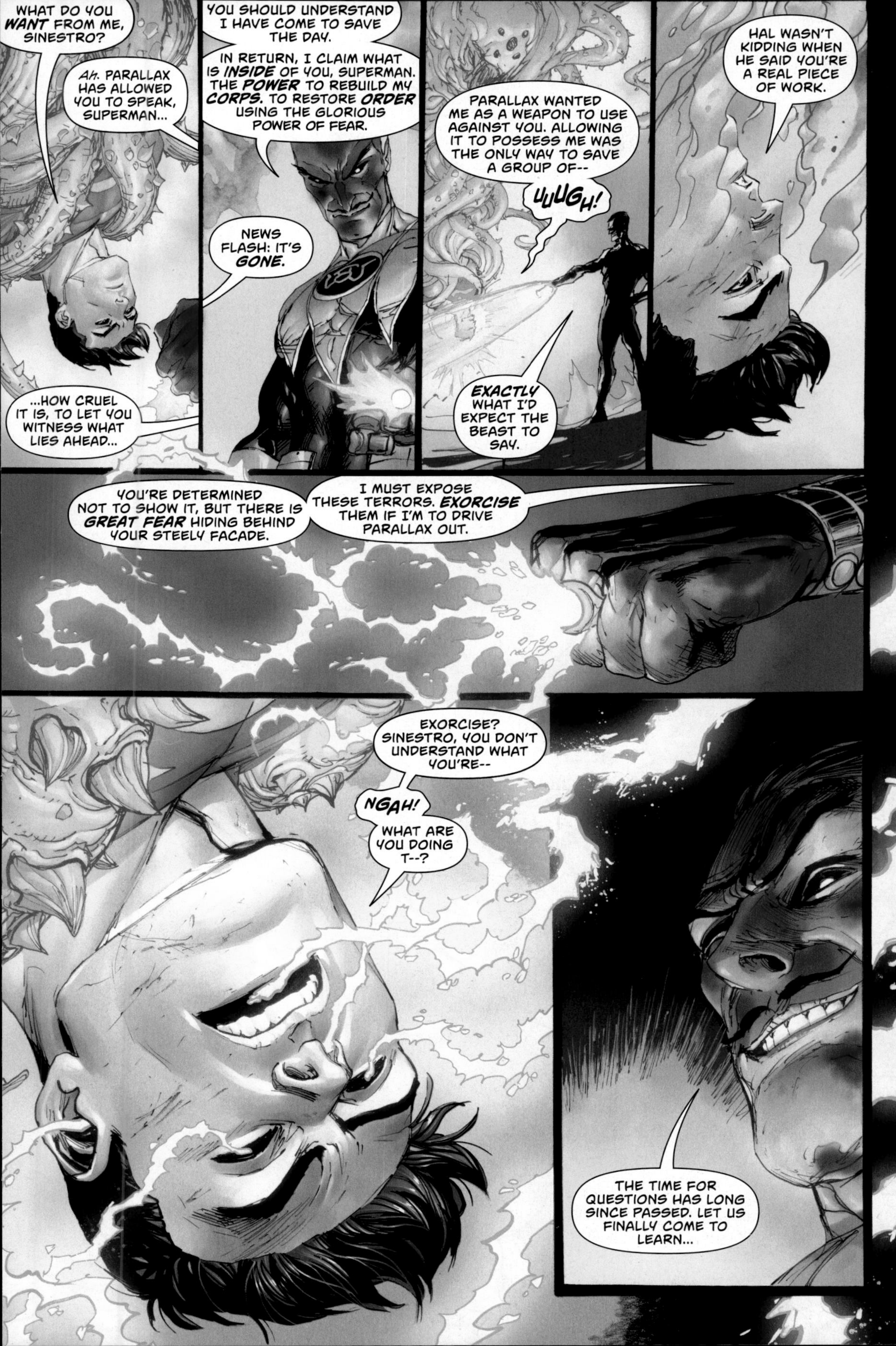
WHAT DO YOU *WANT* FROM ME, SINESTRO?
AH. PARALLAX HAS ALLOWED YOU TO SPEAK, SUPERMAN...
...HOW CRUEL IT IS, TO LET YOU WITNESS WHAT LIES AHEAD...
YOU SHOULD UNDERSTAND I HAVE COME TO SAVE THE DAY.
IN RETURN, I CLAIM WHAT IS *INSIDE* OF YOU, SUPERMAN. THE *POWER* TO REBUILD MY *CORPS.* TO RESTORE *ORDER* USING THE GLORIOUS POWER OF FEAR.
NEWS FLASH: IT'S *GONE.*
PARALLAX WANTED ME AS A WEAPON TO USE AGAINST YOU. ALLOWING IT TO POSSESS ME WAS THE ONLY WAY TO SAVE A GROUP OF--
UUUGH!
EXACTLY WHAT I'D EXPECT THE BEAST TO SAY.
HAL WASN'T KIDDING WHEN HE SAID YOU'RE A REAL PIECE OF WORK.
YOU'RE DETERMINED NOT TO SHOW IT, BUT THERE IS *GREAT FEAR* HIDING BEHIND YOUR STEELY FACADE.
I MUST EXPOSE THESE TERRORS. *EXORCISE* THEM IF I'M TO DRIVE PARALLAX OUT.
EXORCISE? SINESTRO, YOU DON'T UNDERSTAND WHAT YOU'RE--
NGAH!
WHAT ARE YOU DOING T--?
THE TIME FOR QUESTIONS HAS LONG SINCE PASSED. LET US FINALLY COME TO LEARN...

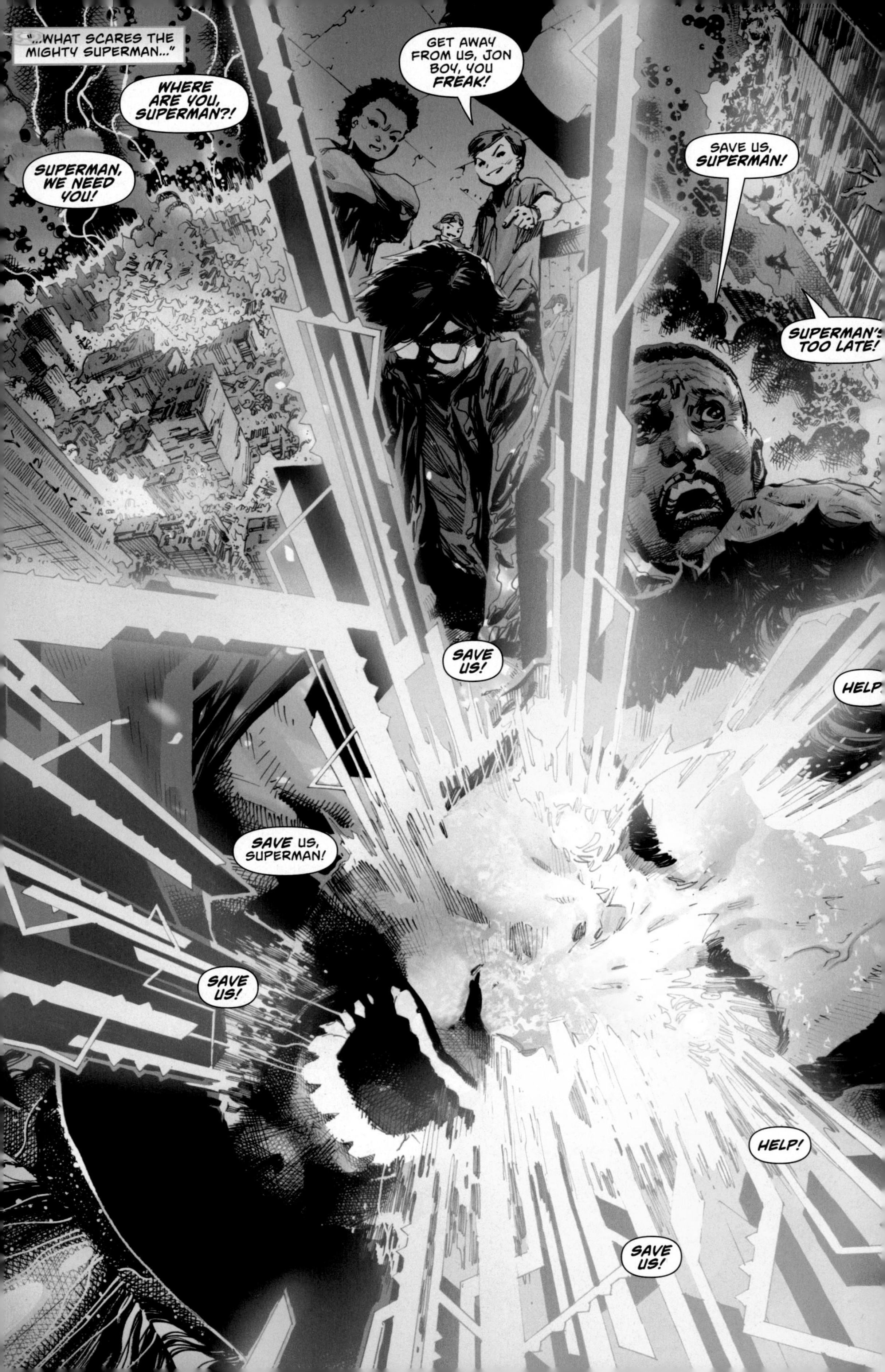
"...WHAT SCARES THE MIGHTY SUPERMAN..."
WHERE ARE YOU, SUPERMAN?!
SUPERMAN, WE NEED YOU!
GET AWAY FROM US, JON BOY, YOU FREAK!
SAVE US, SUPERMAN!
SUPERMAN'S TOO LATE!
SAVE US!
HELP!
SAVE US, SUPERMAN!
SAVE US!
HELP!
SAVE US!

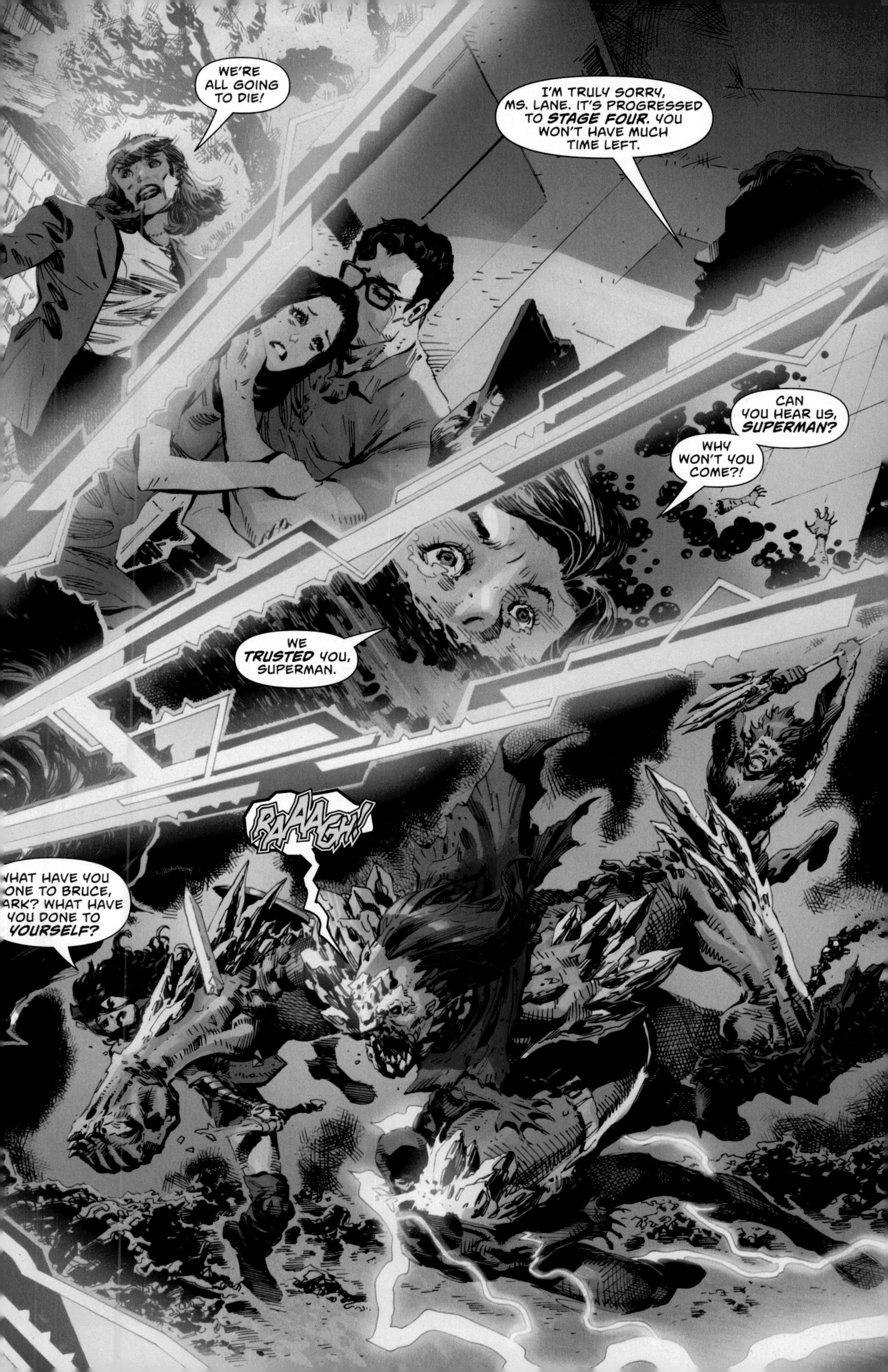
WE'RE ALL GOING TO DIE!
I'M TRULY SORRY, MS. LANE. IT'S PROGRESSED TO STAGE FOUR. YOU WON'T HAVE MUCH TIME LEFT.
CAN YOU HEAR US, SUPERMAN?
WHY WON'T YOU COME?!
WE TRUSTED YOU, SUPERMAN.
RAAAGH!
WHAT HAVE YOU DONE TO BRUCE, ARK? WHAT HAVE YOU DONE TO YOURSELF?

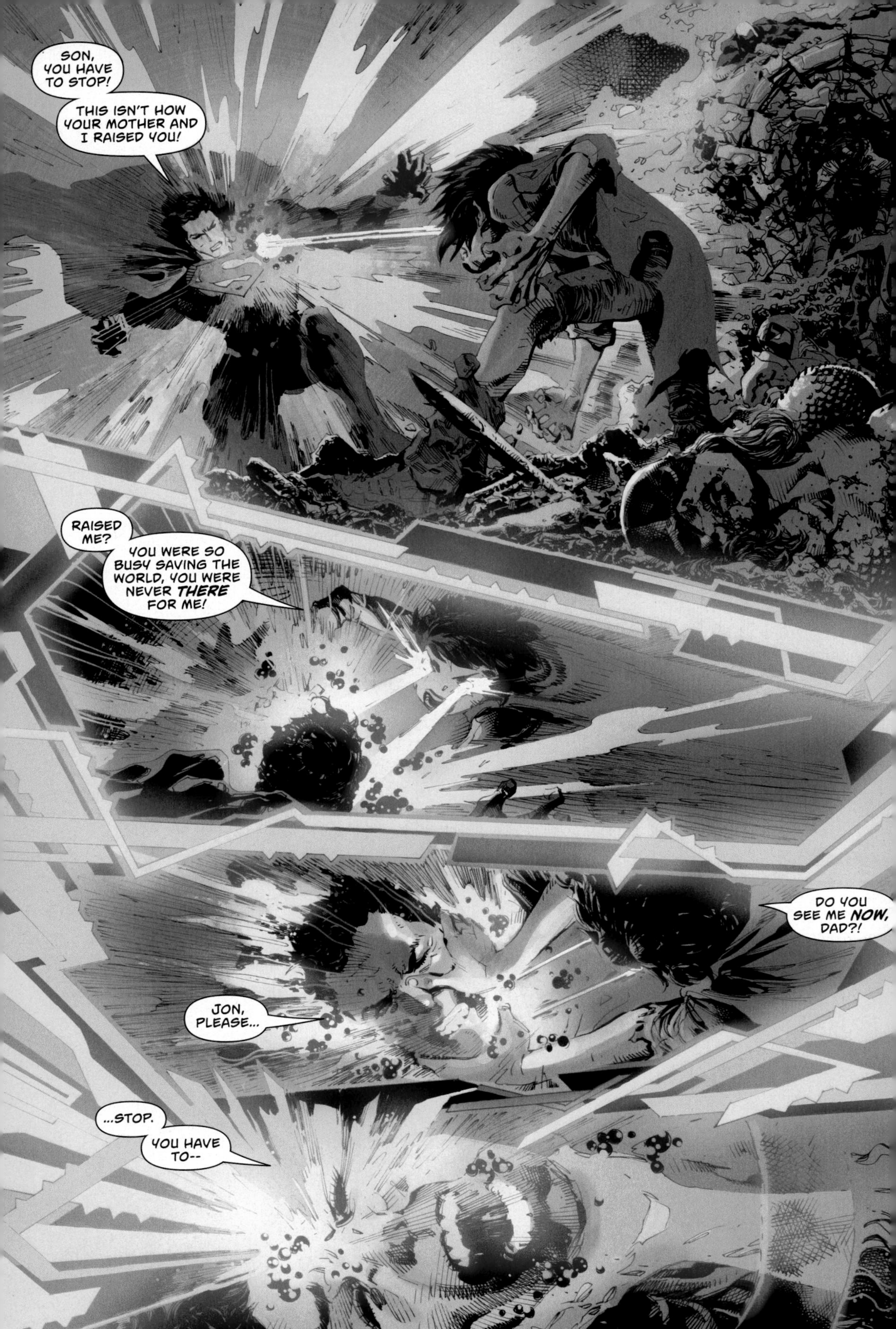
SON, YOU HAVE TO STOP!
THIS ISN'T HOW YOUR MOTHER AND I RAISED YOU!
RAISED ME?
YOU WERE SO BUSY SAVING THE WORLD, YOU WERE NEVER **THERE** FOR ME!
DO YOU SEE ME **NOW,** DAD?!
JON, PLEASE...
...STOP.
YOU HAVE TO--

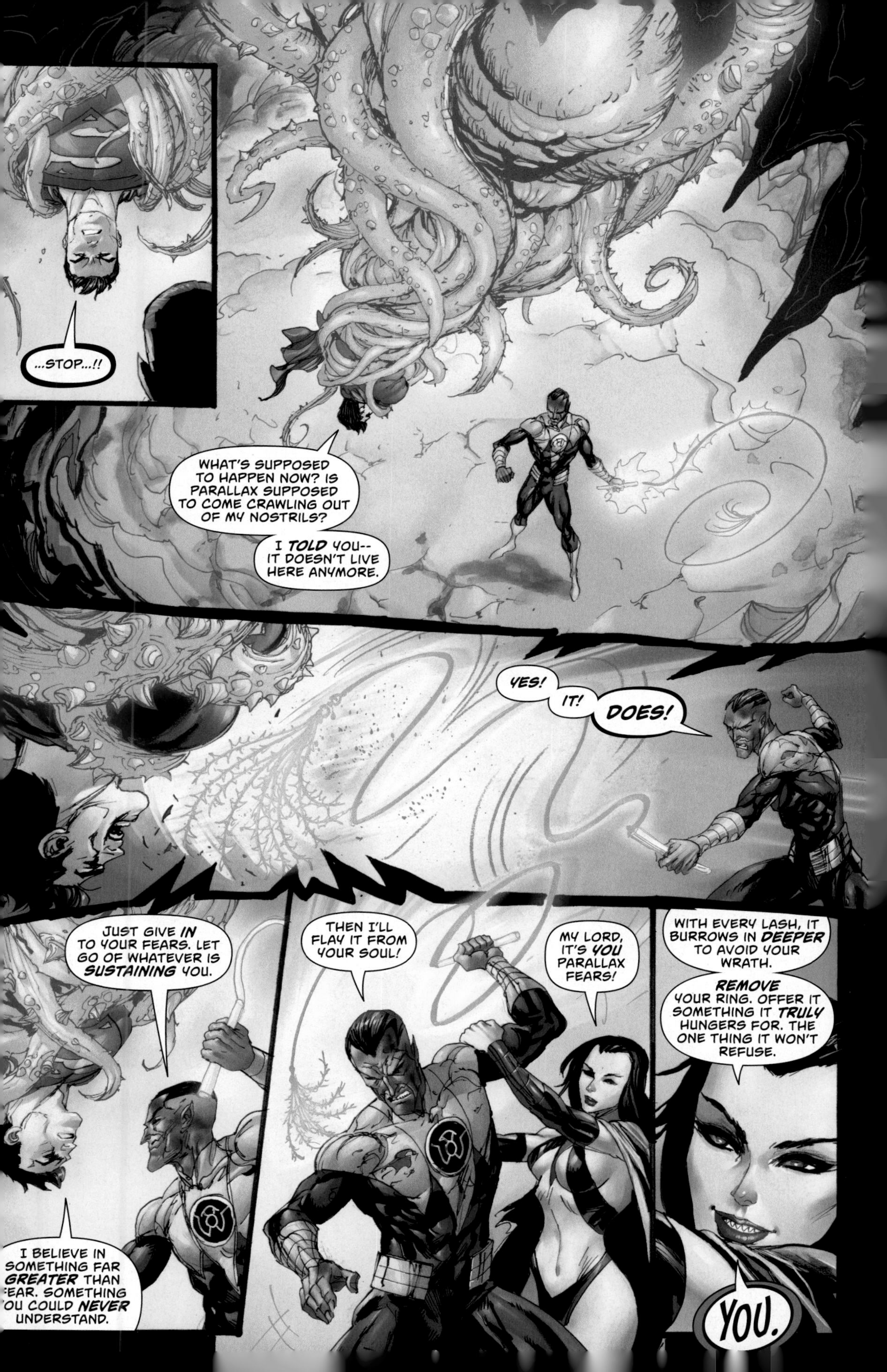
...STOP...!!
WHAT'S SUPPOSED TO HAPPEN NOW? IS PARALLAX SUPPOSED TO COME CRAWLING OUT OF MY NOSTRILS?
I TOLD YOU-- IT DOESN'T LIVE HERE ANYMORE.
YES!
IT!
DOES!
JUST GIVE IN TO YOUR FEARS. LET GO OF WHATEVER IS SUSTAINING YOU.
I BELIEVE IN SOMETHING FAR GREATER THAN FEAR. SOMETHING YOU COULD NEVER UNDERSTAND.
THEN I'LL FLAY IT FROM YOUR SOUL!
MY LORD, IT'S YOU PARALLAX FEARS!
WITH EVERY LASH, IT BURROWS IN DEEPER TO AVOID YOUR WRATH.
REMOVE YOUR RING. OFFER IT SOMETHING IT TRULY HUNGERS FOR. THE ONE THING IT WON'T REFUSE.
YOU.

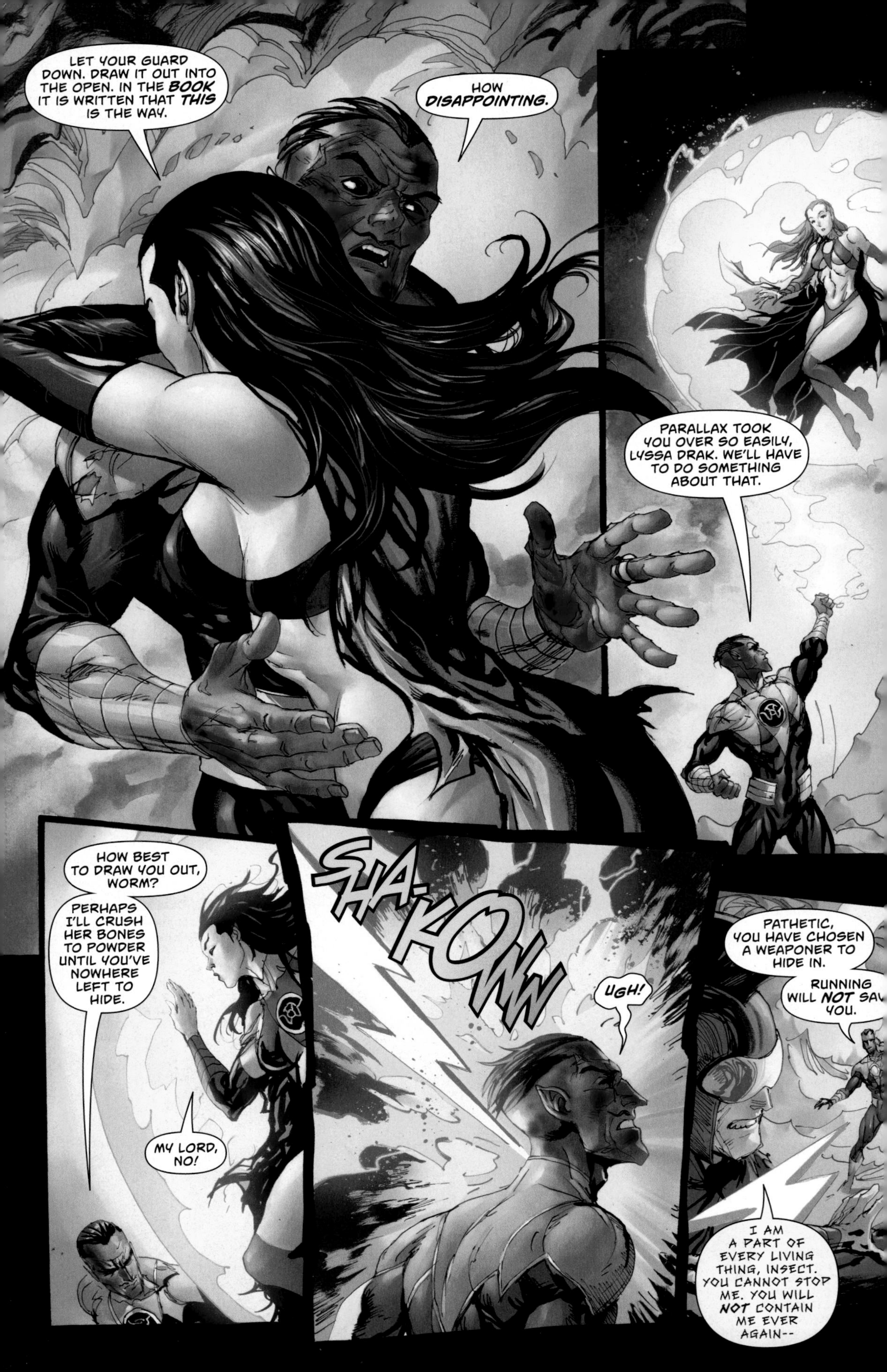
LET YOUR GUARD DOWN. DRAW IT OUT INTO THE OPEN. IN THE BOOK IT IS WRITTEN THAT THIS IS THE WAY.
HOW DISAPPOINTING.
PARALLAX TOOK YOU OVER SO EASILY, LYSSA DRAK. WE'LL HAVE TO DO SOMETHING ABOUT THAT.
HOW BEST TO DRAW YOU OUT, WORM?
PERHAPS I'LL CRUSH HER BONES TO POWDER UNTIL YOU'VE NOWHERE LEFT TO HIDE.
MY LORD, NO!
SHA-KOWW
UGH!
PATHETIC, YOU HAVE CHOSEN A WEAPONER TO HIDE IN.
RUNNING WILL NOT SAV YOU.
I AM A PART OF EVERY LIVING THING, INSECT. YOU CANNOT STOP ME. YOU WILL NOT CONTAIN ME EVER AGAIN--

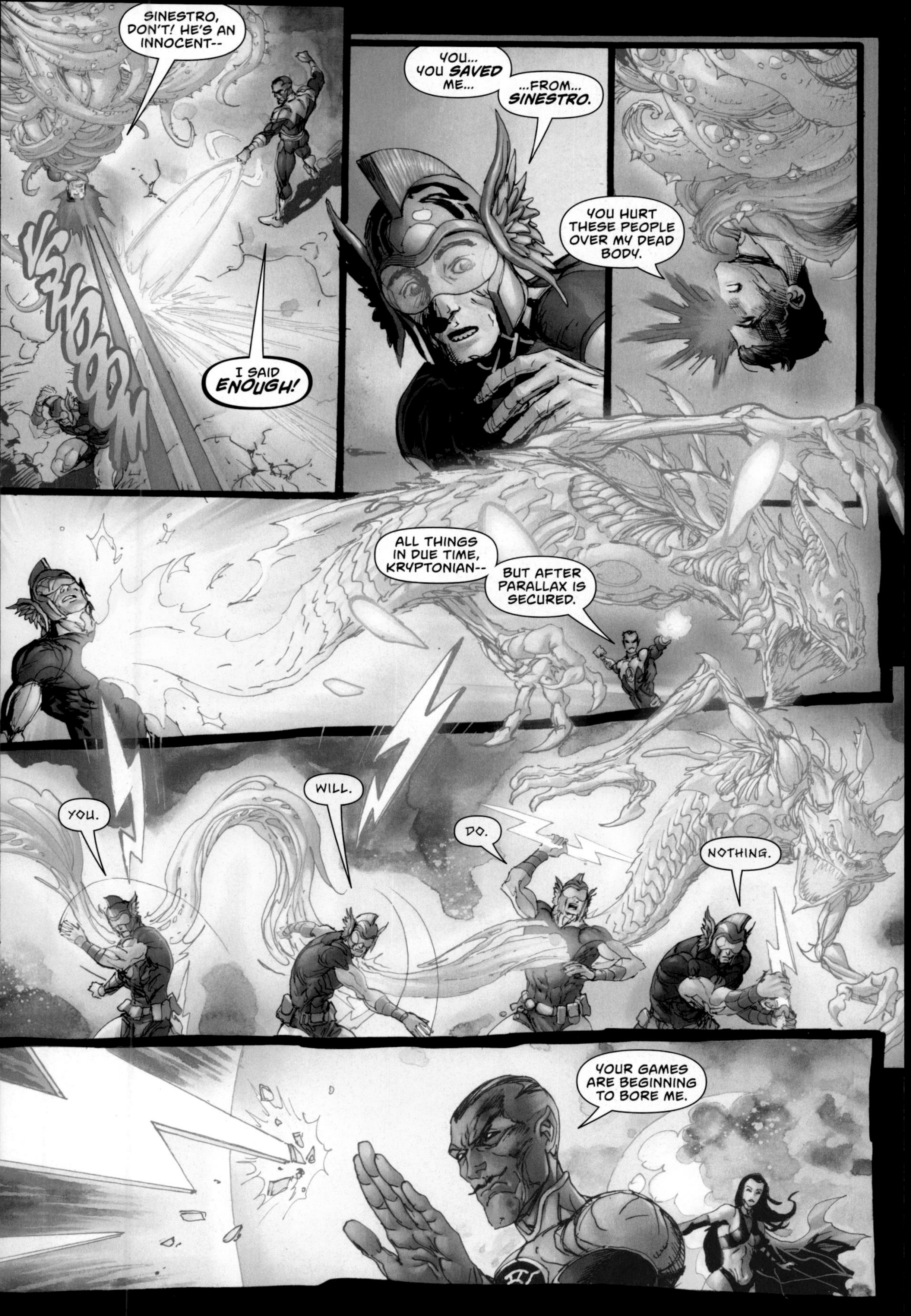
SINESTRO, DON'T! HE'S AN INNOCENT--
KA-BOOM
I SAID ENOUGH!
YOU... YOU SAVED ME...
...FROM... SINESTRO.
YOU HURT THESE PEOPLE OVER MY DEAD BODY.
ALL THINGS IN DUE TIME, KRYPTONIAN--
BUT AFTER PARALLAX IS SECURED.
YOU.
WILL.
DO.
NOTHING.
YOUR GAMES ARE BEGINNING TO BORE ME.

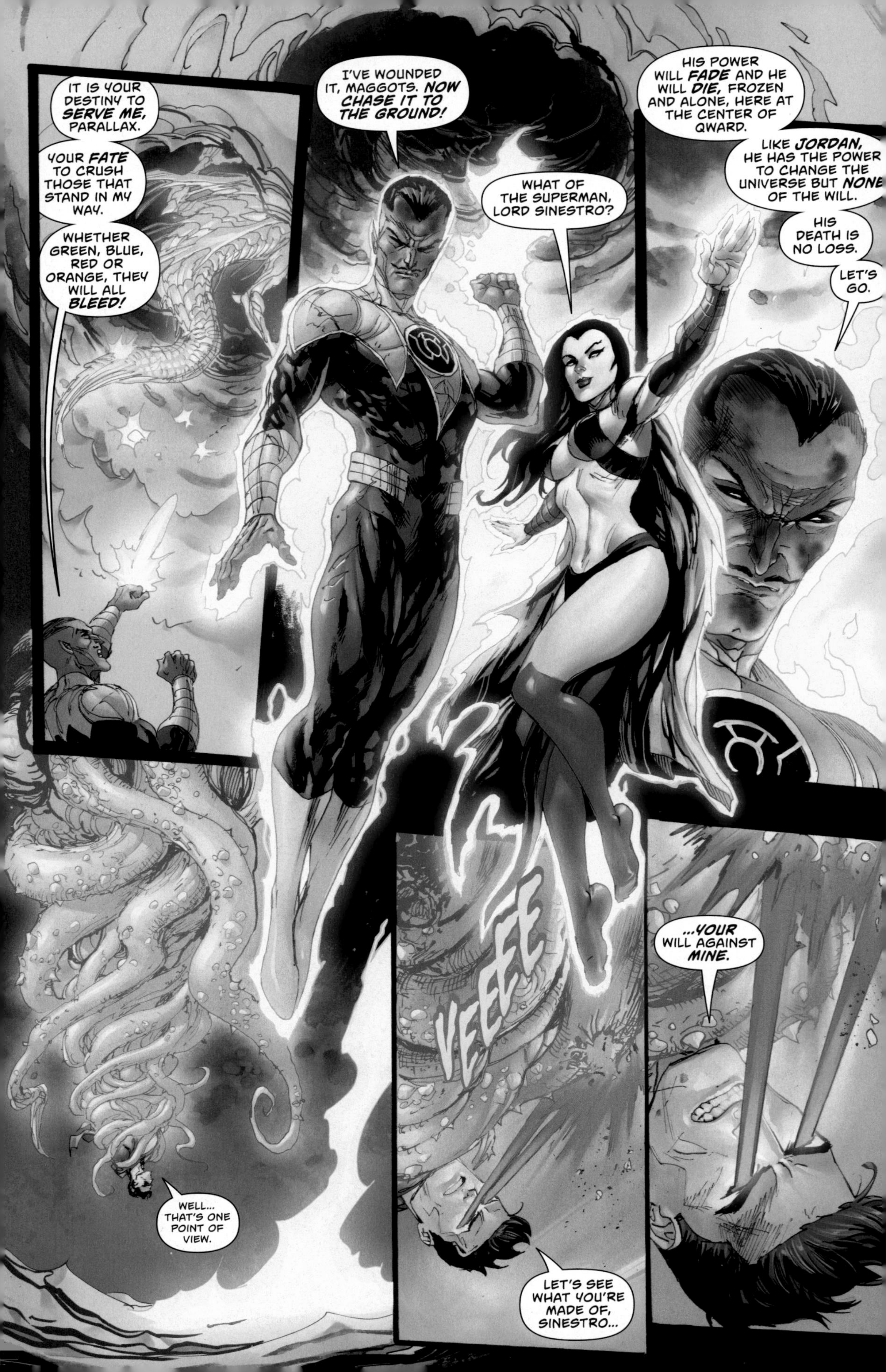

IT IS YOUR DESTINY TO SERVE ME, PARALLAX.
YOUR FATE TO CRUSH THOSE THAT STAND IN MY WAY.
WHETHER GREEN, BLUE, RED OR ORANGE, THEY WILL ALL BLEED!
I'VE WOUNDED IT, MAGGOTS. NOW CHASE IT TO THE GROUND!
WHAT OF THE SUPERMAN, LORD SINESTRO?
HIS POWER WILL FADE AND HE WILL DIE, FROZEN AND ALONE, HERE AT THE CENTER OF QWARD.
LIKE JORDAN, HE HAS THE POWER TO CHANGE THE UNIVERSE BUT NONE OF THE WILL.
HIS DEATH IS NO LOSS.
LET'S GO.
WELL... THAT'S ONE POINT OF VIEW.
VEEEE
LET'S SEE WHAT YOU'RE MADE OF, SINESTRO...
...YOUR WILL AGAINST MINE.

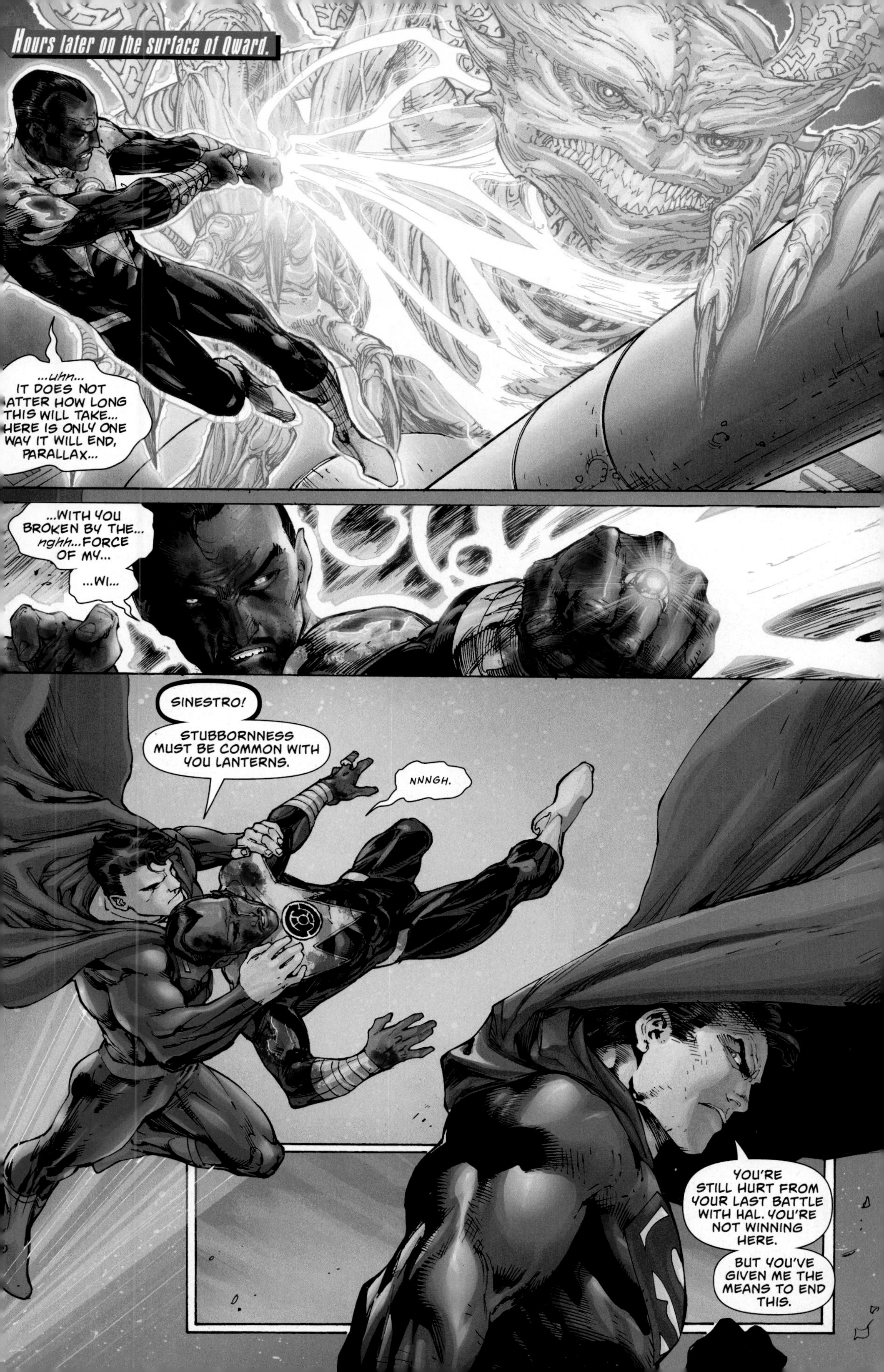
Hours later on the surface of Qward.
...uhn... IT DOES NOT ATTER HOW LONG THIS WILL TAKE... HERE IS ONLY ONE WAY IT WILL END, PARALLAX...
...WITH YOU BROKEN BY THE... nghh...FORCE OF MY...
...WI...
SINESTRO!
STUBBORNNESS MUST BE COMMON WITH YOU LANTERNS.
NNNGH.
YOU'RE STILL HURT FROM YOUR LAST BATTLE WITH HAL. YOU'RE NOT WINNING HERE.
BUT YOU'VE GIVEN ME THE MEANS TO END THIS.

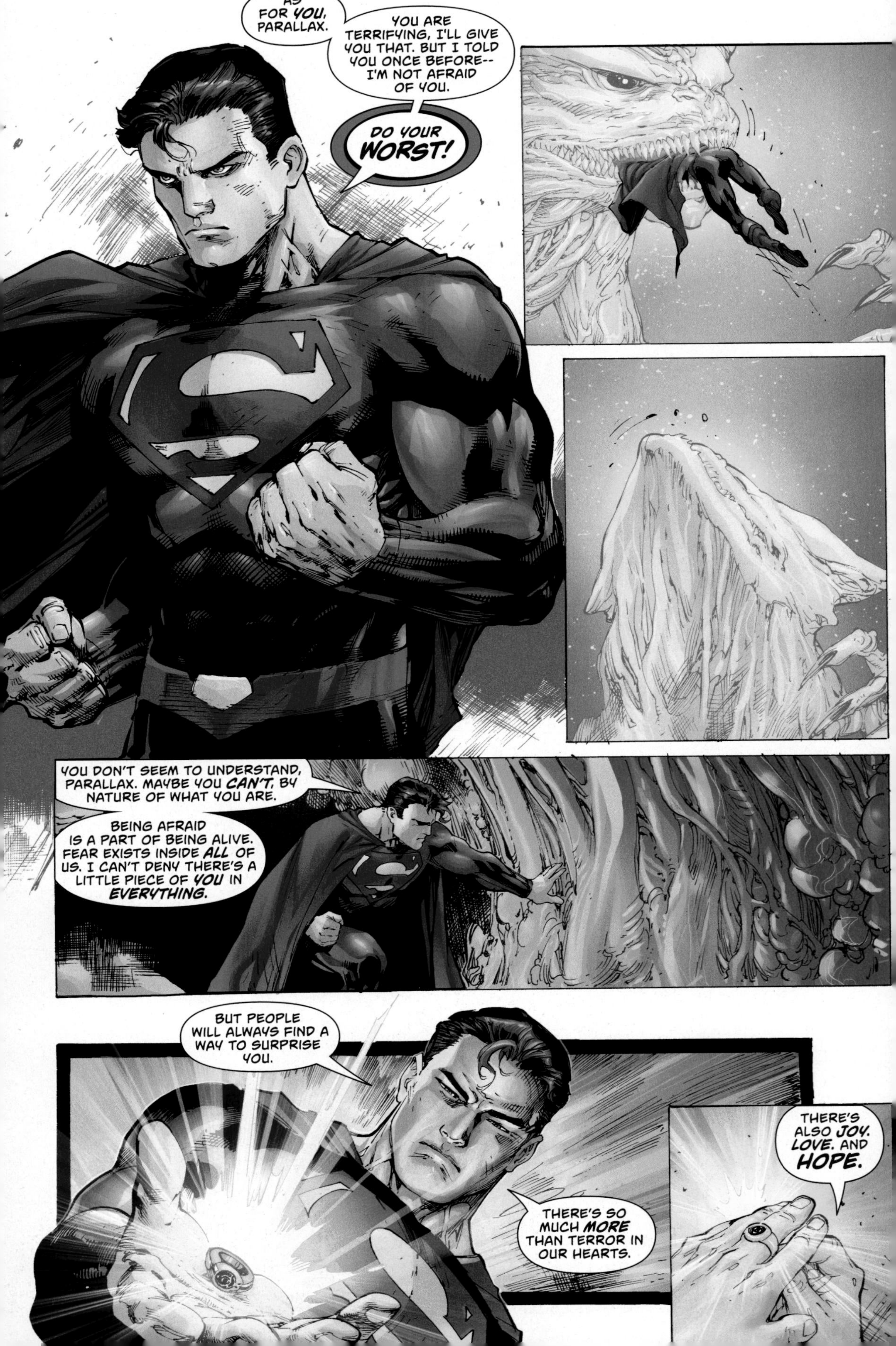
AS FOR YOU, PARALLAX.
YOU ARE TERRIFYING, I'LL GIVE YOU THAT. BUT I TOLD YOU ONCE BEFORE-- I'M NOT AFRAID OF YOU.
DO YOUR WORST!
YOU DON'T SEEM TO UNDERSTAND, PARALLAX. MAYBE YOU CAN'T, BY NATURE OF WHAT YOU ARE.
BEING AFRAID IS A PART OF BEING ALIVE. FEAR EXISTS INSIDE ALL OF US. I CAN'T DENY THERE'S A LITTLE PIECE OF YOU IN EVERYTHING.
BUT PEOPLE WILL ALWAYS FIND A WAY TO SURPRISE YOU.
THERE'S SO MUCH MORE THAN TERROR IN OUR HEARTS.
THERE'S ALSO JOY. LOVE. AND HOPE.

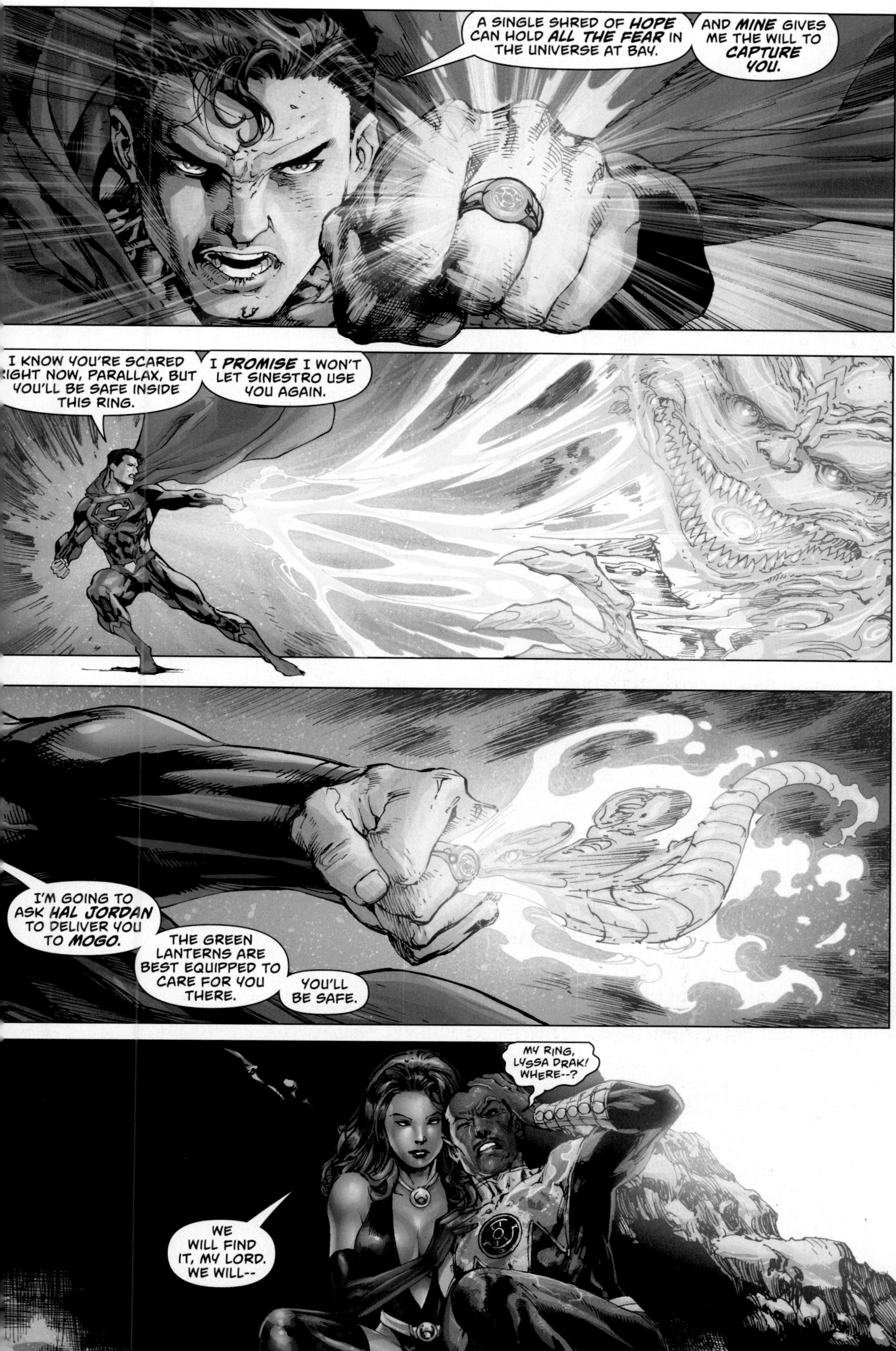
A SINGLE SHRED OF HOPE CAN HOLD ALL THE FEAR IN THE UNIVERSE AT BAY.
AND MINE GIVES ME THE WILL TO CAPTURE YOU.
I KNOW YOU'RE SCARED RIGHT NOW, PARALLAX, BUT YOU'LL BE SAFE INSIDE THIS RING.
I PROMISE I WON'T LET SINESTRO USE YOU AGAIN.
I'M GOING TO ASK HAL JORDAN TO DELIVER YOU TO MOGO.
THE GREEN LANTERNS ARE BEST EQUIPPED TO CARE FOR YOU THERE.
YOU'LL BE SAFE.
MY RING, LYSSA DRAK! WHERE--?
WE WILL FIND IT, MY LORD. WE WILL--

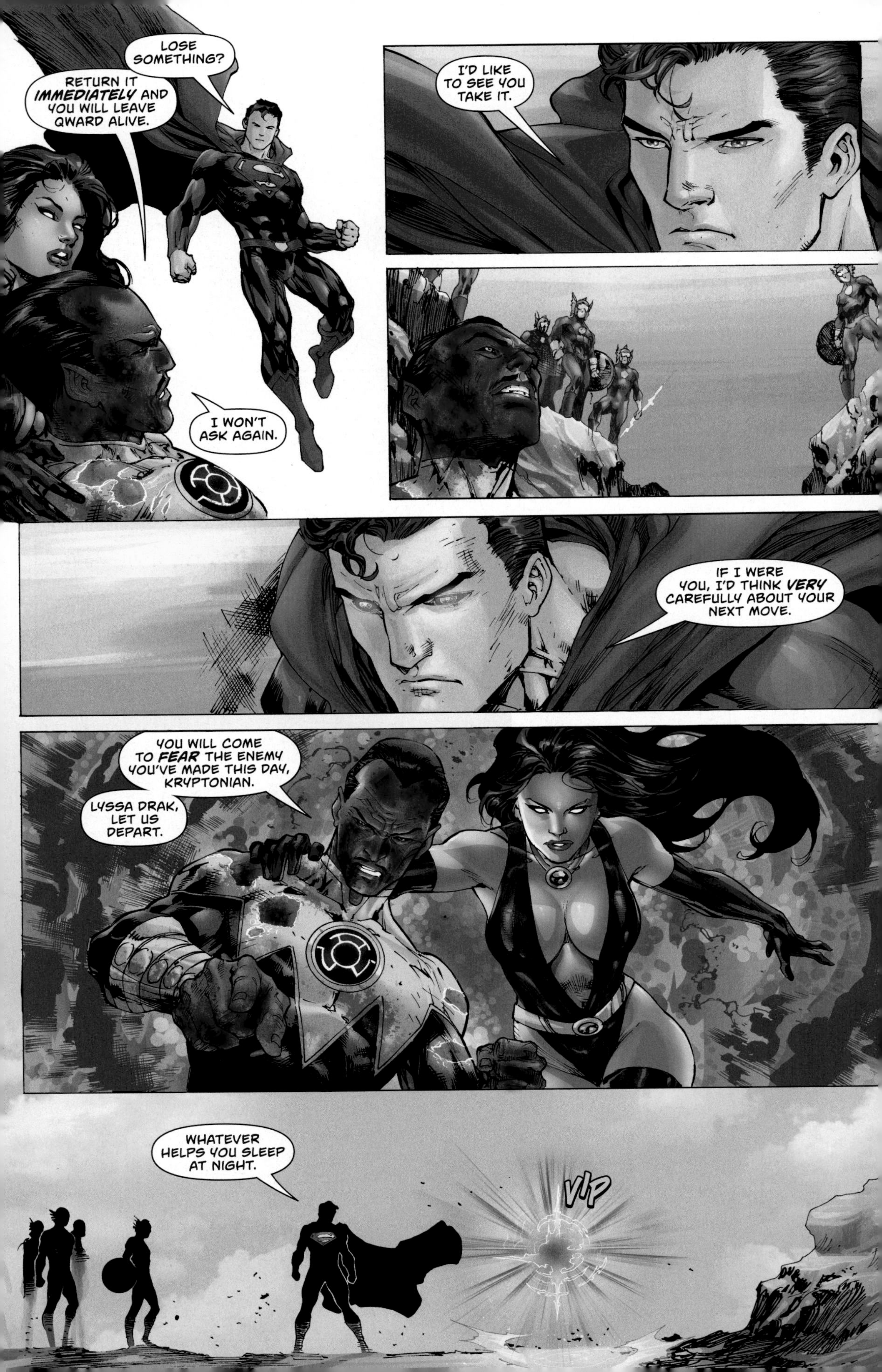

LOSE SOMETHING?
RETURN IT IMMEDIATELY AND YOU WILL LEAVE QWARD ALIVE.
I WON'T ASK AGAIN.
I'D LIKE TO SEE YOU TAKE IT.
IF I WERE YOU, I'D THINK VERY CAREFULLY ABOUT YOUR NEXT MOVE.
YOU WILL COME TO FEAR THE ENEMY YOU'VE MADE THIS DAY, KRYPTONIAN.
LYSSA DRAK, LET US DEPART.
WHATEVER HELPS YOU SLEEP AT NIGHT.
VIP

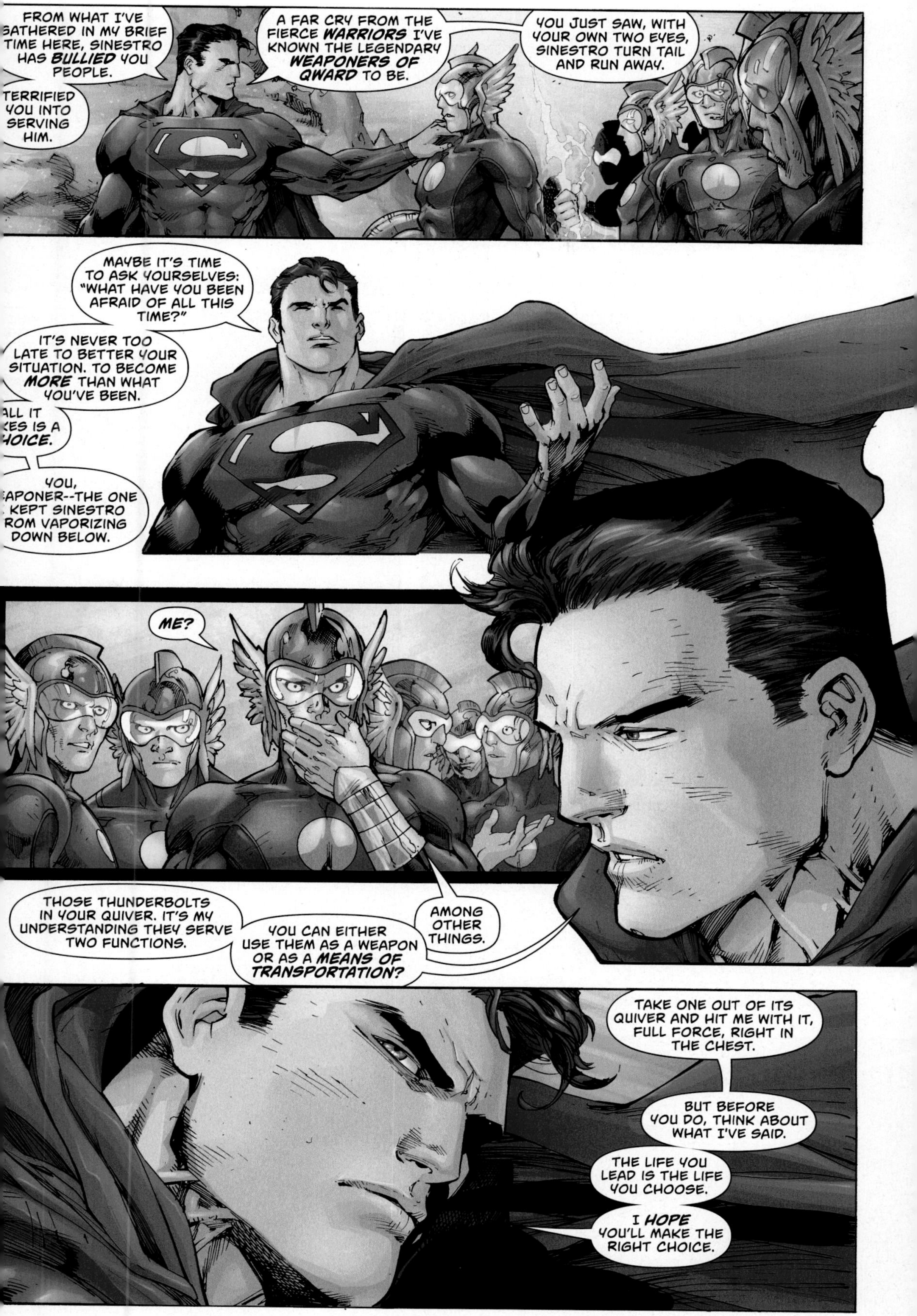

FROM WHAT I'VE GATHERED IN MY BRIEF TIME HERE, SINESTRO HAS BULLIED YOU PEOPLE.
TERRIFIED YOU INTO SERVING HIM.
A FAR CRY FROM THE FIERCE WARRIORS I'VE KNOWN THE LEGENDARY WEAPONERS OF QWARD TO BE.
YOU JUST SAW, WITH YOUR OWN TWO EYES, SINESTRO TURN TAIL AND RUN AWAY.
MAYBE IT'S TIME TO ASK YOURSELVES: "WHAT HAVE YOU BEEN AFRAID OF ALL THIS TIME?"
IT'S NEVER TOO LATE TO BETTER YOUR SITUATION. TO BECOME MORE THAN WHAT YOU'VE BEEN.
ALL IT KES IS A HOICE.
YOU, APONER--THE ONE KEPT SINESTRO ROM VAPORIZING DOWN BELOW.
ME?
THOSE THUNDERBOLTS IN YOUR QUIVER. IT'S MY UNDERSTANDING THEY SERVE TWO FUNCTIONS.
YOU CAN EITHER USE THEM AS A WEAPON OR AS A MEANS OF TRANSPORTATION?
AMONG OTHER THINGS.
TAKE ONE OUT OF ITS QUIVER AND HIT ME WITH IT, FULL FORCE, RIGHT IN THE CHEST.
BUT BEFORE YOU DO, THINK ABOUT WHAT I'VE SAID.
THE LIFE YOU LEAD IS THE LIFE YOU CHOOSE.
I HOPE YOU'LL MAKE THE RIGHT CHOICE.

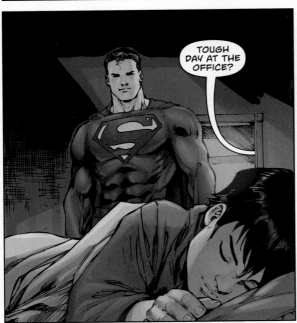

TOUGH DAY AT THE OFFICE?

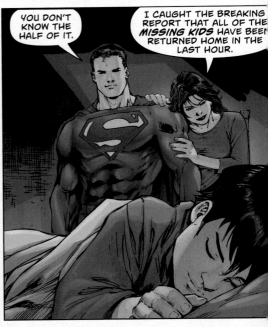

YOU DON'T KNOW THE HALF OF IT.

I CAUGHT THE BREAKING REPORT THAT ALL OF THE *MISSING KIDS* HAVE BEEN RETURNED HOME IN THE LAST HOUR.

THANK YOU FOR HELPING THEM.

HOW ABOUT I HEAT YOU UP SOME PIE AND YOU CAN TELL ME ALL ABOUT IT.

I'LL MEET YOU IN THE LIVING ROOM, LOIS...

...RIGHT NOW, IT FEELS GOOD TO JUST STAND HERE AND *BREATHE*...

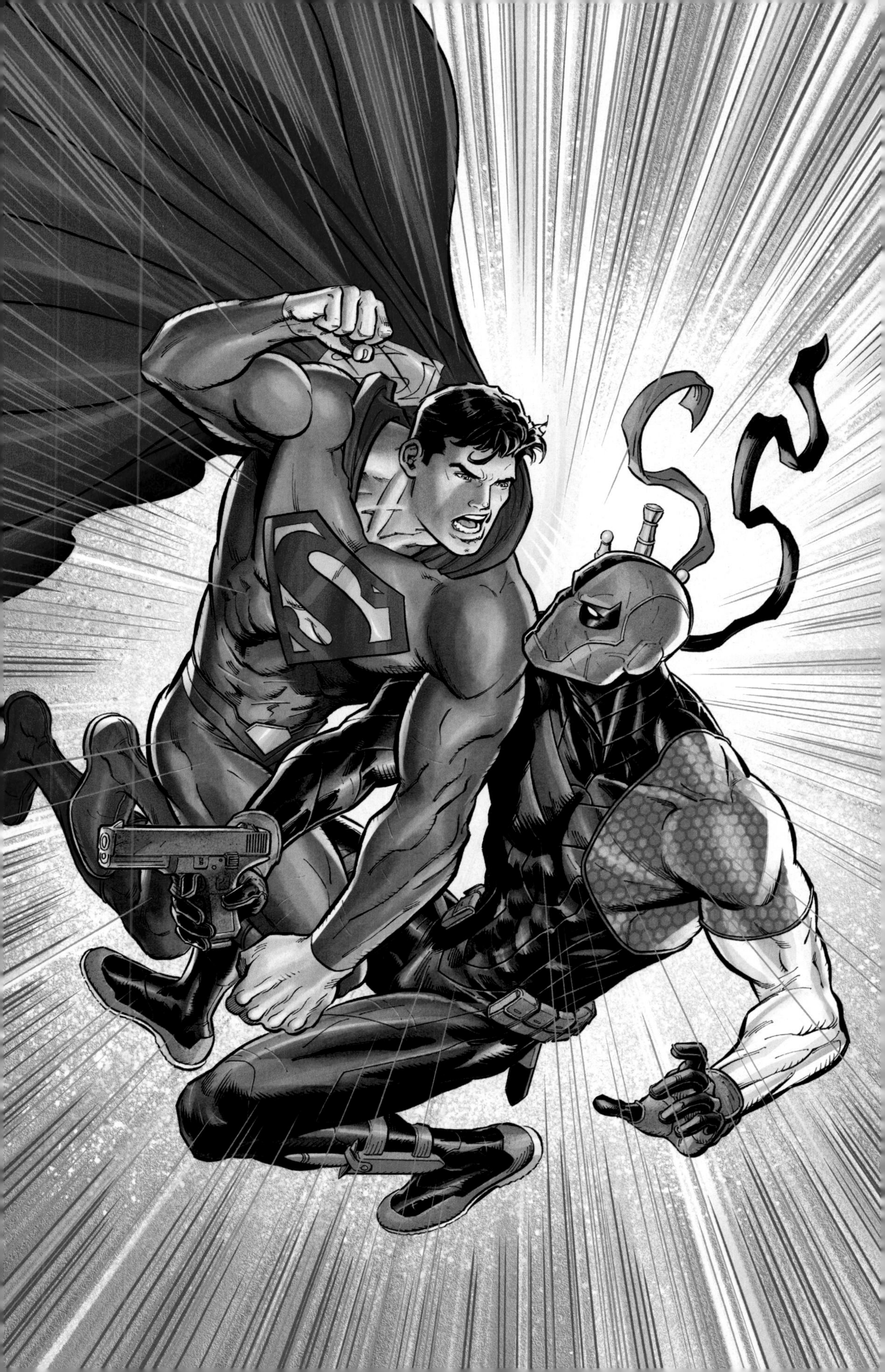

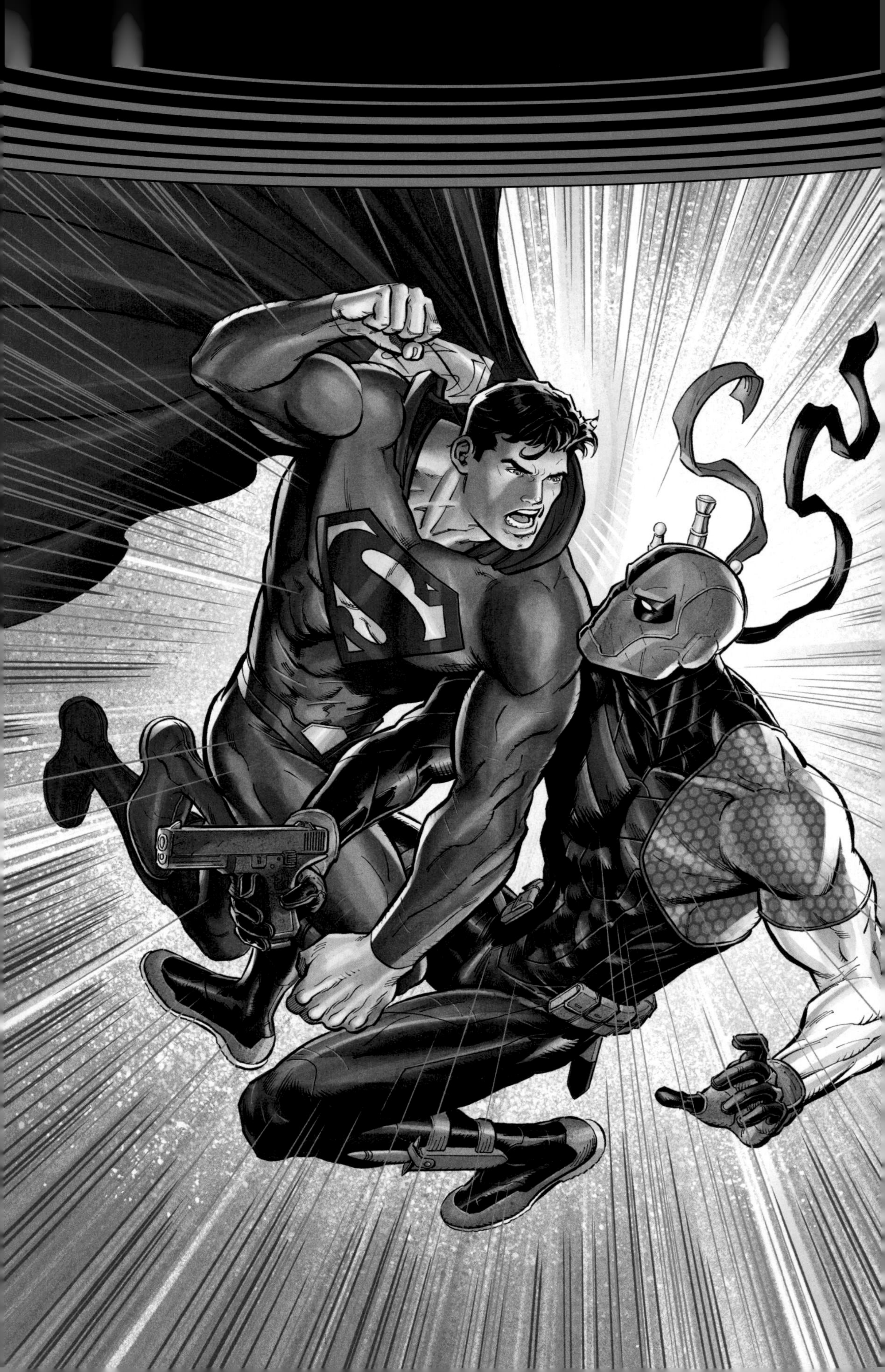

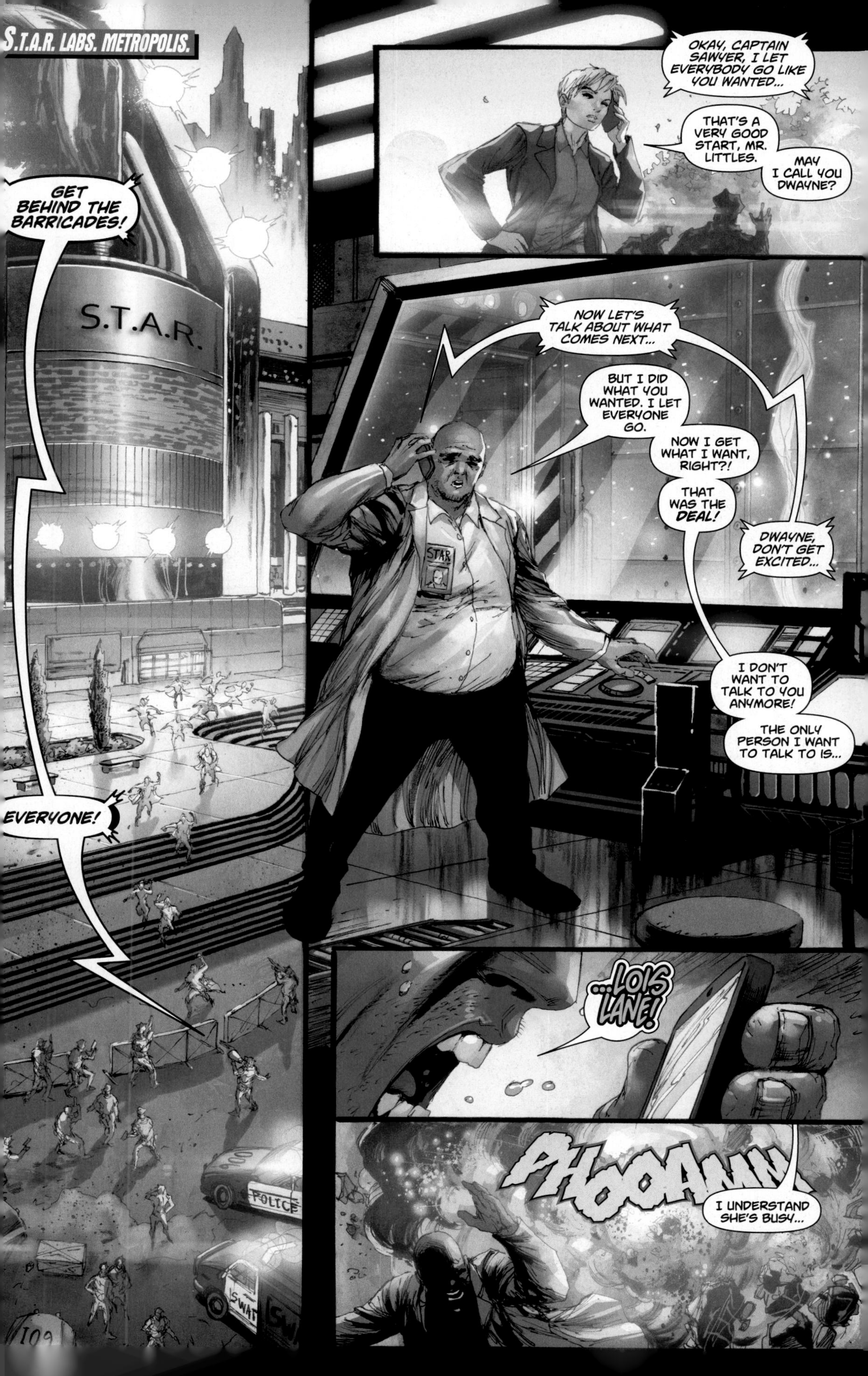
S.T.A.R. LABS. METROPOLIS.
GET BEHIND THE BARRICADES!
EVERYONE!
S.T.A.R.
OKAY, CAPTAIN SAWYER, I LET EVERYBODY GO LIKE YOU WANTED...
THAT'S A VERY GOOD START, MR. LITTLES.
MAY I CALL YOU DWAYNE?
NOW LET'S TALK ABOUT WHAT COMES NEXT...
BUT I DID WHAT YOU WANTED. I LET EVERYONE GO.
NOW I GET WHAT I WANT, RIGHT?!
THAT WAS THE DEAL!
DWAYNE, DON'T GET EXCITED...
I DON'T WANT TO TALK TO YOU ANYMORE!
THE ONLY PERSON I WANT TO TALK TO IS...
...LOIS LANE!
PHOOAMM
I UNDERSTAND SHE'S BUSY...
POLICE
SWAT

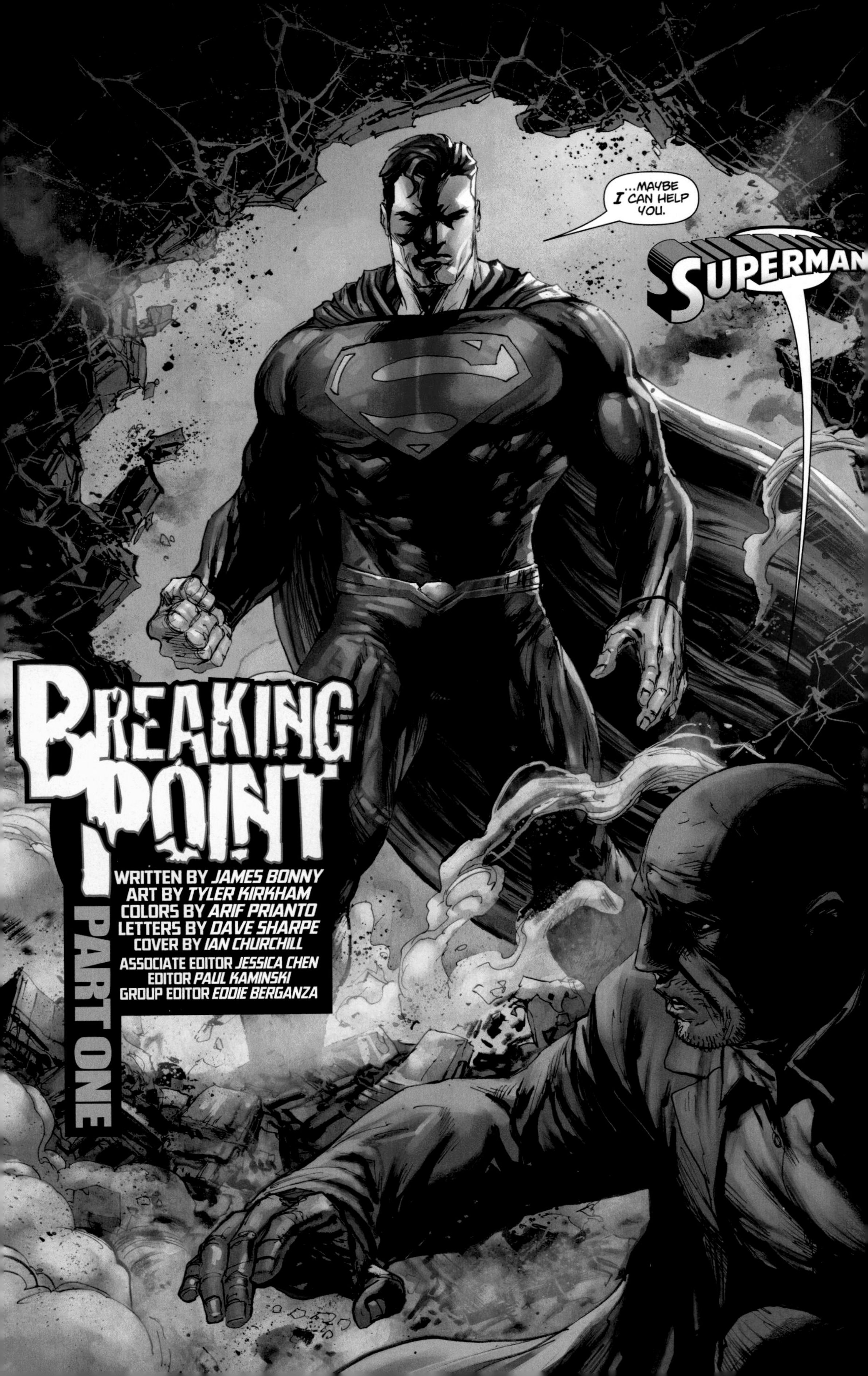

...MAYBE I CAN HELP YOU.
SUPERMAN
BREAKING POINT
PART ONE
WRITTEN BY JAMES BONNY
ART BY TYLER KIRKHAM
COLORS BY ARIF PRIANTO
LETTERS BY DAVE SHARPE
COVER BY IAN CHURCHILL
ASSOCIATE EDITOR JESSICA CHEN
EDITOR PAUL KAMINSKI
GROUP EDITOR EDDIE BERGANZA

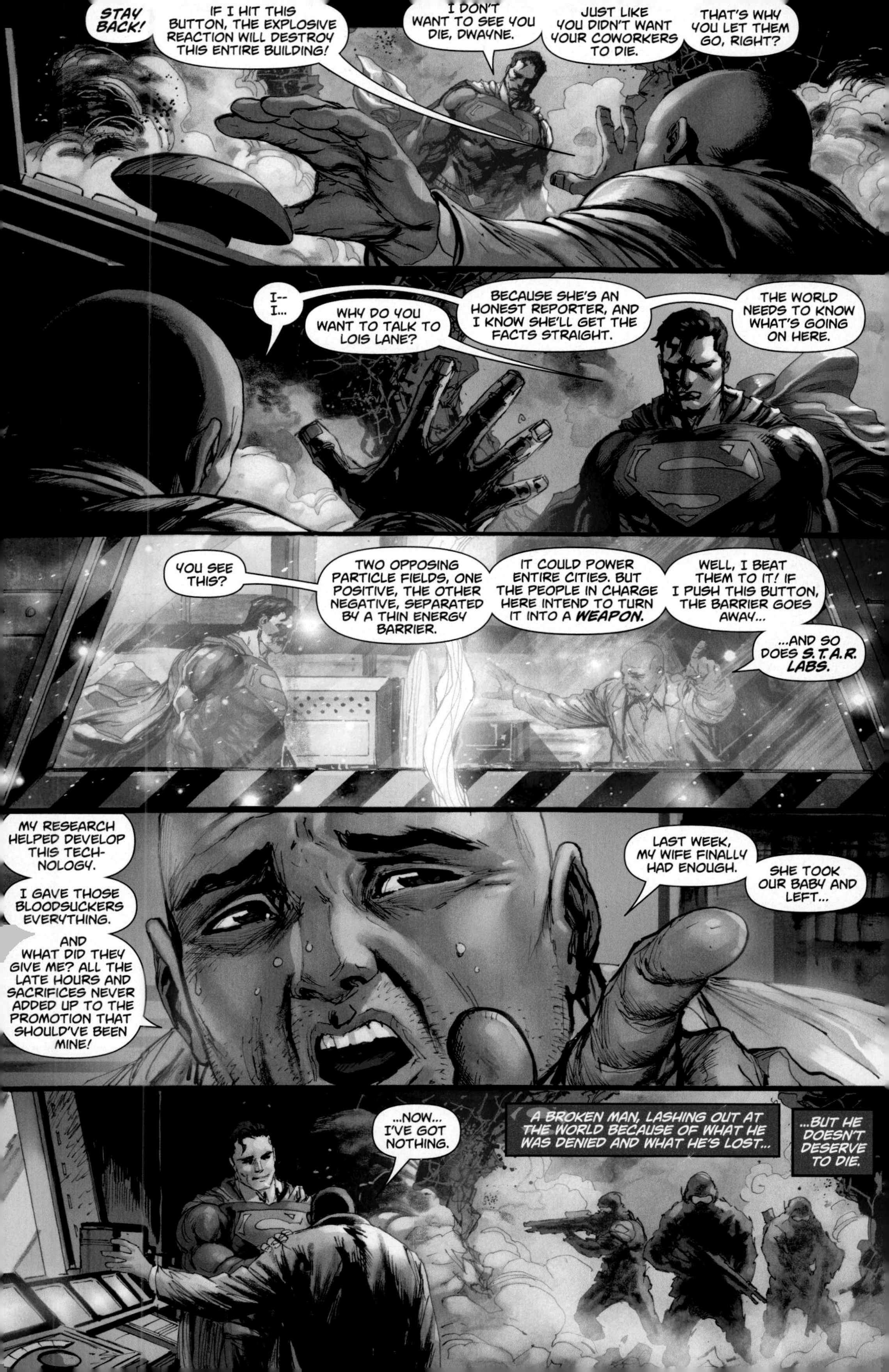

STAY BACK!
IF I HIT THIS BUTTON, THE EXPLOSIVE REACTION WILL DESTROY THIS ENTIRE BUILDING!
I DON'T WANT TO SEE YOU DIE, DWAYNE.
JUST LIKE YOU DIDN'T WANT YOUR COWORKERS TO DIE.
THAT'S WHY YOU LET THEM GO, RIGHT?
I-- I...
WHY DO YOU WANT TO TALK TO LOIS LANE?
BECAUSE SHE'S AN HONEST REPORTER, AND I KNOW SHE'LL GET THE FACTS STRAIGHT.
THE WORLD NEEDS TO KNOW WHAT'S GOING ON HERE.
YOU SEE THIS?
TWO OPPOSING PARTICLE FIELDS, ONE POSITIVE, THE OTHER NEGATIVE, SEPARATED BY A THIN ENERGY BARRIER.
IT COULD POWER ENTIRE CITIES. BUT THE PEOPLE IN CHARGE HERE INTEND TO TURN IT INTO A WEAPON.
WELL, I BEAT THEM TO IT! IF I PUSH THIS BUTTON, THE BARRIER GOES AWAY...
...AND SO DOES S.T.A.R. LABS.
MY RESEARCH HELPED DEVELOP THIS TECH-NOLOGY.
I GAVE THOSE BLOODSUCKERS EVERYTHING.
AND WHAT DID THEY GIVE ME? ALL THE LATE HOURS AND SACRIFICES NEVER ADDED UP TO THE PROMOTION THAT SHOULD'VE BEEN MINE!
LAST WEEK, MY WIFE FINALLY HAD ENOUGH.
SHE TOOK OUR BABY AND LEFT...
...NOW... I'VE GOT NOTHING.
A BROKEN MAN, LASHING OUT AT THE WORLD BECAUSE OF WHAT HE WAS DENIED AND WHAT HE'S LOST...
...BUT HE DOESN'T DESERVE TO DIE.

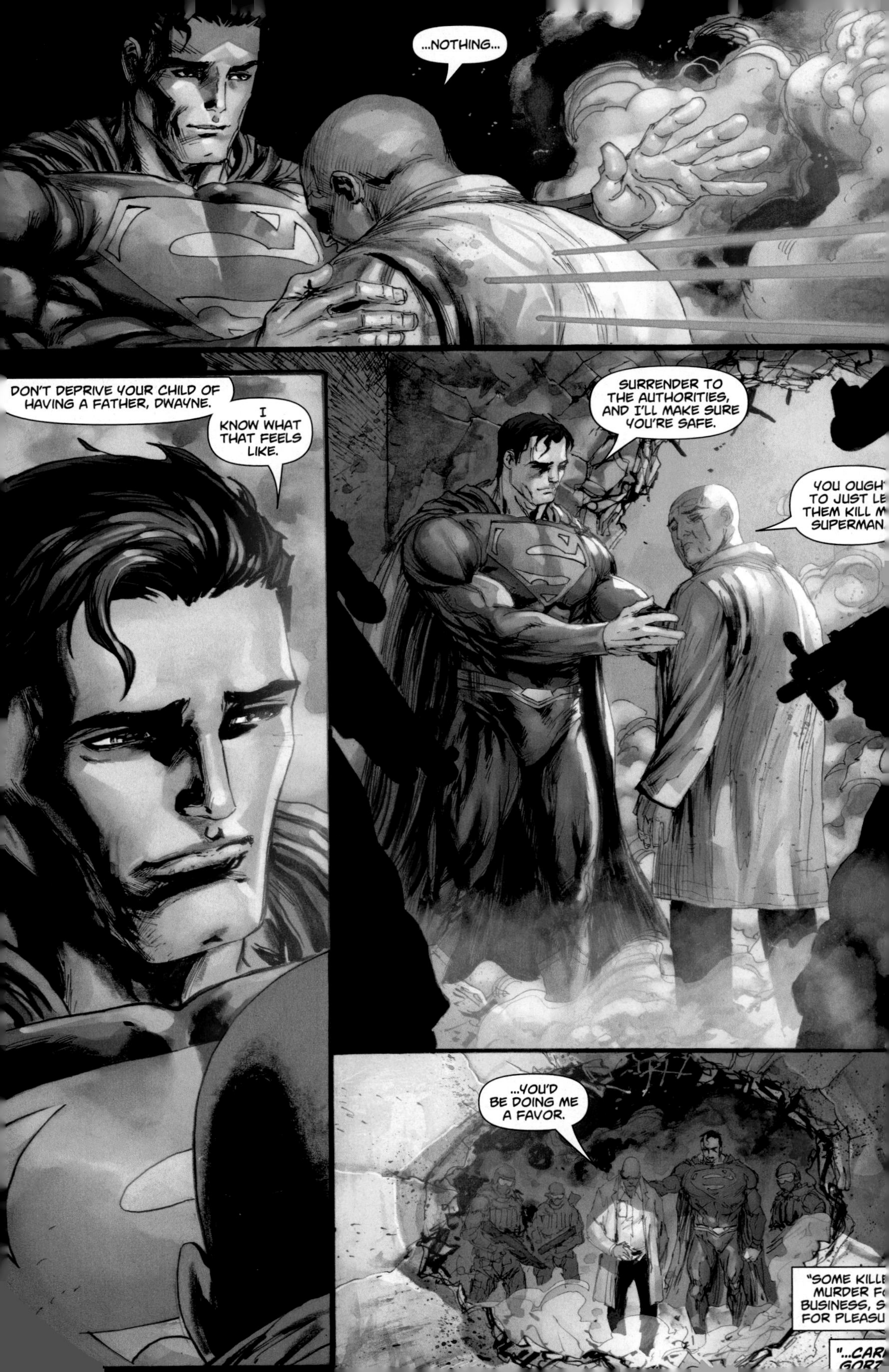

...NOTHING...
DON'T DEPRIVE YOUR CHILD OF HAVING A FATHER, DWAYNE.
I KNOW WHAT THAT FEELS LIKE.
SURRENDER TO THE AUTHORITIES, AND I'LL MAKE SURE YOU'RE SAFE.
YOU OUGH TO JUST LE THEM KILL M SUPERMAN
...YOU'D BE DOING ME A FAVOR.
"SOME KILLE MURDER F BUSINESS, S FOR PLEASU
"...CAR GORZ

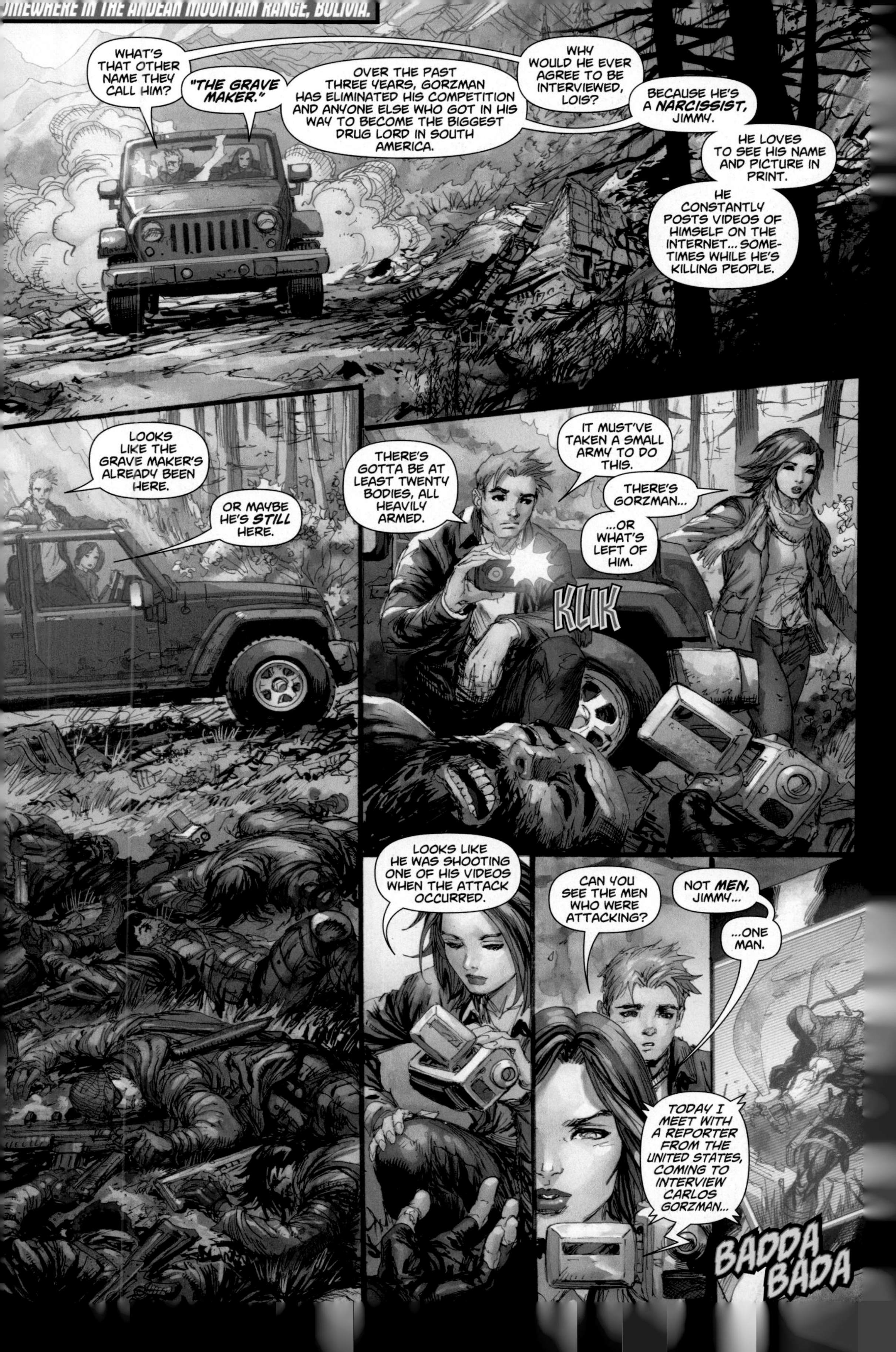
SOMEWHERE IN THE ANDEAN MOUNTAIN RANGE, BOLIVIA.
WHAT'S THAT OTHER NAME THEY CALL HIM?
"THE GRAVE MAKER."
OVER THE PAST THREE YEARS, GORZMAN HAS ELIMINATED HIS COMPETITION AND ANYONE ELSE WHO GOT IN HIS WAY TO BECOME THE BIGGEST DRUG LORD IN SOUTH AMERICA.
WHY WOULD HE EVER AGREE TO BE INTERVIEWED, LOIS?
BECAUSE HE'S A NARCISSIST, JIMMY.
HE LOVES TO SEE HIS NAME AND PICTURE IN PRINT.
HE CONSTANTLY POSTS VIDEOS OF HIMSELF ON THE INTERNET... SOMETIMES WHILE HE'S KILLING PEOPLE.
LOOKS LIKE THE GRAVE MAKER'S ALREADY BEEN HERE.
OR MAYBE HE'S STILL HERE.
THERE'S GOTTA BE AT LEAST TWENTY BODIES, ALL HEAVILY ARMED.
IT MUST'VE TAKEN A SMALL ARMY TO DO THIS.
THERE'S GORZMAN...
...OR WHAT'S LEFT OF HIM.
KLIK
LOOKS LIKE HE WAS SHOOTING ONE OF HIS VIDEOS WHEN THE ATTACK OCCURRED.
CAN YOU SEE THE MEN WHO WERE ATTACKING?
NOT MEN, JIMMY...
...ONE MAN.
TODAY I MEET WITH A REPORTER FROM THE UNITED STATES, COMING TO INTERVIEW CARLOS GORZMAN...
BADDA BADA

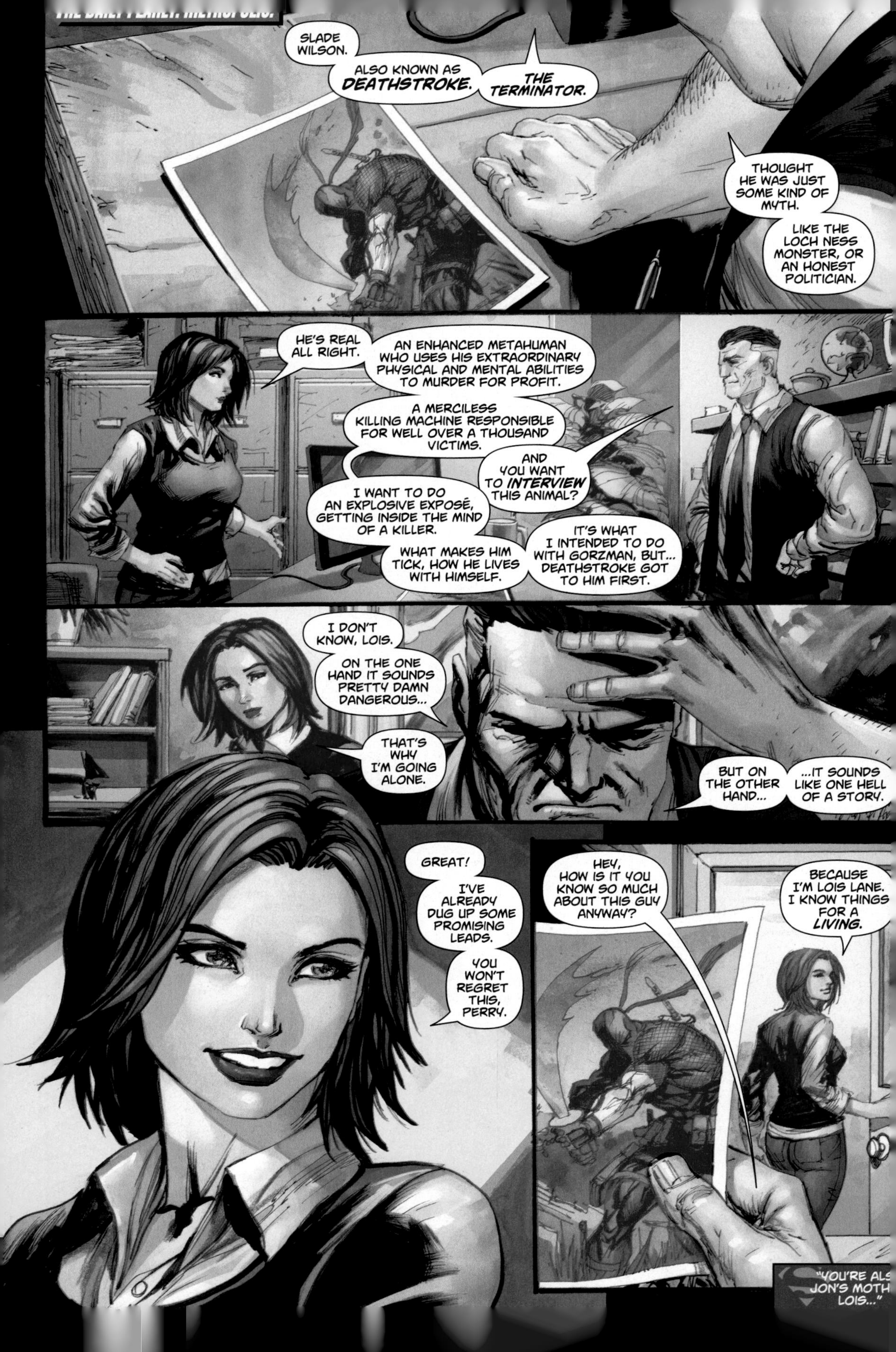
SLADE WILSON.
ALSO KNOWN AS DEATHSTROKE.
THE TERMINATOR.
THOUGHT HE WAS JUST SOME KIND OF MYTH.
LIKE THE LOCH NESS MONSTER, OR AN HONEST POLITICIAN.
HE'S REAL ALL RIGHT.
AN ENHANCED METAHUMAN WHO USES HIS EXTRAORDINARY PHYSICAL AND MENTAL ABILITIES TO MURDER FOR PROFIT.
A MERCILESS KILLING MACHINE RESPONSIBLE FOR WELL OVER A THOUSAND VICTIMS.
AND YOU WANT TO INTERVIEW THIS ANIMAL?
I WANT TO DO AN EXPLOSIVE EXPOSÉ, GETTING INSIDE THE MIND OF A KILLER.
WHAT MAKES HIM TICK, HOW HE LIVES WITH HIMSELF.
IT'S WHAT I INTENDED TO DO WITH GORZMAN, BUT... DEATHSTROKE GOT TO HIM FIRST.
I DON'T KNOW, LOIS.
ON THE ONE HAND IT SOUNDS PRETTY DAMN DANGEROUS...
THAT'S WHY I'M GOING ALONE.
BUT ON THE OTHER HAND...
...IT SOUNDS LIKE ONE HELL OF A STORY.
GREAT!
I'VE ALREADY DUG UP SOME PROMISING LEADS.
YOU WON'T REGRET THIS, PERRY.
HEY, HOW IS IT YOU KNOW SO MUCH ABOUT THIS GUY ANYWAY?
BECAUSE I'M LOIS LANE. I KNOW THINGS FOR A LIVING.

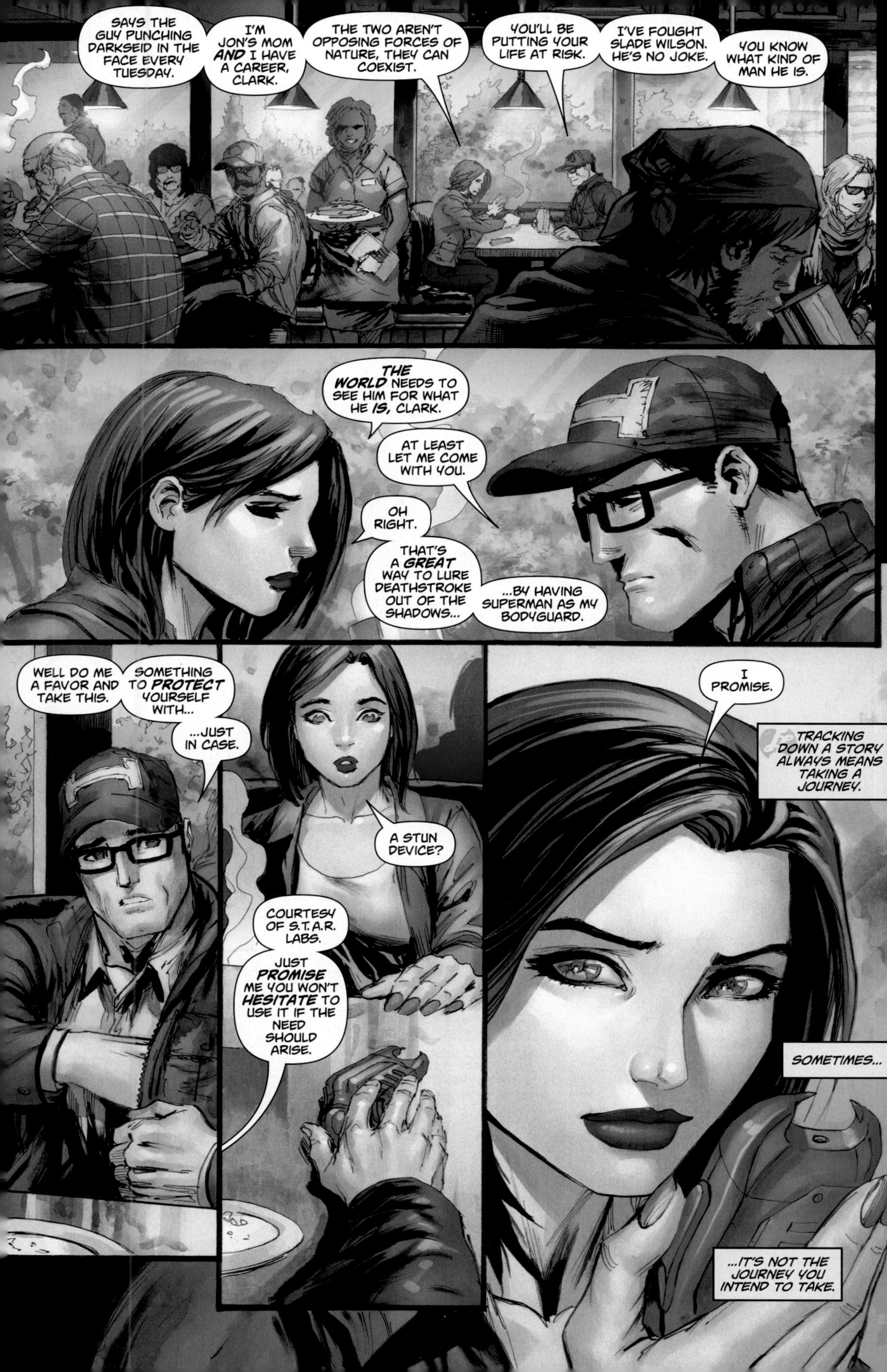
SAYS THE GUY PUNCHING DARKSEID IN THE FACE EVERY TUESDAY.
I'M JON'S MOM AND I HAVE A CAREER, CLARK.
THE TWO AREN'T OPPOSING FORCES OF NATURE, THEY CAN COEXIST.
YOU'LL BE PUTTING YOUR LIFE AT RISK.
I'VE FOUGHT SLADE WILSON. HE'S NO JOKE.
YOU KNOW WHAT KIND OF MAN HE IS.
THE WORLD NEEDS TO SEE HIM FOR WHAT HE IS, CLARK.
AT LEAST LET ME COME WITH YOU.
OH RIGHT.
THAT'S A GREAT WAY TO LURE DEATHSTROKE OUT OF THE SHADOWS...
...BY HAVING SUPERMAN AS MY BODYGUARD.
WELL DO ME A FAVOR AND TAKE THIS.
SOMETHING TO PROTECT YOURSELF WITH...
...JUST IN CASE.
A STUN DEVICE?
COURTESY OF S.T.A.R. LABS.
JUST PROMISE ME YOU WON'T HESITATE TO USE IT IF THE NEED SHOULD ARISE.
I PROMISE.
TRACKING DOWN A STORY ALWAYS MEANS TAKING A JOURNEY.
SOMETIMES...
...IT'S NOT THE JOURNEY YOU INTEND TO TAKE.

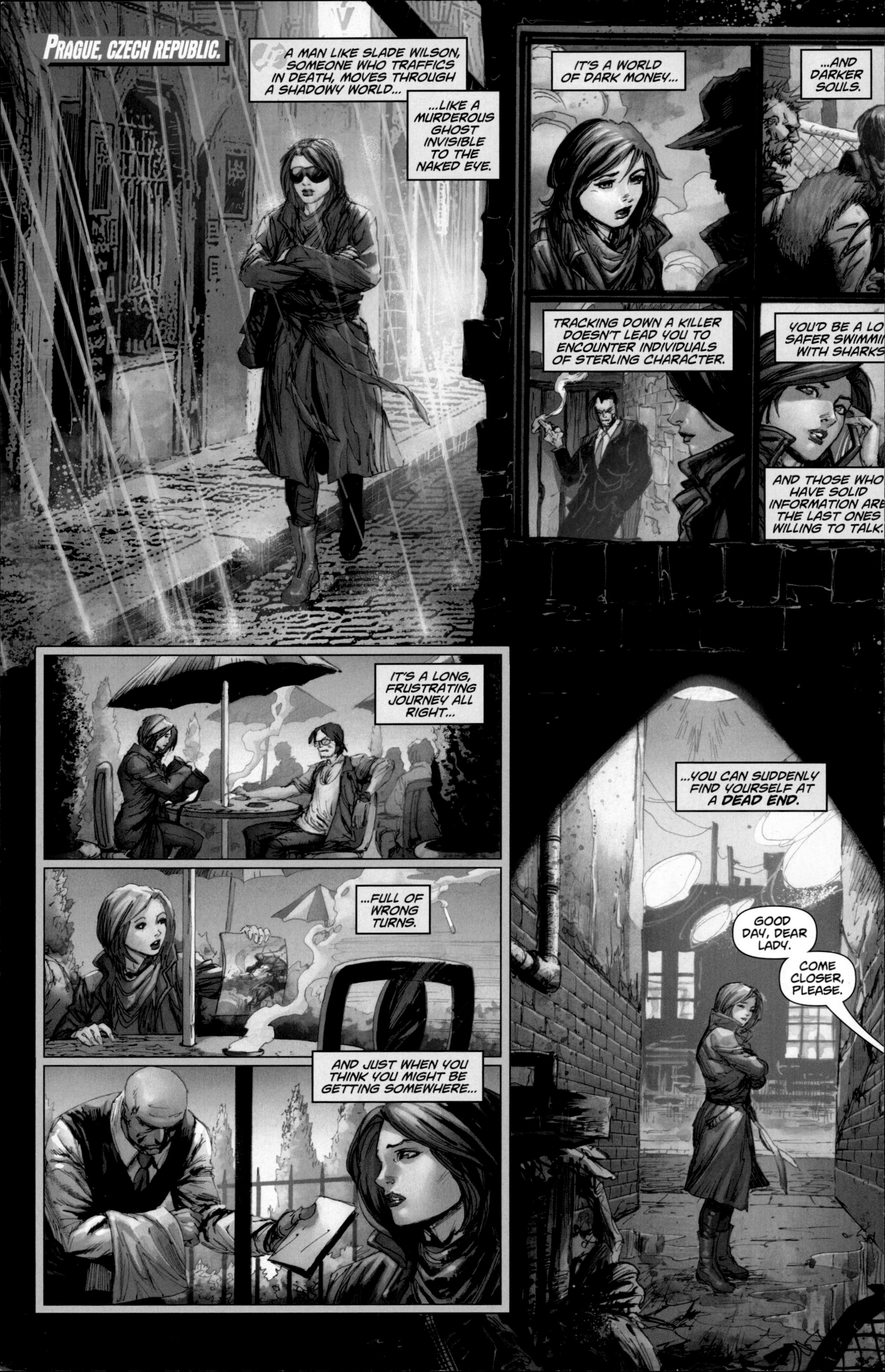
PRAGUE, CZECH REPUBLIC.
A MAN LIKE SLADE WILSON, SOMEONE WHO TRAFFICS IN DEATH, MOVES THROUGH A SHADOWY WORLD...
...LIKE A MURDEROUS GHOST INVISIBLE TO THE NAKED EYE.
IT'S A WORLD OF DARK MONEY...
...AND DARKER SOULS.
TRACKING DOWN A KILLER DOESN'T LEAD YOU TO ENCOUNTER INDIVIDUALS OF STERLING CHARACTER.
YOU'D BE A LO SAFER SWIMMIN WITH SHARKS
AND THOSE WHO HAVE SOLID INFORMATION ARE THE LAST ONES WILLING TO TALK.
IT'S A LONG, FRUSTRATING JOURNEY ALL RIGHT...
...FULL OF WRONG TURNS.
AND JUST WHEN YOU THINK YOU MIGHT BE GETTING SOMEWHERE...
...YOU CAN SUDDENLY FIND YOURSELF AT A DEAD END.
GOOD DAY, DEAR LADY.
COME CLOSER, PLEASE.

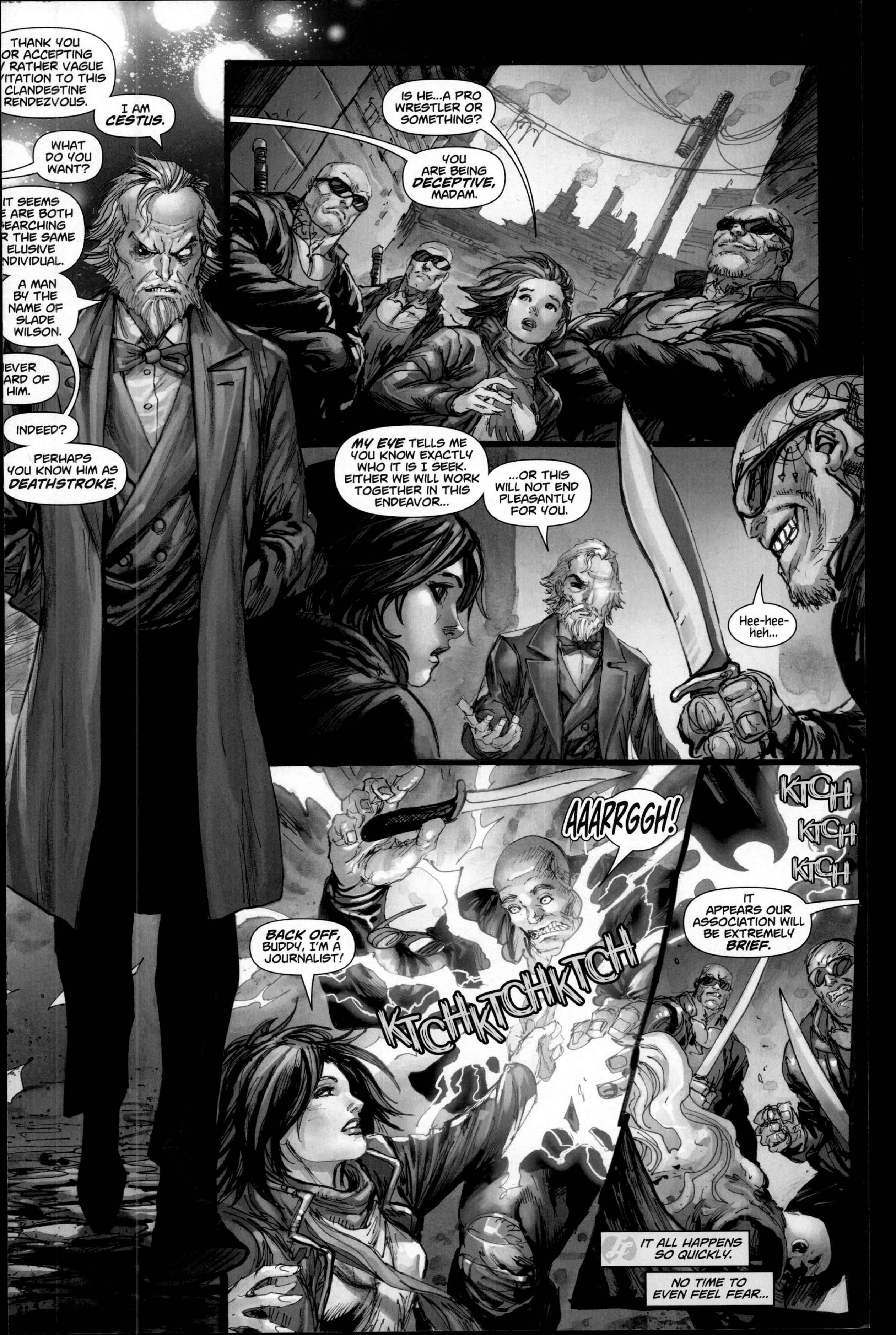
THANK YOU OR ACCEPTING Y RATHER VAGUE VITATION TO THIS CLANDESTINE RENDEZVOUS.
I AM CESTUS.
WHAT DO YOU WANT?
IT SEEMS E ARE BOTH EARCHING R THE SAME ELUSIVE NDIVIDUAL.
A MAN BY THE NAME OF SLADE WILSON.
EVER ARD OF HIM.
INDEED?
PERHAPS YOU KNOW HIM AS DEATHSTROKE.
IS HE...A PRO WRESTLER OR SOMETHING?
YOU ARE BEING DECEPTIVE, MADAM.
MY EYE TELLS ME YOU KNOW EXACTLY WHO IT IS I SEEK. EITHER WE WILL WORK TOGETHER IN THIS ENDEAVOR...
...OR THIS WILL NOT END PLEASANTLY FOR YOU.
Hee-hee-heh...
AAARRGGH!
BACK OFF, BUDDY, I'M A JOURNALIST!
KTCHKTCHKTCH
KTCH
KTCH
KTCH
IT APPEARS OUR ASSOCIATION WILL BE EXTREMELY BRIEF.
IT ALL HAPPENS SO QUICKLY.
NO TIME TO EVEN FEEL FEAR...

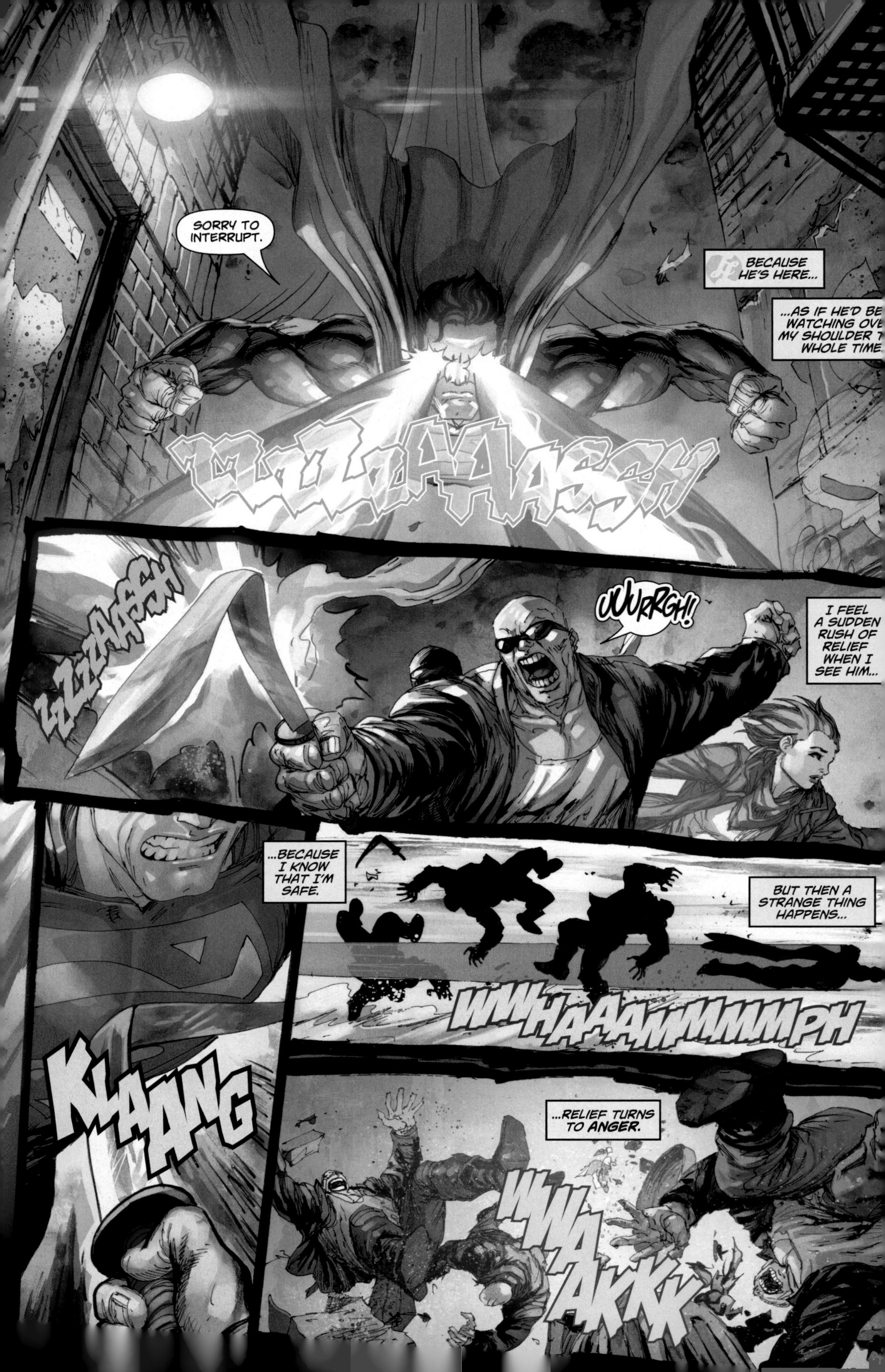
SORRY TO INTERRUPT.
BECAUSE HE'S HERE...
...AS IF HE'D BE WATCHING OVE MY SHOULDER T WHOLE TIME.
UUURRGH!
I FEEL A SUDDEN RUSH OF RELIEF WHEN I SEE HIM...
...BECAUSE I KNOW THAT I'M SAFE.
BUT THEN A STRANGE THING HAPPENS...
WWHAAAMMMMMPH
KLAANG
...RELIEF TURNS TO ANGER.

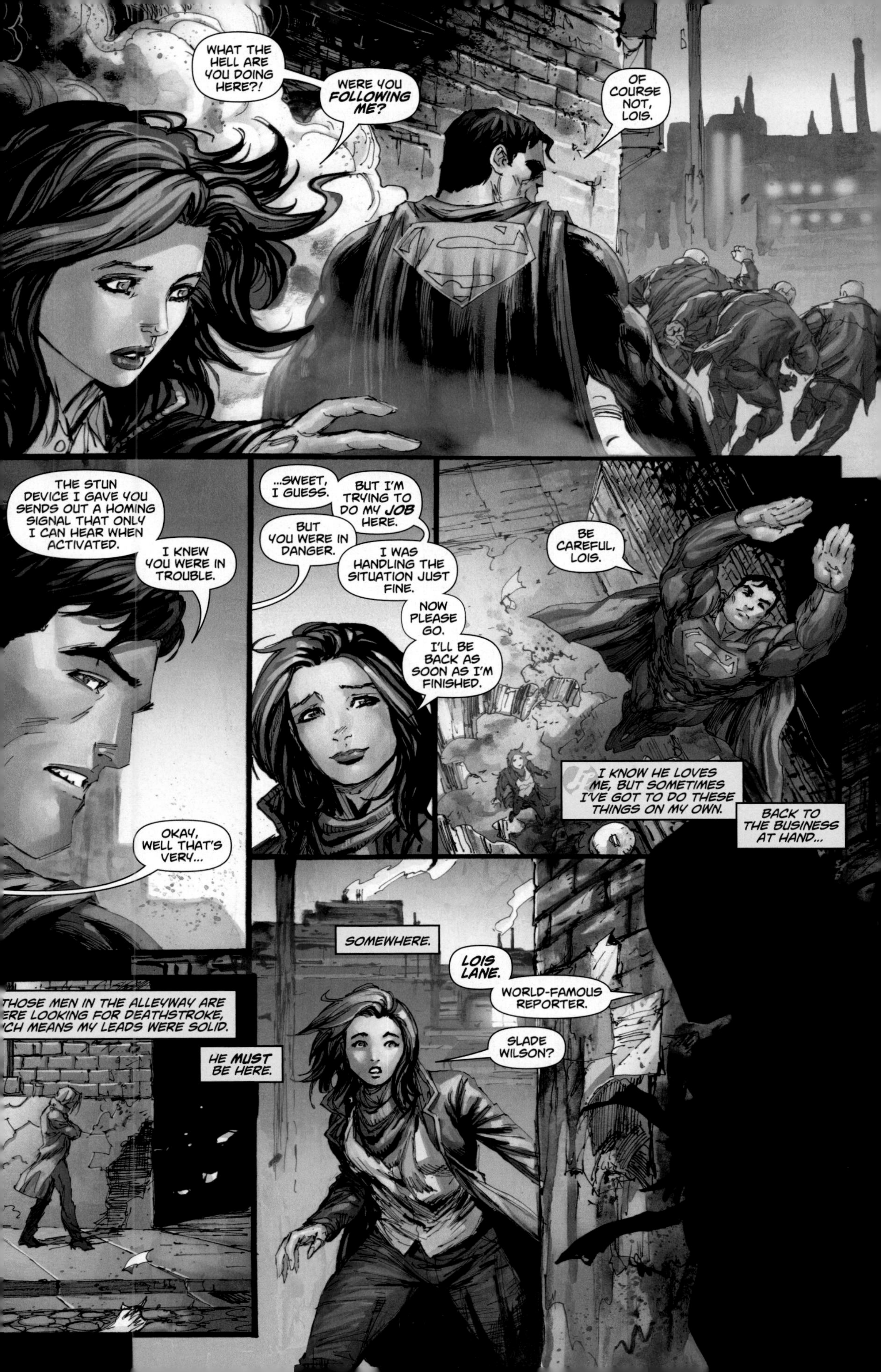

WHAT THE HELL ARE YOU DOING HERE?!
WERE YOU FOLLOWING ME?
OF COURSE NOT, LOIS.
THE STUN DEVICE I GAVE YOU SENDS OUT A HOMING SIGNAL THAT ONLY I CAN HEAR WHEN ACTIVATED.
I KNEW YOU WERE IN TROUBLE.
OKAY, WELL THAT'S VERY...
...SWEET, I GUESS.
BUT I'M TRYING TO DO MY JOB HERE.
BUT YOU WERE IN DANGER.
I WAS HANDLING THE SITUATION JUST FINE.
NOW PLEASE GO.
I'LL BE BACK AS SOON AS I'M FINISHED.
BE CAREFUL, LOIS.
I KNOW HE LOVES ME, BUT SOMETIMES I'VE GOT TO DO THESE THINGS ON MY OWN.
BACK TO THE BUSINESS AT HAND...
THOSE MEN IN THE ALLEYWAY ARE ERE LOOKING FOR DEATHSTROKE, ICH MEANS MY LEADS WERE SOLID.
HE MUST BE HERE.
SOMEWHERE.
LOIS LANE.
WORLD-FAMOUS REPORTER.
SLADE WILSON?

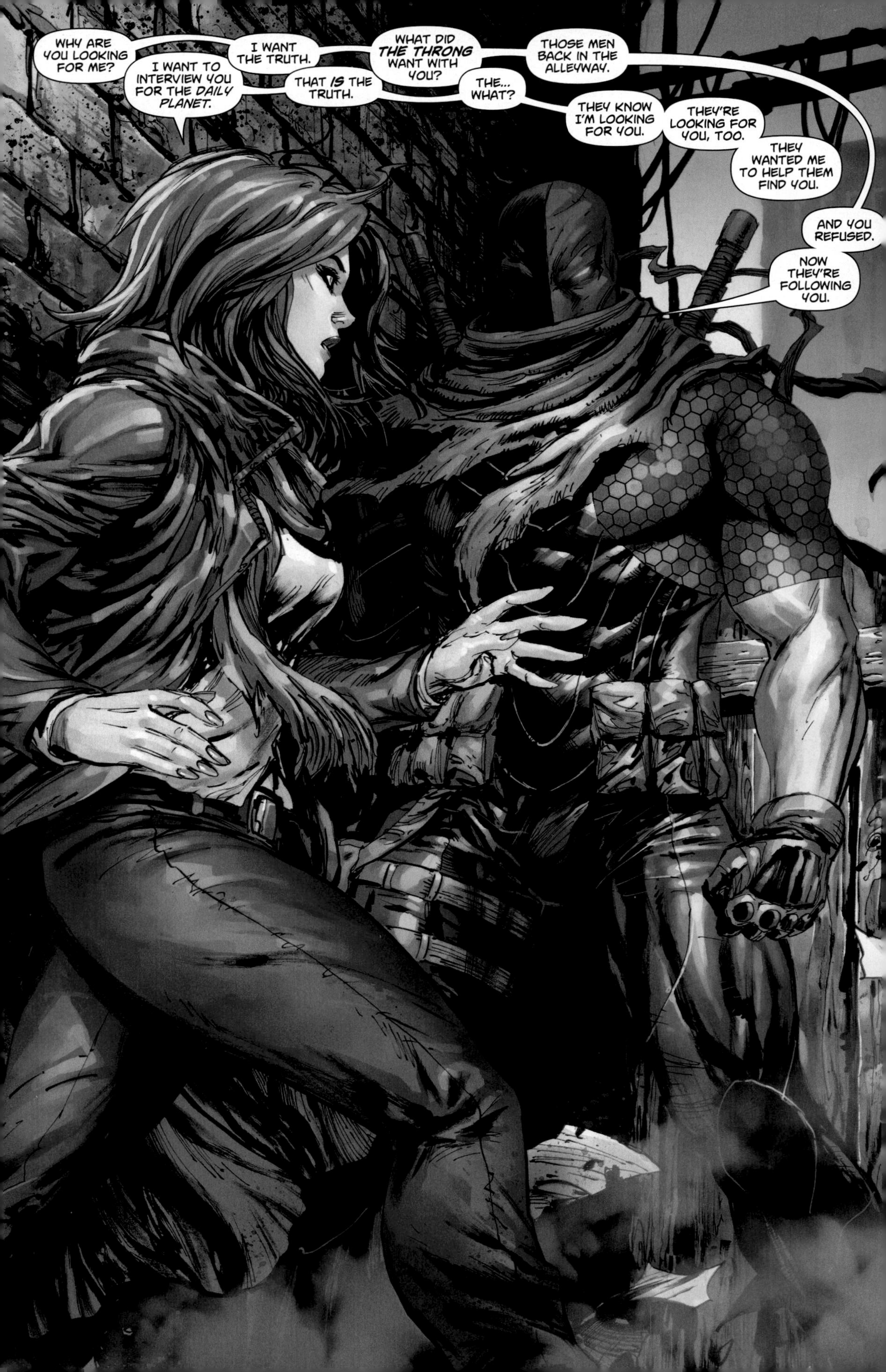
WHY ARE YOU LOOKING FOR ME?
I WANT TO INTERVIEW YOU FOR THE *DAILY PLANET*.
I WANT THE TRUTH.
THAT *IS* THE TRUTH.
WHAT DID *THE THRONG* WANT WITH YOU?
THE... WHAT?
THOSE MEN BACK IN THE ALLEYWAY.
THEY KNOW I'M LOOKING FOR YOU.
THEY'RE LOOKING FOR YOU, TOO.
THEY WANTED ME TO HELP THEM FIND YOU.
AND YOU REFUSED.
NOW THEY'RE FOLLOWING YOU.

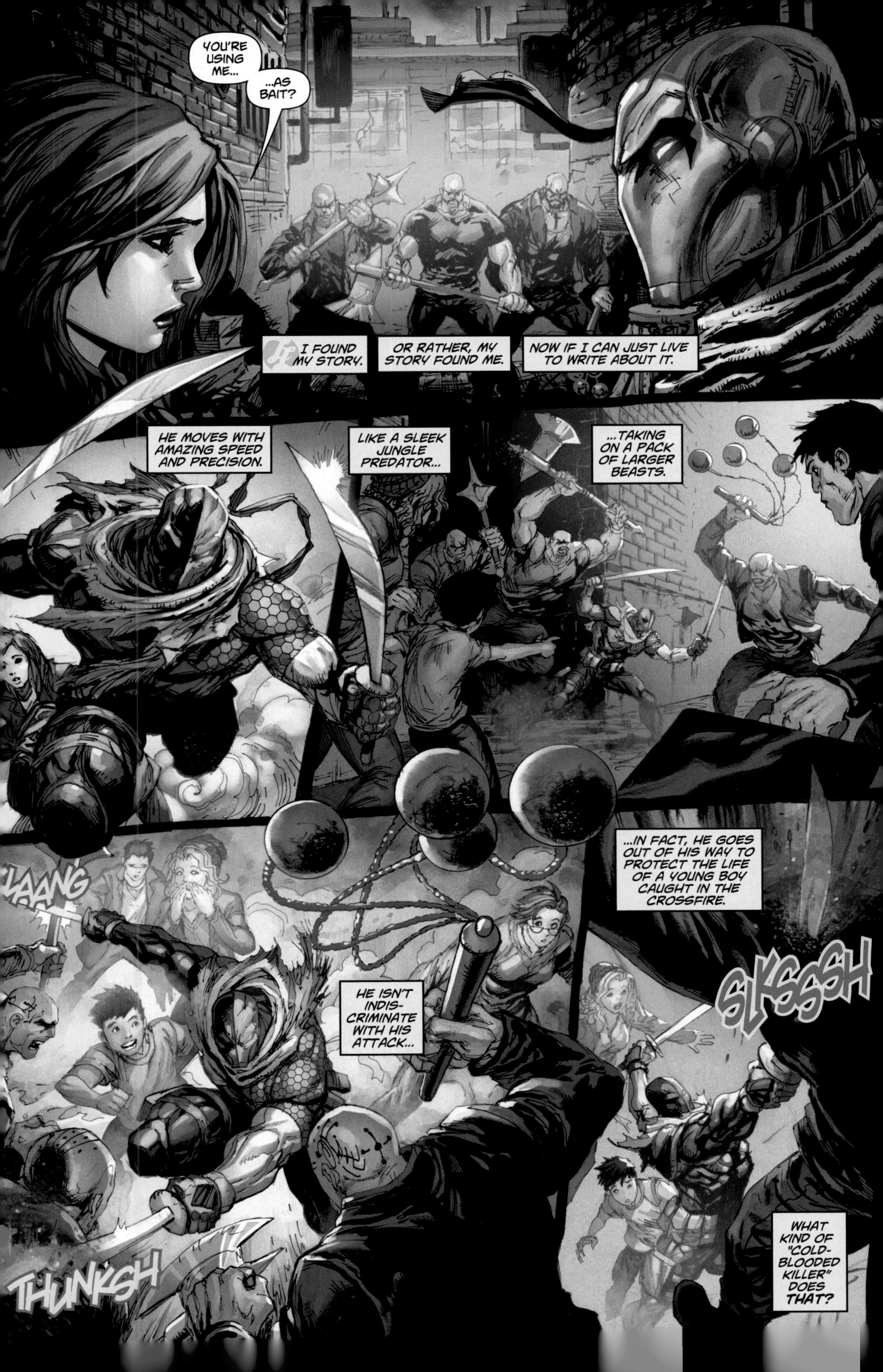

YOU'RE USING ME...
...AS BAIT?
I FOUND MY STORY.
OR RATHER, MY STORY FOUND ME.
NOW IF I CAN JUST LIVE TO WRITE ABOUT IT.
HE MOVES WITH AMAZING SPEED AND PRECISION.
LIKE A SLEEK JUNGLE PREDATOR...
...TAKING ON A PACK OF LARGER BEASTS.
CLAANG
HE ISN'T INDIS-CRIMINATE WITH HIS ATTACK...
THUNKSH
...IN FACT, HE GOES OUT OF HIS WAY TO PROTECT THE LIFE OF A YOUNG BOY CAUGHT IN THE CROSSFIRE.
SLKSSSH
WHAT KIND OF "COLD-BLOODED KILLER" DOES THAT?

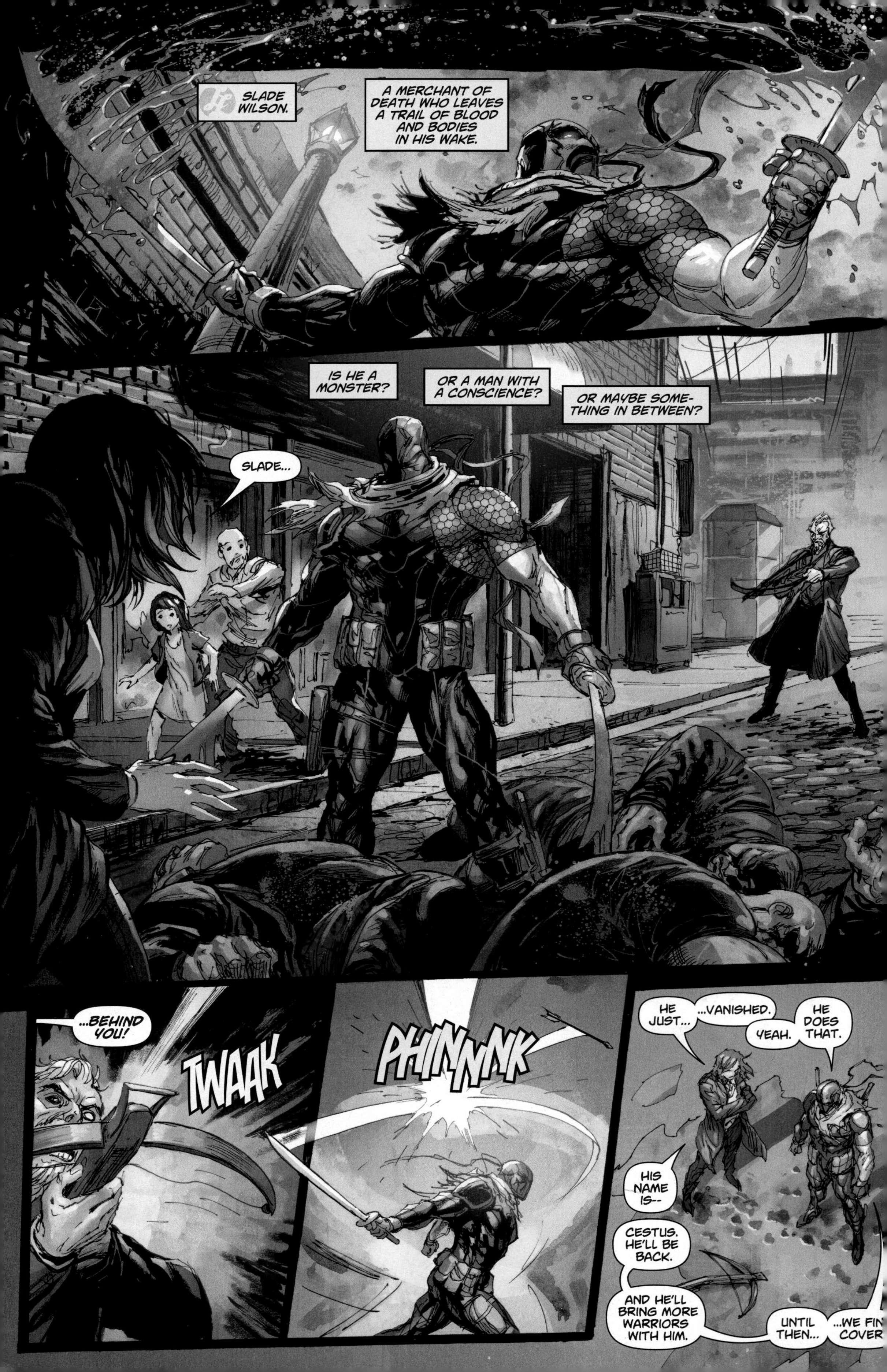

SLADE WILSON.
A MERCHANT OF DEATH WHO LEAVES A TRAIL OF BLOOD AND BODIES IN HIS WAKE.
IS HE A MONSTER?
OR A MAN WITH A CONSCIENCE?
OR MAYBE SOME-THING IN BETWEEN?
SLADE...
...BEHIND YOU!
TWAAK
PHINNNK
HE JUST...
...VANISHED.
YEAH.
HE DOES THAT.
HIS NAME IS--
CESTUS. HE'LL BE BACK.
AND HE'LL BRING MORE WARRIORS WITH HIM.
UNTIL THEN...

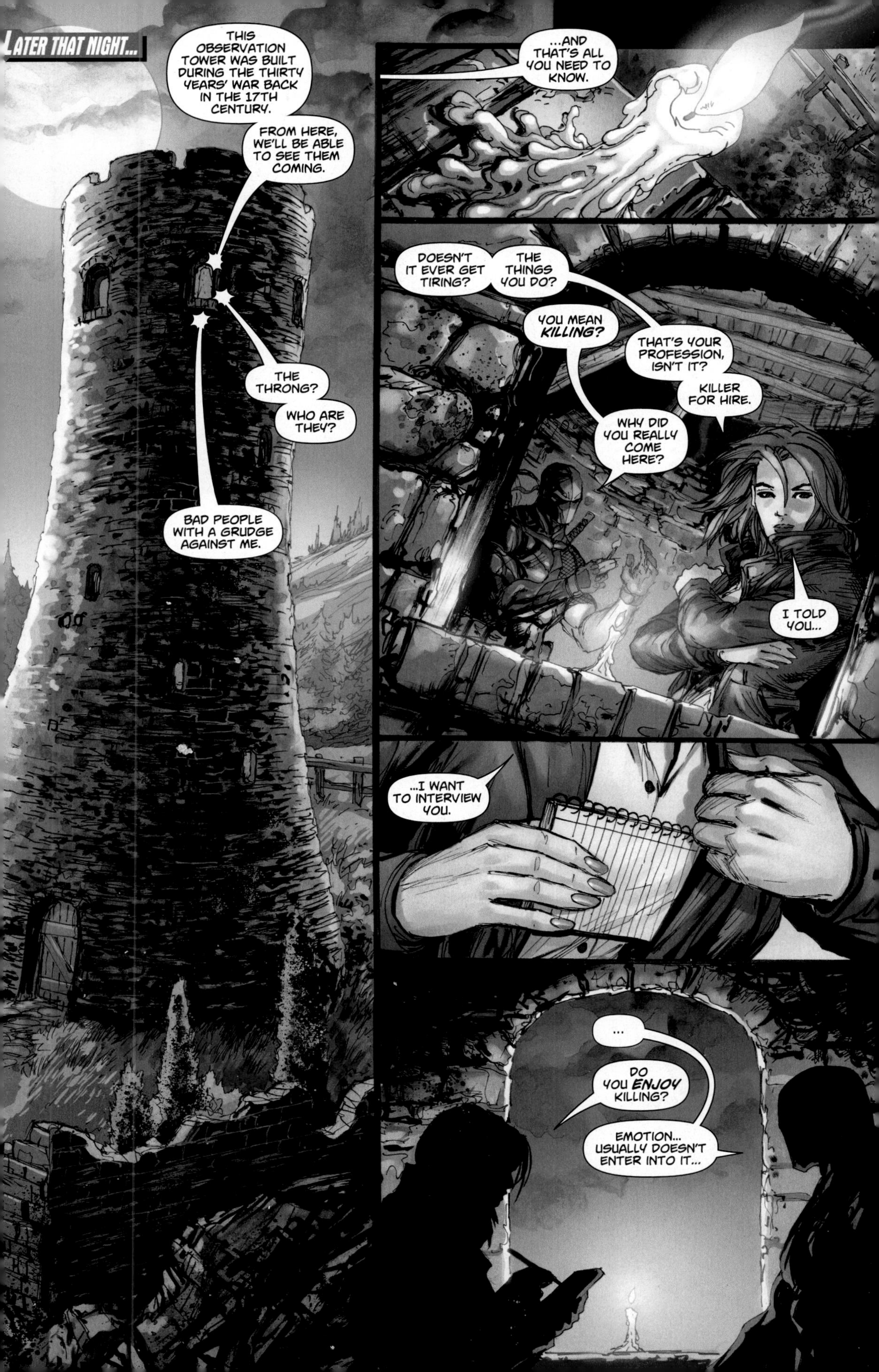
LATER THAT NIGHT...
THIS OBSERVATION TOWER WAS BUILT DURING THE THIRTY YEARS' WAR BACK IN THE 17TH CENTURY.
FROM HERE, WE'LL BE ABLE TO SEE THEM COMING.
THE THRONG?
WHO ARE THEY?
BAD PEOPLE WITH A GRUDGE AGAINST ME.
...AND THAT'S ALL YOU NEED TO KNOW.
DOESN'T IT EVER GET TIRING?
THE THINGS YOU DO?
YOU MEAN KILLING?
THAT'S YOUR PROFESSION, ISN'T IT?
KILLER FOR HIRE.
WHY DID YOU REALLY COME HERE?
I TOLD YOU...
...I WANT TO INTERVIEW YOU.
...
DO YOU ENJOY KILLING?
EMOTION... USUALLY DOESN'T ENTER INTO IT...

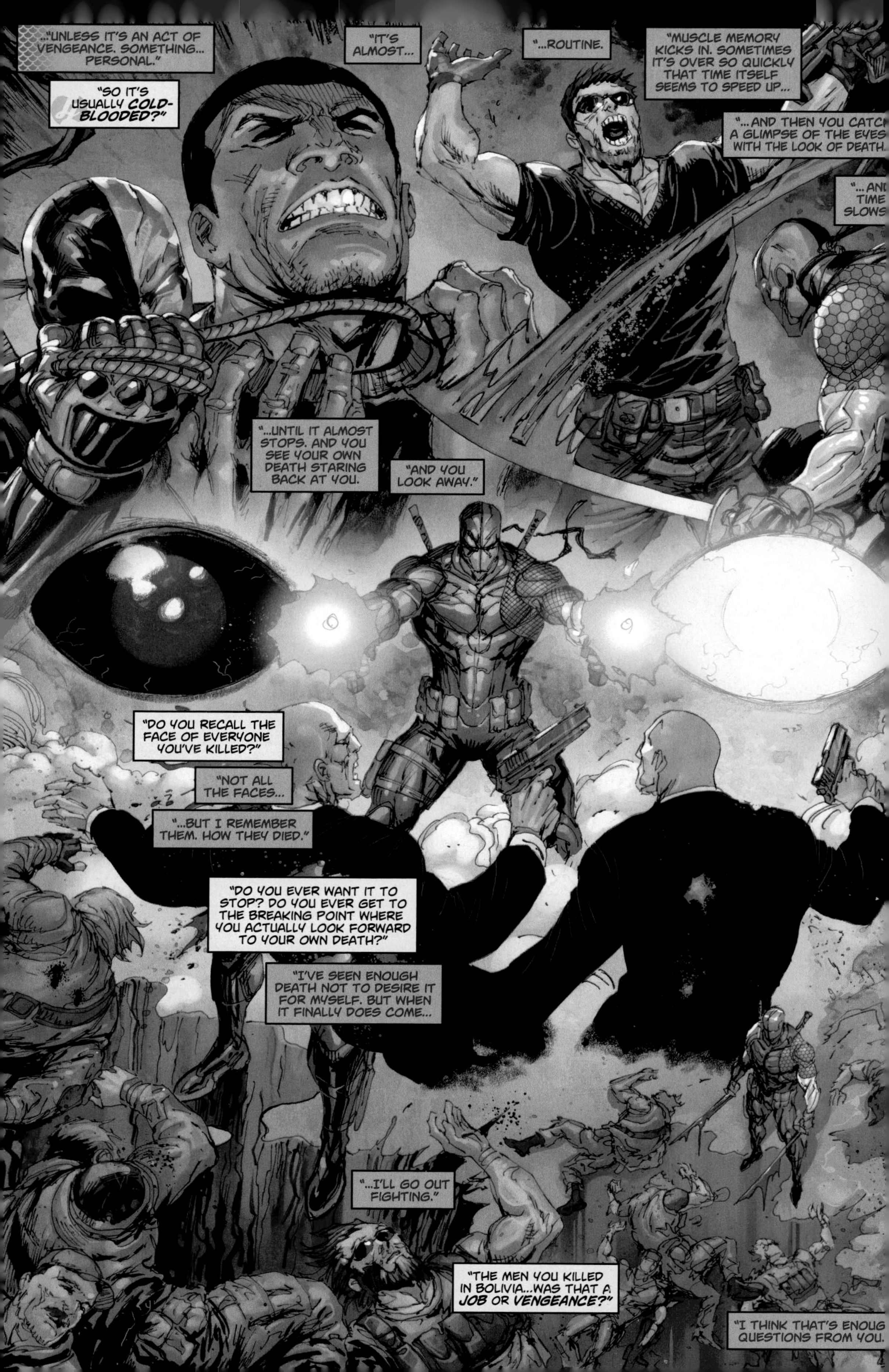
"...UNLESS IT'S AN ACT OF VENGEANCE. SOMETHING... PERSONAL."
"SO IT'S USUALLY COLD-BLOODED?"
"IT'S ALMOST...
"...ROUTINE.
"MUSCLE MEMORY KICKS IN. SOMETIMES IT'S OVER SO QUICKLY THAT TIME ITSELF SEEMS TO SPEED UP...
"...AND THEN YOU CATCH A GLIMPSE OF THE EYES WITH THE LOOK OF DEATH.
"...AND TIME SLOWS
"...UNTIL IT ALMOST STOPS. AND YOU SEE YOUR OWN DEATH STARING BACK AT YOU.
"AND YOU LOOK AWAY."
"DO YOU RECALL THE FACE OF EVERYONE YOU'VE KILLED?"
"NOT ALL THE FACES...
"...BUT I REMEMBER THEM. HOW THEY DIED."
"DO YOU EVER WANT IT TO STOP? DO YOU EVER GET TO THE BREAKING POINT WHERE YOU ACTUALLY LOOK FORWARD TO YOUR OWN DEATH?"
"I'VE SEEN ENOUGH DEATH NOT TO DESIRE IT FOR MYSELF. BUT WHEN IT FINALLY DOES COME...
"...I'LL GO OUT FIGHTING."
"THE MEN YOU KILLED IN BOLIVIA...WAS THAT A JOB OR VENGEANCE?"
"I THINK THAT'S ENOUGH QUESTIONS FROM YOU.

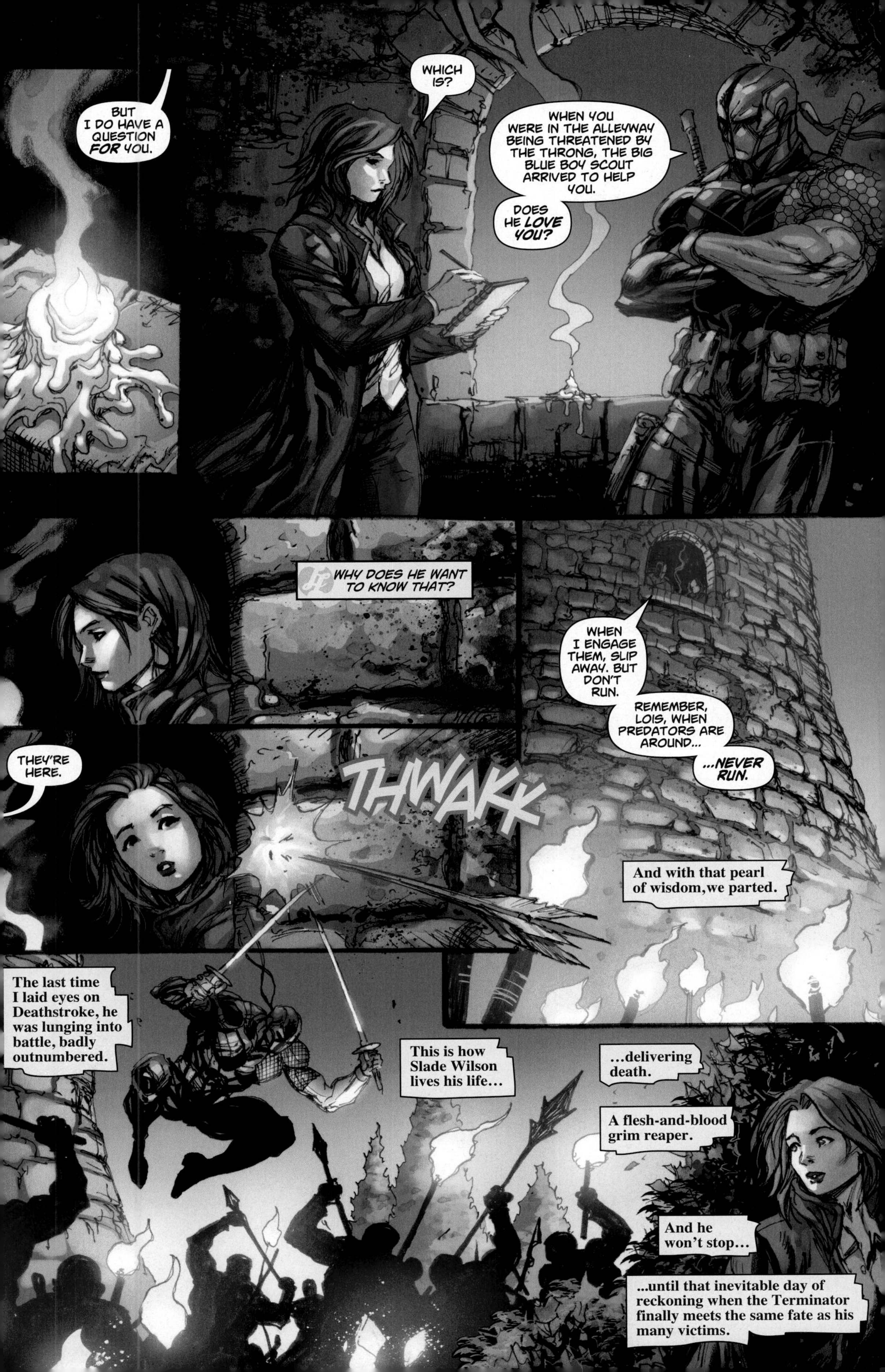

BUT I DO HAVE A QUESTION FOR YOU.
WHICH IS?
WHEN YOU WERE IN THE ALLEYWAY BEING THREATENED BY THE THRONG, THE BIG BLUE BOY SCOUT ARRIVED TO HELP YOU.
DOES HE LOVE YOU?
WHY DOES HE WANT TO KNOW THAT?
THEY'RE HERE.
THWAKK
WHEN I ENGAGE THEM, SLIP AWAY. BUT DON'T RUN.
REMEMBER, LOIS, WHEN PREDATORS ARE AROUND...
...NEVER RUN.
And with that pearl of wisdom, we parted.
The last time I laid eyes on Deathstroke, he was lunging into battle, badly outnumbered.
This is how Slade Wilson lives his life...
...delivering death.
A flesh-and-blood grim reaper.
And he won't stop...
...until that inevitable day of reckoning when the Terminator finally meets the same fate as his many victims.

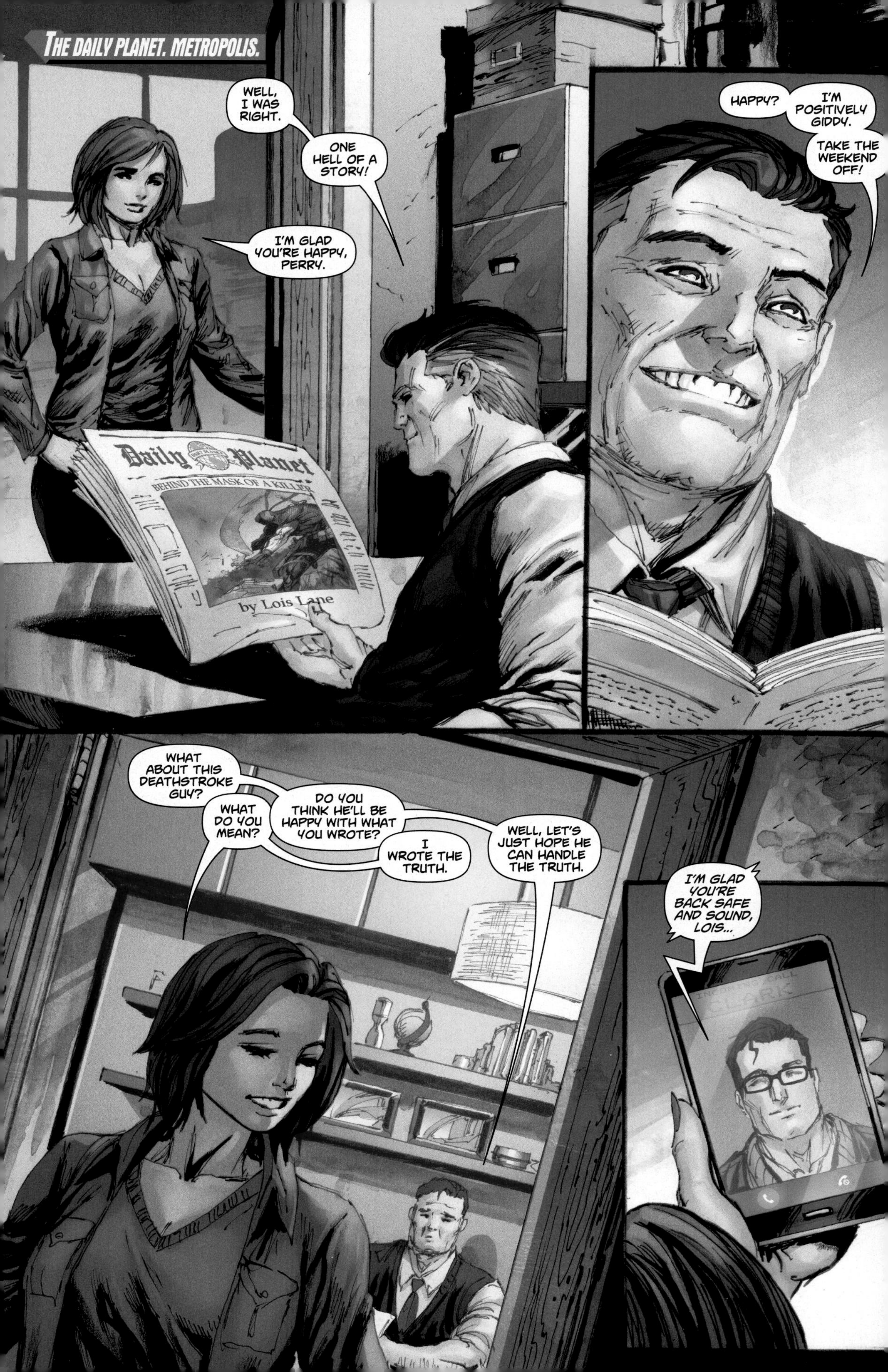
THE DAILY PLANET. METROPOLIS.
WELL, I WAS RIGHT.
ONE HELL OF A STORY!
I'M GLAD YOU'RE HAPPY, PERRY.
Daily Planet
BEHIND THE MASK OF A KILLER
by Lois Lane
HAPPY?
I'M POSITIVELY GIDDY.
TAKE THE WEEKEND OFF!
WHAT ABOUT THIS DEATHSTROKE GUY?
WHAT DO YOU MEAN?
DO YOU THINK HE'LL BE HAPPY WITH WHAT YOU WROTE?
I WROTE THE TRUTH.
WELL, LET'S JUST HOPE HE CAN HANDLE THE TRUTH.
I'M GLAD YOU'RE BACK SAFE AND SOUND, LOIS...
INCOMING CALL
CLARK

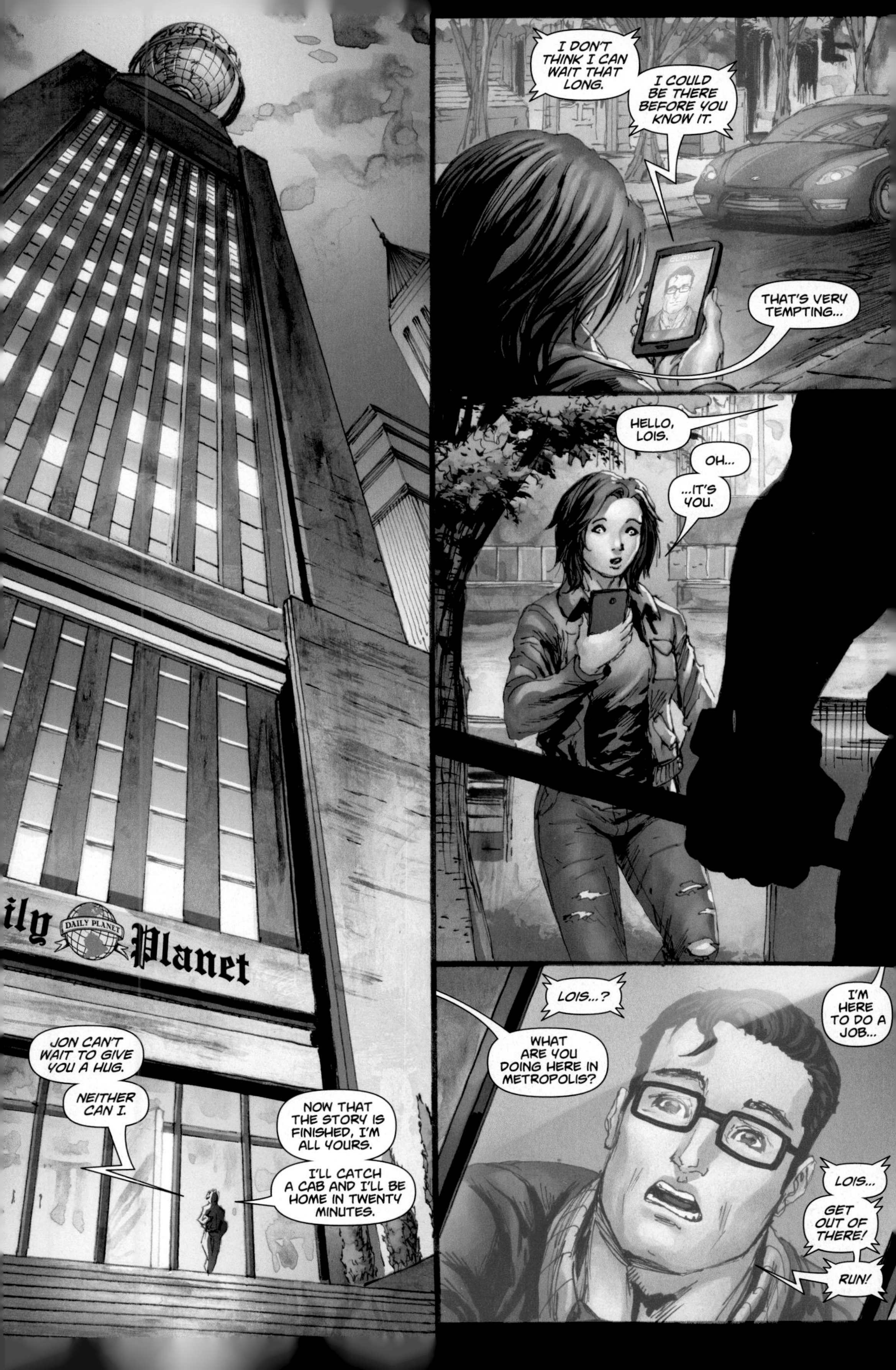

ily DAILY PLANET Planet
JON CAN'T WAIT TO GIVE YOU A HUG.
NEITHER CAN I.
NOW THAT THE STORY IS FINISHED, I'M ALL YOURS.
I'LL CATCH A CAB AND I'LL BE HOME IN TWENTY MINUTES.
I DON'T THINK I CAN WAIT THAT LONG.
I COULD BE THERE BEFORE YOU KNOW IT.
CLARK
THAT'S VERY TEMPTING...
HELLO, LOIS.
OH...
...IT'S YOU.
LOIS...?
WHAT ARE YOU DOING HERE IN METROPOLIS?
I'M HERE TO DO A JOB...
LOIS...
GET OUT OF THERE!
RUN!

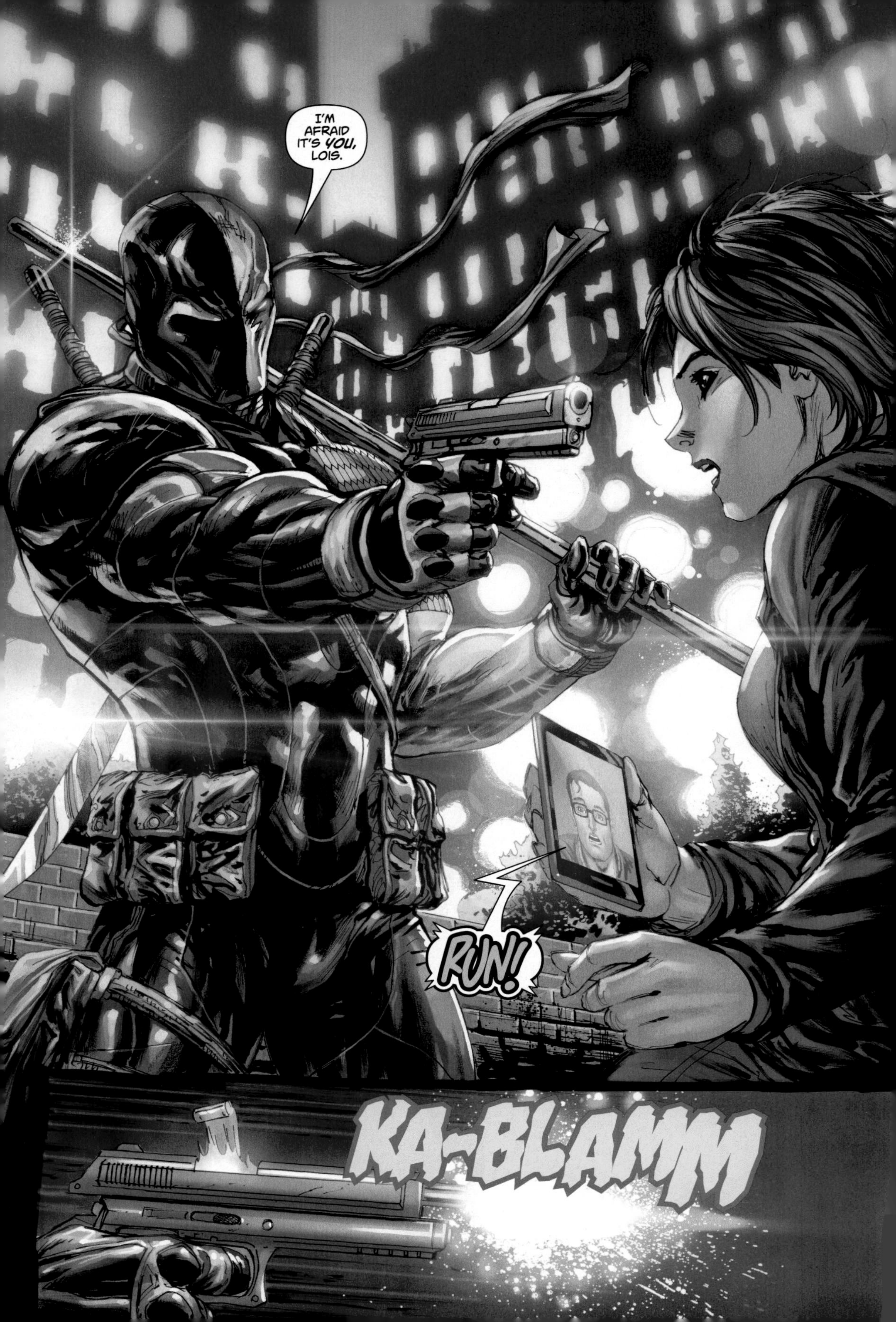
I'M AFRAID IT'S YOU, LOIS.
RUN!
KA-BLAMM

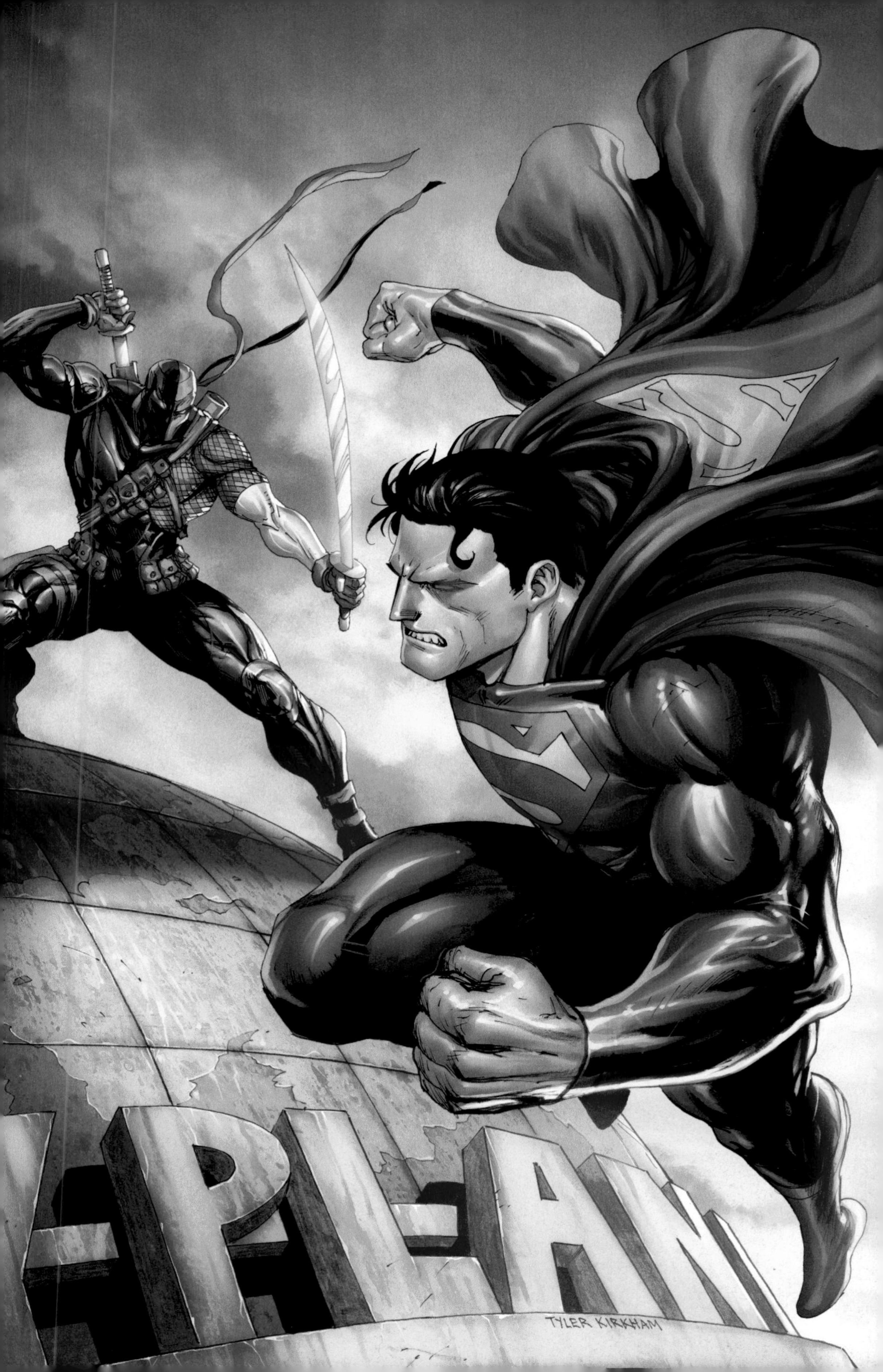
PLAN
TYLER KIRKHAM

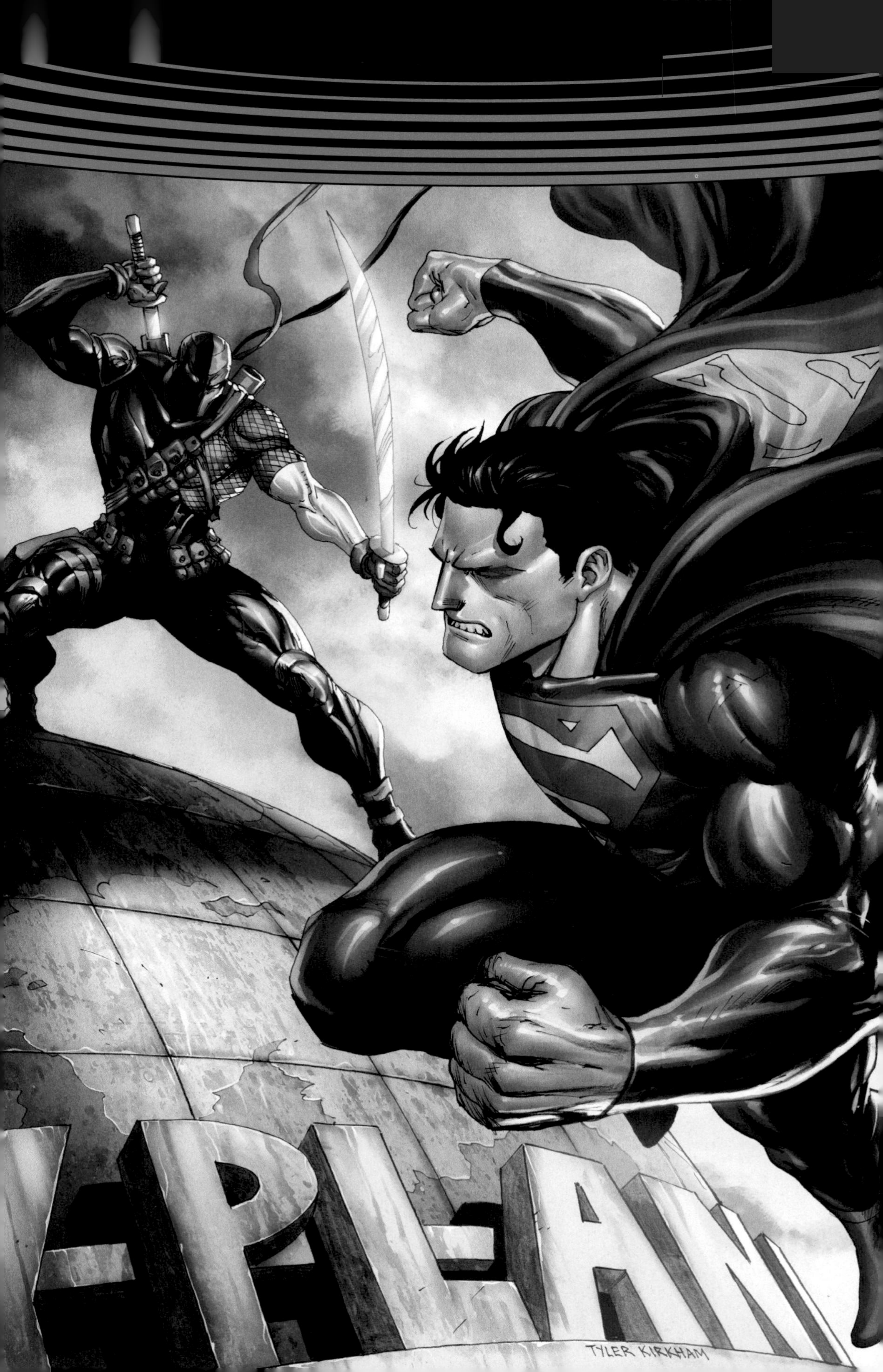
TYLER KIRKHAM

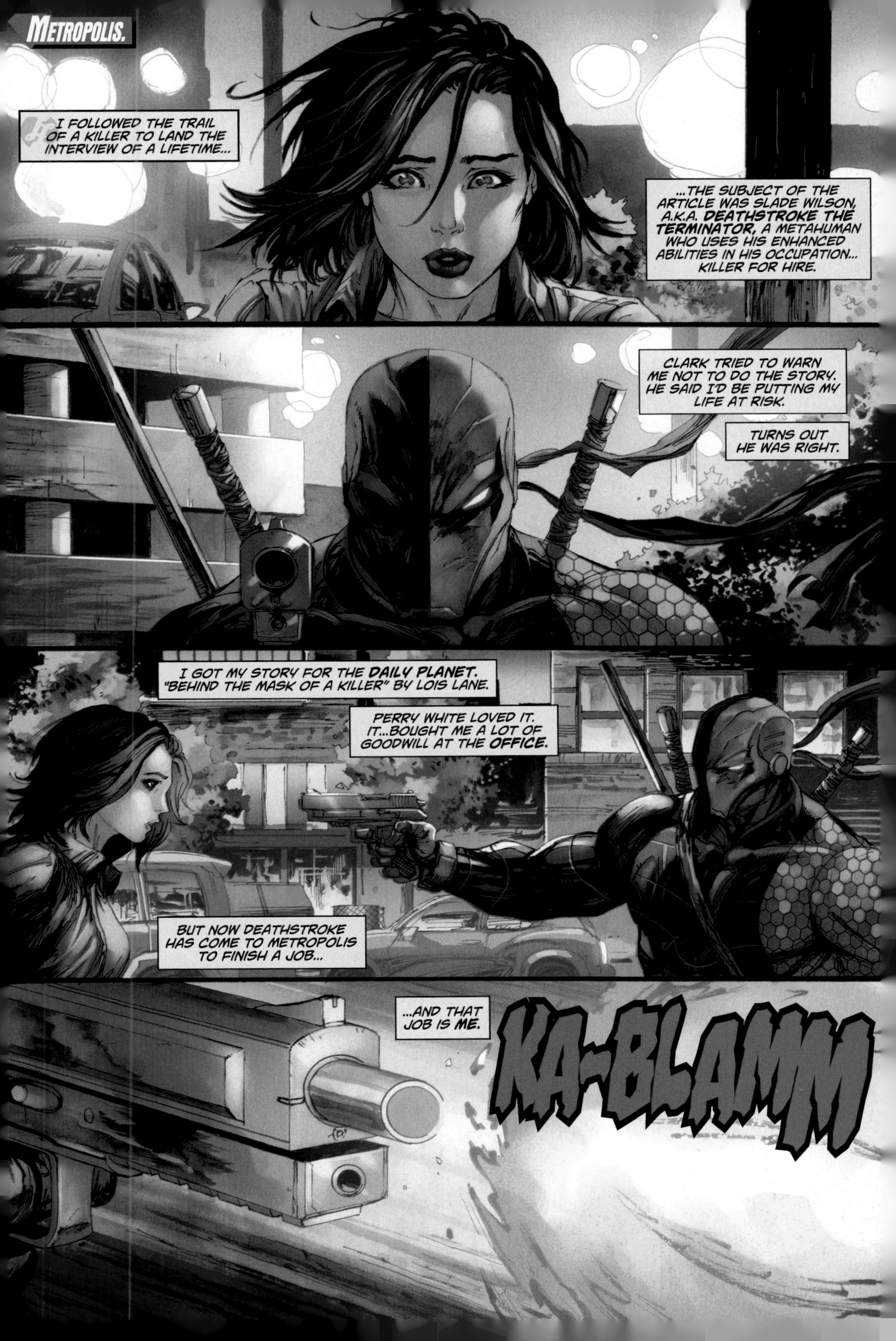
METROPOLIS.
I FOLLOWED THE TRAIL OF A KILLER TO LAND THE INTERVIEW OF A LIFETIME...
...THE SUBJECT OF THE ARTICLE WAS SLADE WILSON, A.K.A. DEATHSTROKE THE TERMINATOR, A METAHUMAN WHO USES HIS ENHANCED ABILITIES IN HIS OCCUPATION... KILLER FOR HIRE.
CLARK TRIED TO WARN ME NOT TO DO THE STORY. HE SAID I'D BE PUTTING MY LIFE AT RISK.
TURNS OUT HE WAS RIGHT.
I GOT MY STORY FOR THE DAILY PLANET. "BEHIND THE MASK OF A KILLER" BY LOIS LANE.
PERRY WHITE LOVED IT. IT...BOUGHT ME A LOT OF GOODWILL AT THE OFFICE.
BUT NOW DEATHSTROKE HAS COME TO METROPOLIS TO FINISH A JOB...
...AND THAT JOB IS ME.
KA-BLAMM

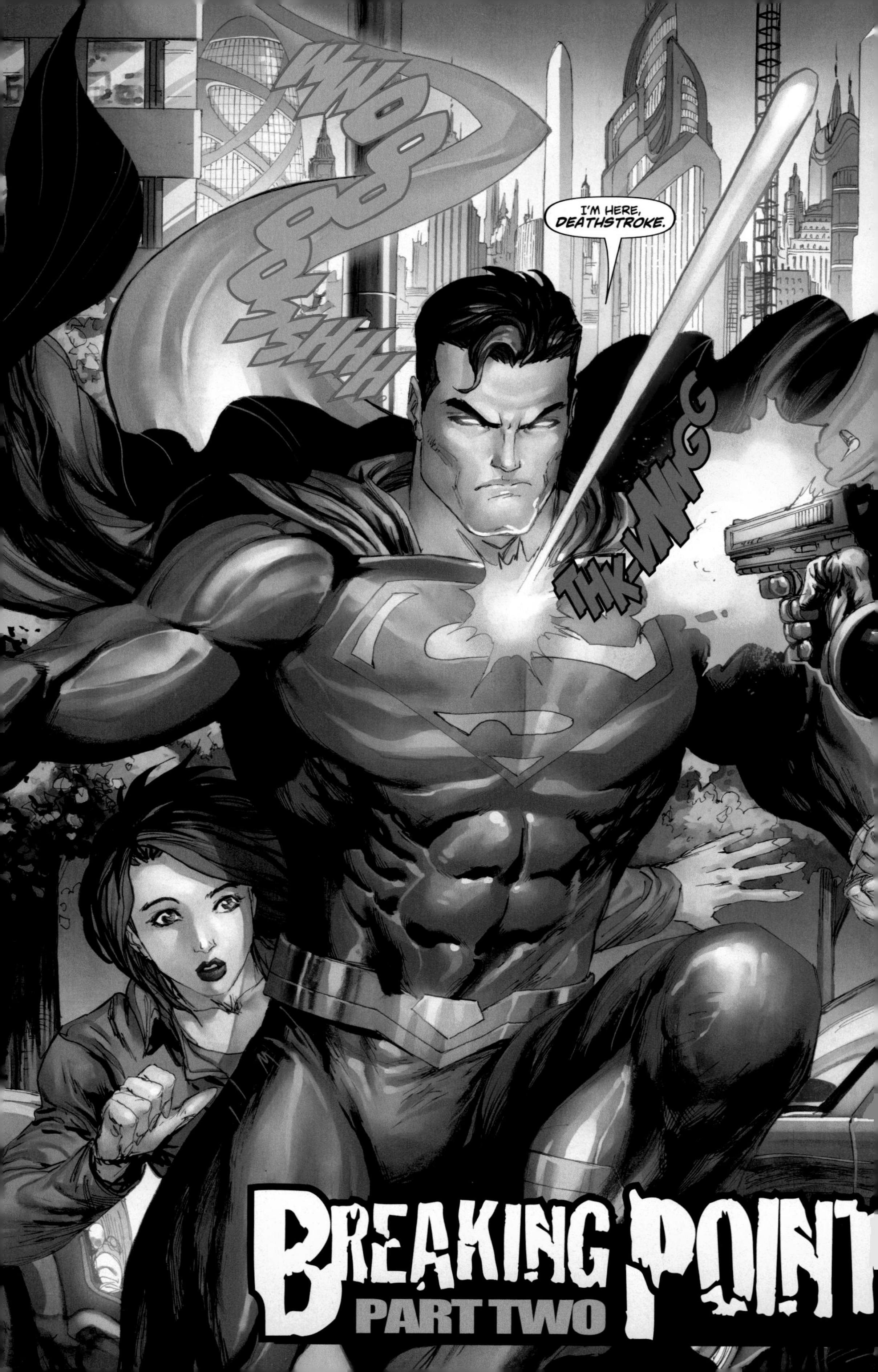

BOOM
BOOSHHH
I'M HERE, DEATHSTROKE.
THK-VMMGG
BREAKING POINT
PART TWO

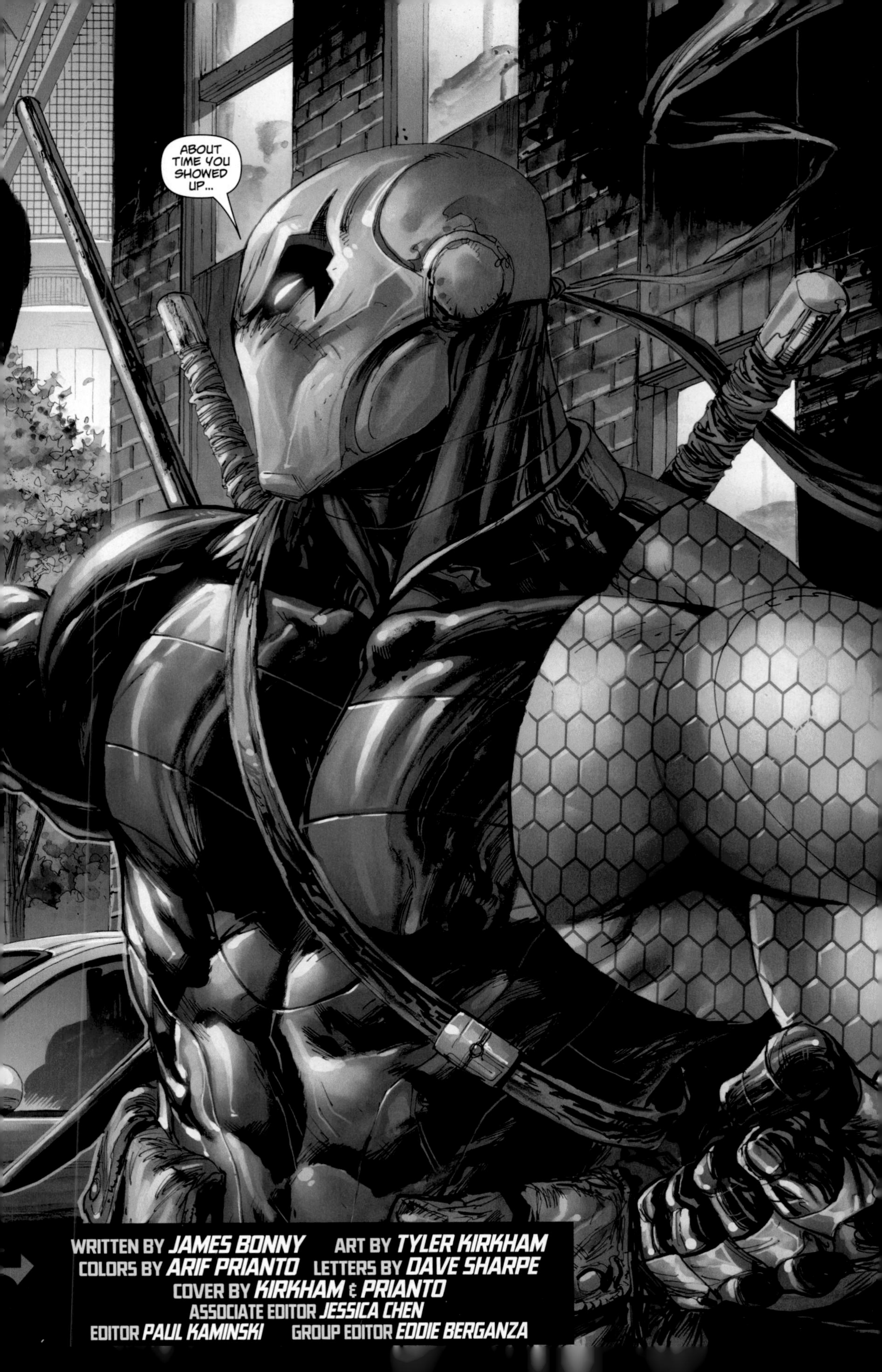

ABOUT TIME YOU SHOWED UP...
WRITTEN BY JAMES BONNY ART BY TYLER KIRKHAM
COLORS BY ARIF PRIANTO LETTERS BY DAVE SHARPE
COVER BY KIRKHAM & PRIANTO
ASSOCIATE EDITOR JESSICA CHEN
EDITOR PAUL KAMINSKI GROUP EDITOR EDDIE BERGANZA

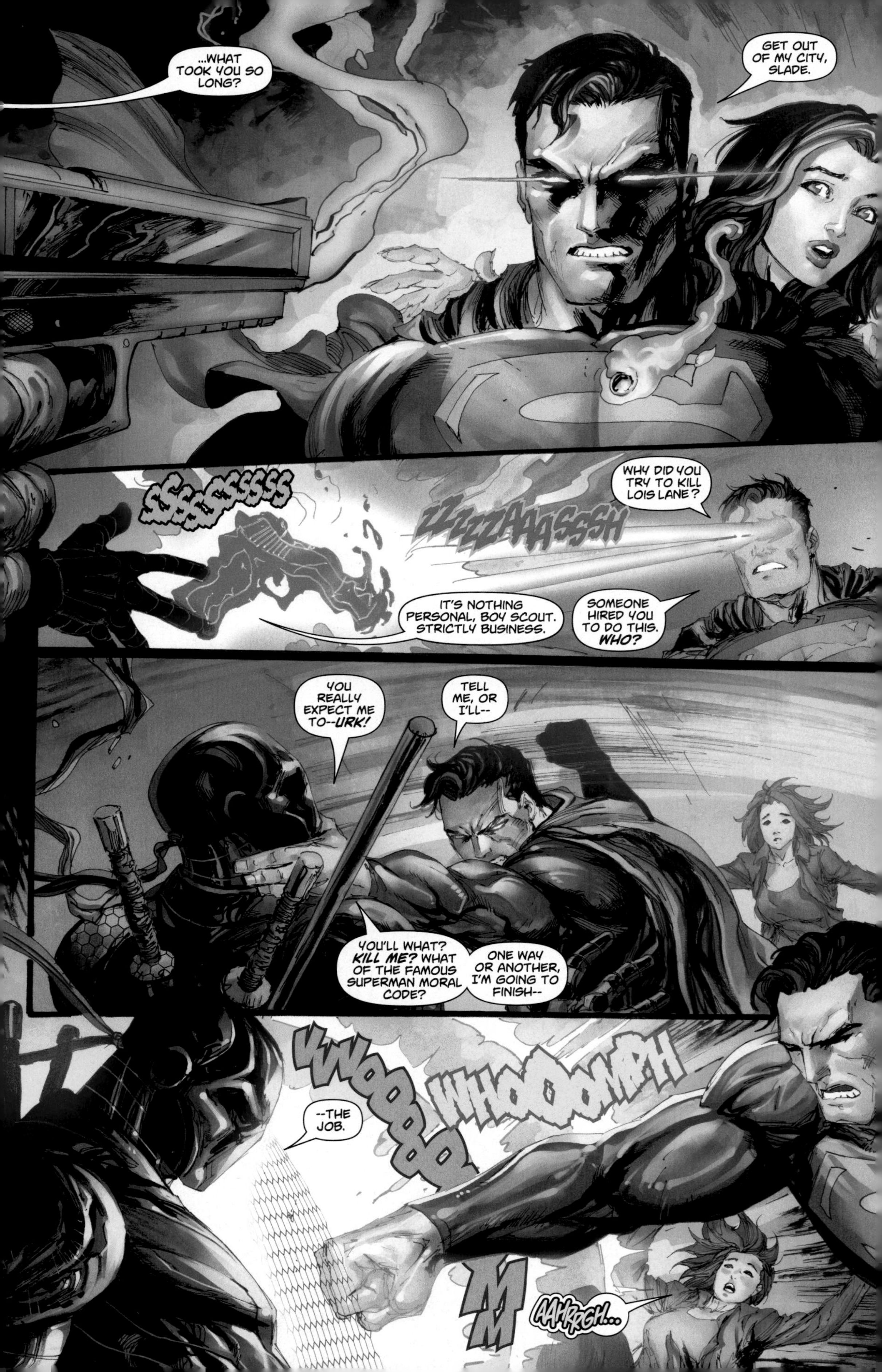

...WHAT TOOK YOU SO LONG?
GET OUT OF MY CITY, SLADE.
SSSSSSSSSS
WHY DID YOU TRY TO KILL LOIS LANE?
ZZZZZAAAASSSH
IT'S NOTHING PERSONAL, BOY SCOUT. STRICTLY BUSINESS.
SOMEONE HIRED YOU TO DO THIS. WHO?
YOU REALLY EXPECT ME TO--URK!
TELL ME, OR I'LL--
YOU'LL WHAT? KILL ME? WHAT OF THE FAMOUS SUPERMAN MORAL CODE?
ONE WAY OR ANOTHER, I'M GOING TO FINISH--
VWOOOOOOOM
WHOOOMPH
--THE JOB.
AAHRRGH...

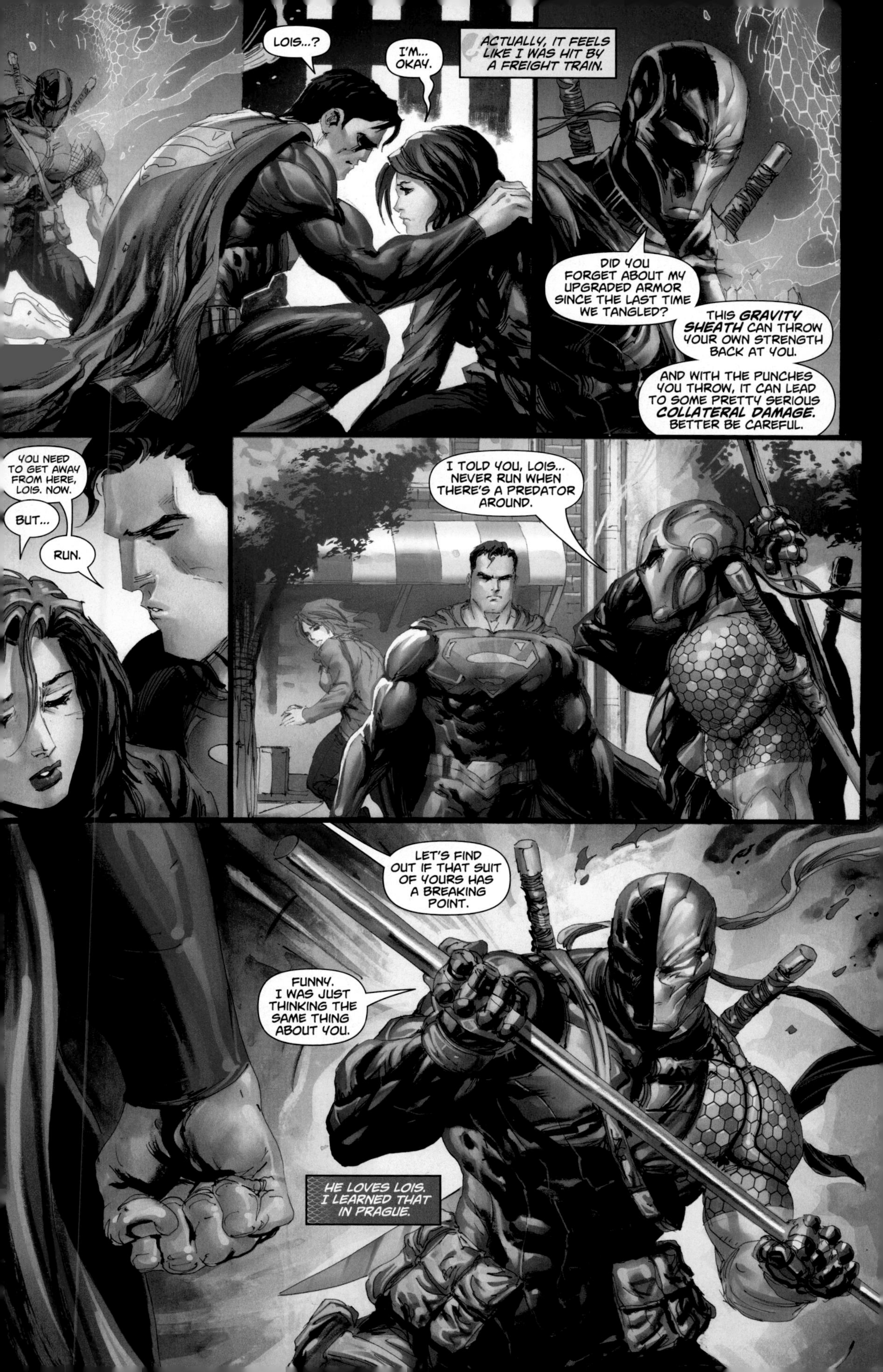
LOIS...?
I'M... OKAY.
ACTUALLY, IT FEELS LIKE I WAS HIT BY A FREIGHT TRAIN.
DID YOU FORGET ABOUT MY UPGRADED ARMOR SINCE THE LAST TIME WE TANGLED?
THIS GRAVITY SHEATH CAN THROW YOUR OWN STRENGTH BACK AT YOU.
AND WITH THE PUNCHES YOU THROW, IT CAN LEAD TO SOME PRETTY SERIOUS COLLATERAL DAMAGE. BETTER BE CAREFUL.
YOU NEED TO GET AWAY FROM HERE, LOIS. NOW.
BUT...
RUN.
I TOLD YOU, LOIS... NEVER RUN WHEN THERE'S A PREDATOR AROUND.
LET'S FIND OUT IF THAT SUIT OF YOURS HAS A BREAKING POINT.
FUNNY. I WAS JUST THINKING THE SAME THING ABOUT YOU.
HE LOVES LOIS. I LEARNED THAT IN PRAGUE.

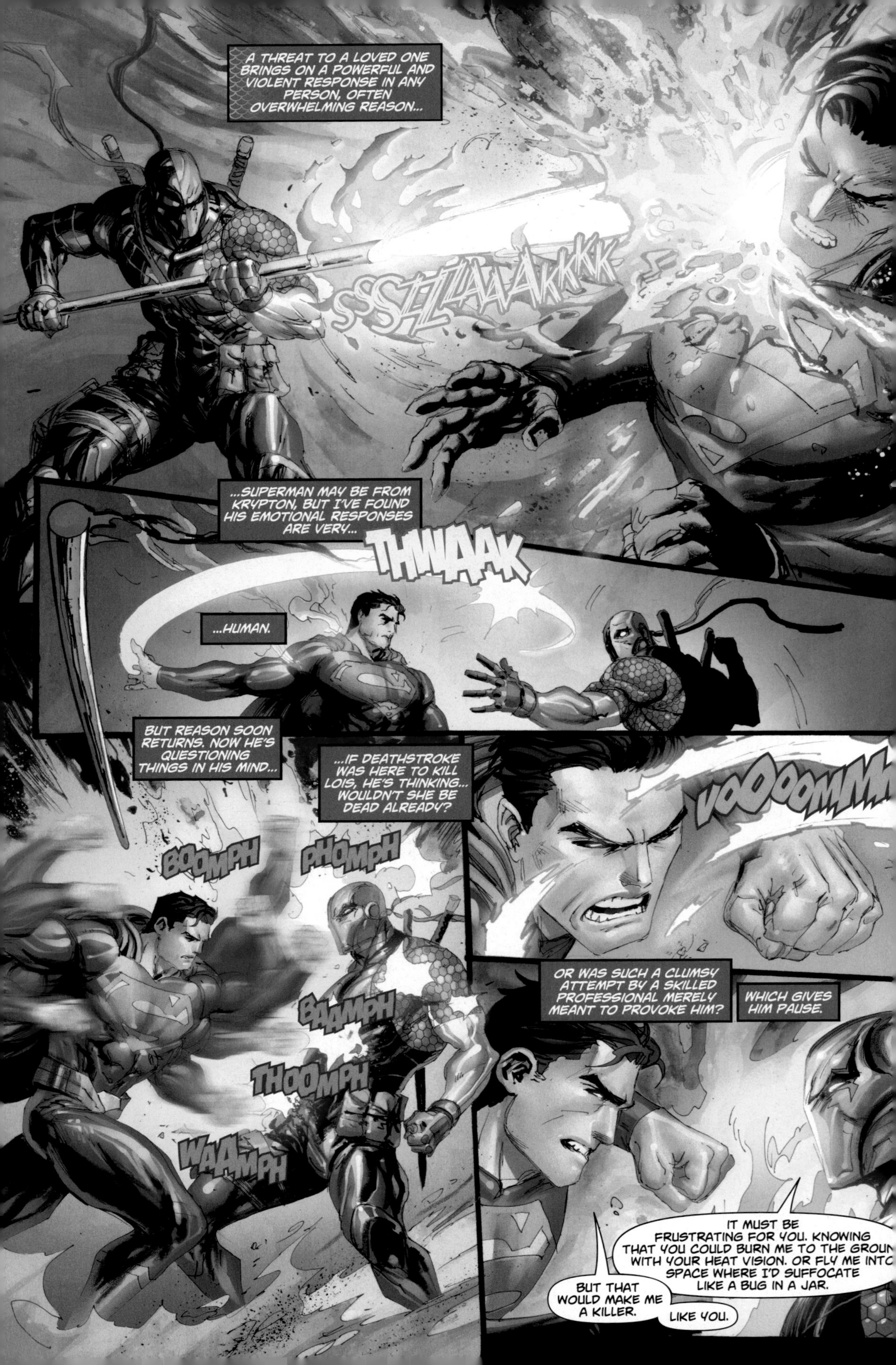
A THREAT TO A LOVED ONE BRINGS ON A POWERFUL AND VIOLENT RESPONSE IN ANY PERSON, OFTEN OVERWHELMING REASON...
SSSHLLAAAKKKK
...SUPERMAN MAY BE FROM KRYPTON, BUT I'VE FOUND HIS EMOTIONAL RESPONSES ARE VERY...
THWAAK
...HUMAN.
BUT REASON SOON RETURNS. NOW HE'S QUESTIONING THINGS IN HIS MIND...
...IF DEATHSTROKE WAS HERE TO KILL LOIS, HE'S THINKING... WOULDN'T SHE BE DEAD ALREADY?
BOOMPH
PHOMPH
BAAMPH
THOOMPH
WAAMPH
VOOOOMMM
OR WAS SUCH A CLUMSY ATTEMPT BY A SKILLED PROFESSIONAL MERELY MEANT TO PROVOKE HIM?
WHICH GIVES HIM PAUSE.
IT MUST BE FRUSTRATING FOR YOU. KNOWING THAT YOU COULD BURN ME TO THE GROUN WITH YOUR HEAT VISION. OR FLY ME INTO SPACE WHERE I'D SUFFOCATE LIKE A BUG IN A JAR.
BUT THAT WOULD MAKE ME A KILLER.
LIKE YOU.

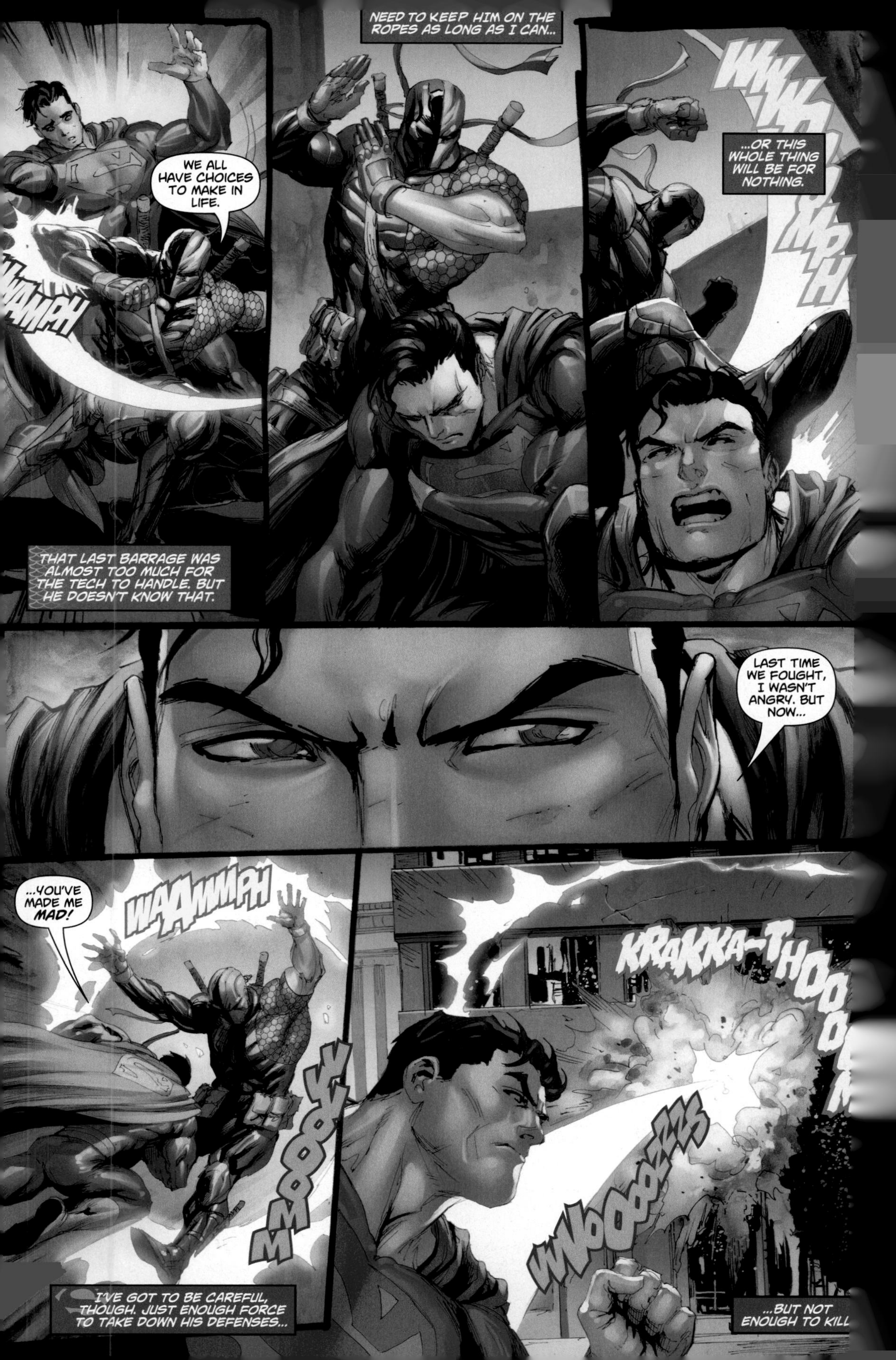
WE ALL HAVE CHOICES TO MAKE IN LIFE.
WHAMPH
THAT LAST BARRAGE WAS ALMOST TOO MUCH FOR THE TECH TO HANDLE. BUT HE DOESN'T KNOW THAT.
NEED TO KEEP HIM ON THE ROPES AS LONG AS I CAN...
...OR THIS WHOLE THING WILL BE FOR NOTHING.
WWOMPH
LAST TIME WE FOUGHT, I WASN'T ANGRY. BUT NOW...
...YOU'VE MADE ME MAD!
WAAMMMPH
VOOOOOMMM
I'VE GOT TO BE CAREFUL, THOUGH. JUST ENOUGH FORCE TO TAKE DOWN HIS DEFENSES...
KRAKKA-THOOOM
WHOOOOZZZS
...BUT NOT ENOUGH TO KILL

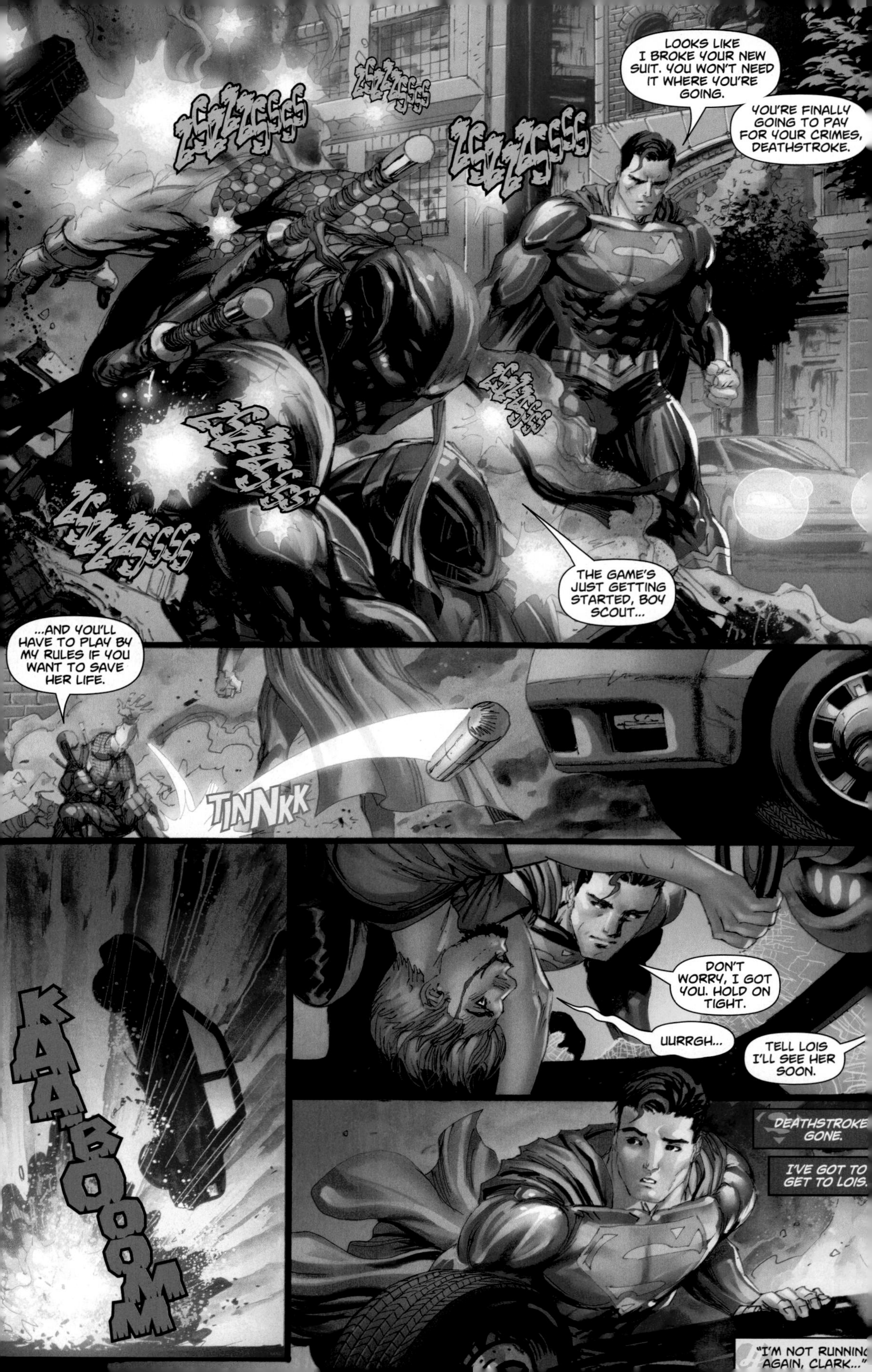
LOOKS LIKE I BROKE YOUR NEW SUIT. YOU WON'T NEED IT WHERE YOU'RE GOING.
YOU'RE FINALLY GOING TO PAY FOR YOUR CRIMES, DEATHSTROKE.
THE GAME'S JUST GETTING STARTED, BOY SCOUT...
...AND YOU'LL HAVE TO PLAY BY MY RULES IF YOU WANT TO SAVE HER LIFE.
TINNKK
KA-BOOOM
DON'T WORRY, I GOT YOU. HOLD ON TIGHT.
UURRGH...
TELL LOIS I'LL SEE HER SOON.
DEATHSTROKE GONE.
I'VE GOT TO GET TO LOIS.
"I'M NOT RUNNING AGAIN, CLARK..."

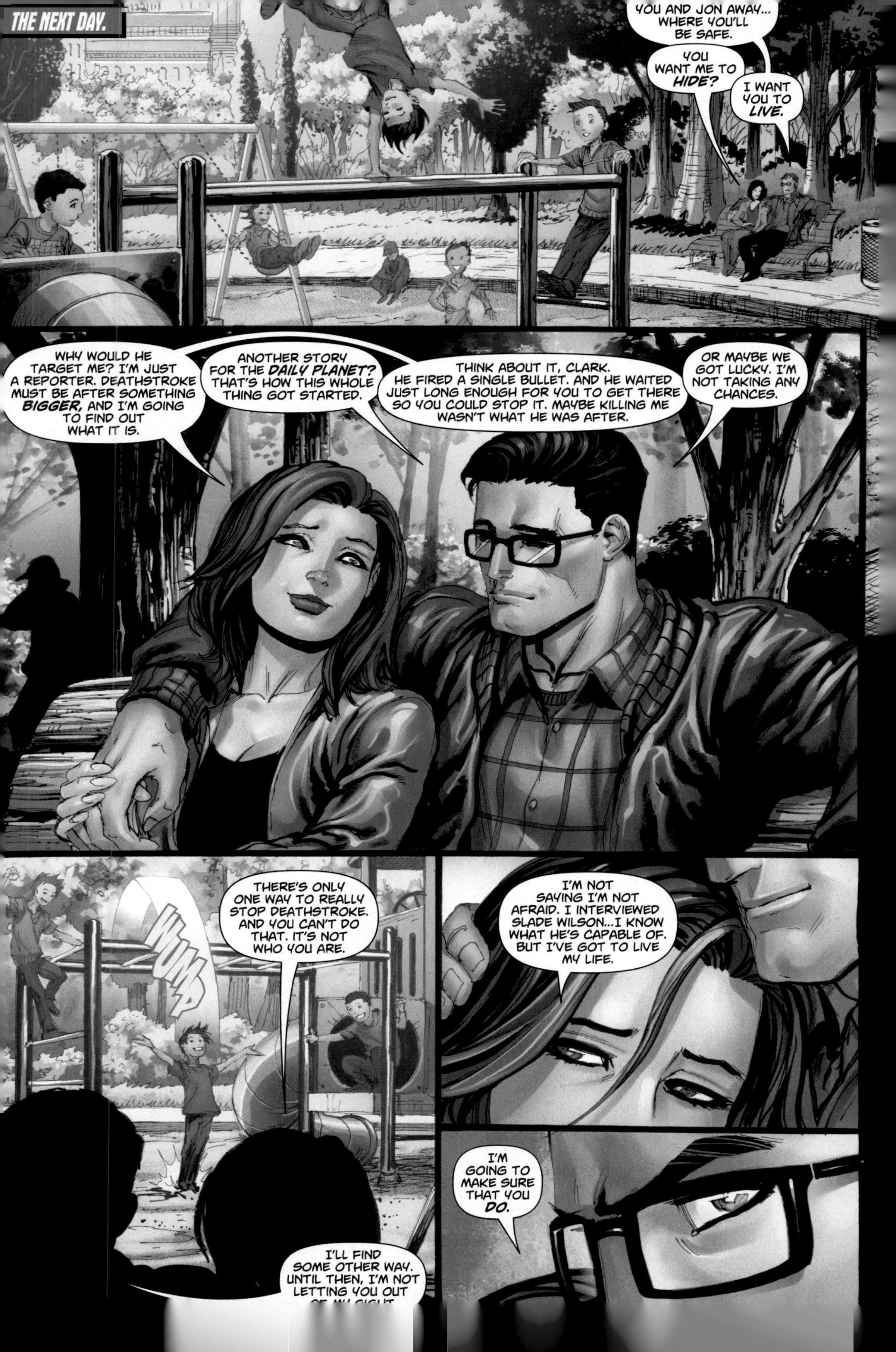
THE NEXT DAY.
YOU AND JON AWAY... WHERE YOU'LL BE SAFE.
YOU WANT ME TO HIDE?
I WANT YOU TO LIVE.
WHY WOULD HE TARGET ME? I'M JUST A REPORTER. DEATHSTROKE MUST BE AFTER SOMETHING BIGGER, AND I'M GOING TO FIND OUT WHAT IT IS.
ANOTHER STORY FOR THE DAILY PLANET? THAT'S HOW THIS WHOLE THING GOT STARTED.
THINK ABOUT IT, CLARK. HE FIRED A SINGLE BULLET. AND HE WAITED JUST LONG ENOUGH FOR YOU TO GET THERE SO YOU COULD STOP IT. MAYBE KILLING ME WASN'T WHAT HE WAS AFTER.
OR MAYBE WE GOT LUCKY. I'M NOT TAKING ANY CHANCES.
THERE'S ONLY ONE WAY TO REALLY STOP DEATHSTROKE. AND YOU CAN'T DO THAT. IT'S NOT WHO YOU ARE.
WUMP
I'LL FIND SOME OTHER WAY. UNTIL THEN, I'M NOT LETTING YOU OUT
I'M NOT SAYING I'M NOT AFRAID. I INTERVIEWED SLADE WILSON...I KNOW WHAT HE'S CAPABLE OF. BUT I'VE GOT TO LIVE MY LIFE.
I'M GOING TO MAKE SURE THAT YOU DO.

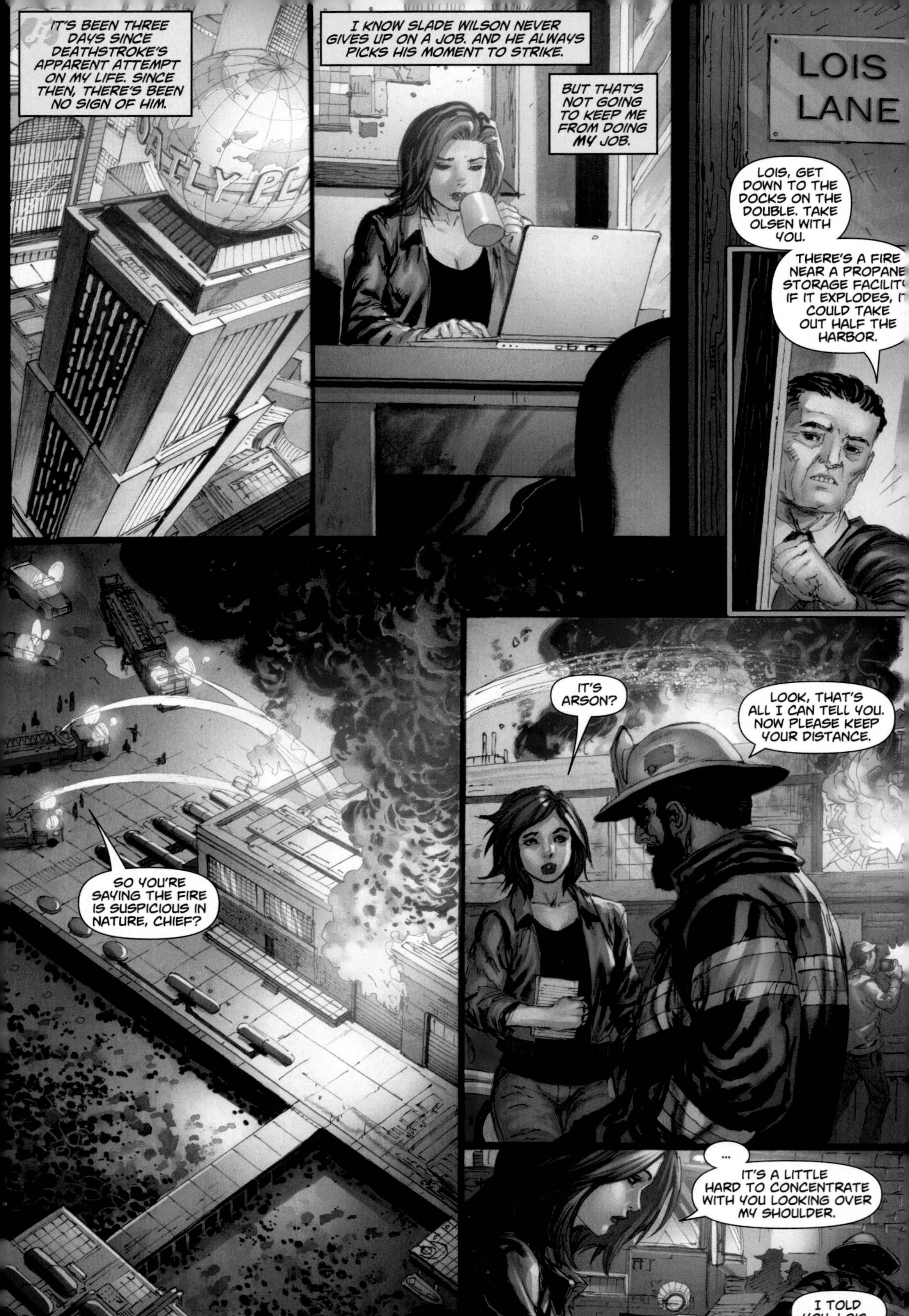
IT'S BEEN THREE DAYS SINCE DEATHSTROKE'S APPARENT ATTEMPT ON MY LIFE. SINCE THEN, THERE'S BEEN NO SIGN OF HIM.
I KNOW SLADE WILSON NEVER GIVES UP ON A JOB. AND HE ALWAYS PICKS HIS MOMENT TO STRIKE.
BUT THAT'S NOT GOING TO KEEP ME FROM DOING MY JOB.
LOIS LANE
LOIS, GET DOWN TO THE DOCKS ON THE DOUBLE. TAKE OLSEN WITH YOU.
THERE'S A FIRE NEAR A PROPANE STORAGE FACILITY. IF IT EXPLODES, IT COULD TAKE OUT HALF THE HARBOR.
SO YOU'RE SAYING THE FIRE IS SUSPICIOUS IN NATURE, CHIEF?
IT'S ARSON?
LOOK, THAT'S ALL I CAN TELL YOU. NOW PLEASE KEEP YOUR DISTANCE.
...
IT'S A LITTLE HARD TO CONCENTRATE WITH YOU LOOKING OVER MY SHOULDER.
I TOLD YOU, LOIS...

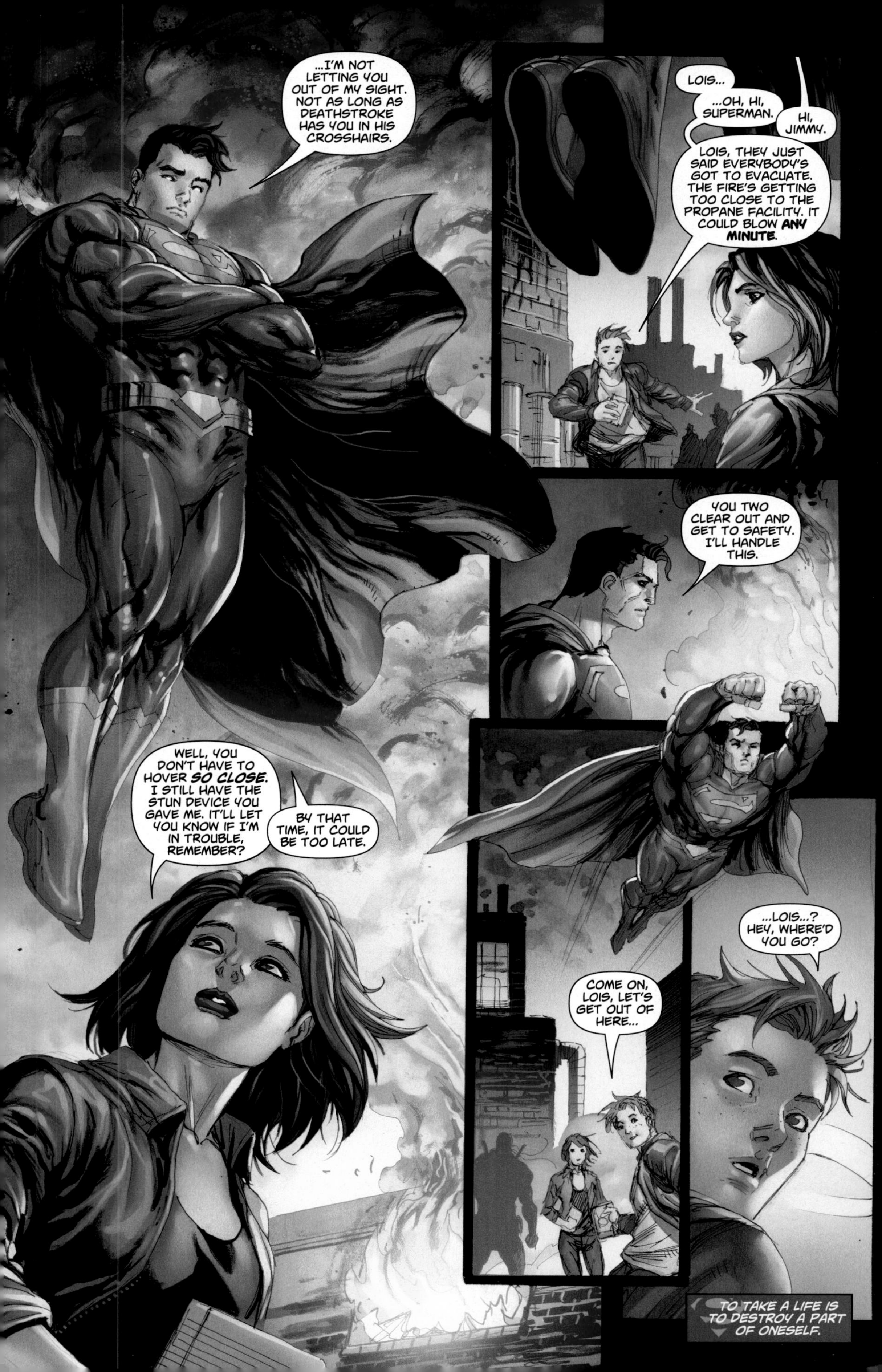
...I'M NOT LETTING YOU OUT OF MY SIGHT. NOT AS LONG AS DEATHSTROKE HAS YOU IN HIS CROSSHAIRS.
WELL, YOU DON'T HAVE TO HOVER SO CLOSE. I STILL HAVE THE STUN DEVICE YOU GAVE ME. IT'LL LET YOU KNOW IF I'M IN TROUBLE, REMEMBER?
BY THAT TIME, IT COULD BE TOO LATE.
LOIS...
...OH, HI, SUPERMAN.
HI, JIMMY.
LOIS, THEY JUST SAID EVERYBODY'S GOT TO EVACUATE. THE FIRE'S GETTING TOO CLOSE TO THE PROPANE FACILITY. IT COULD BLOW ANY MINUTE.
YOU TWO CLEAR OUT AND GET TO SAFETY. I'LL HANDLE THIS.
COME ON, LOIS, LET'S GET OUT OF HERE...
...LOIS...? HEY, WHERE'D YOU GO?
TO TAKE A LIFE IS TO DESTROY A PART OF ONESELF.

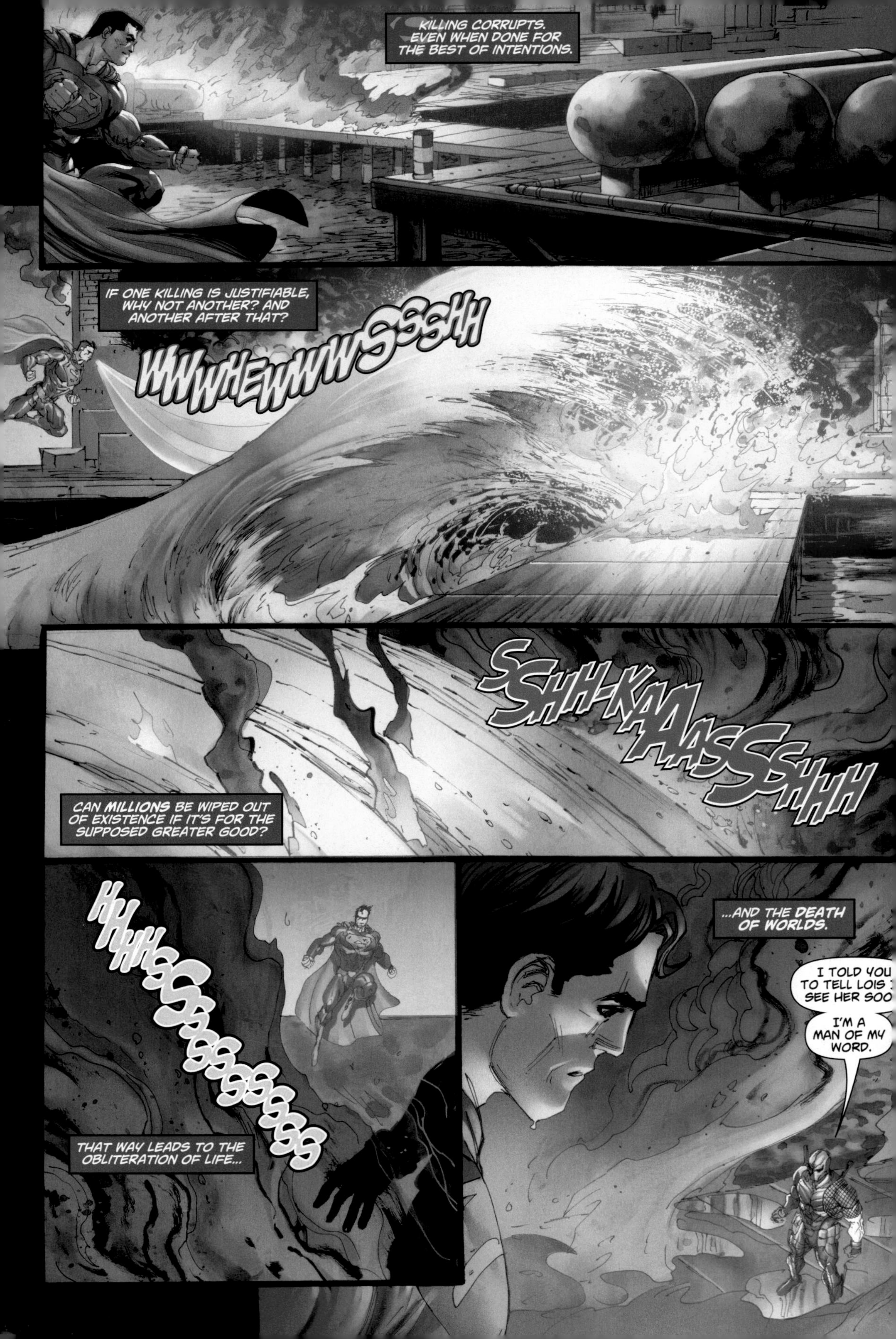
KILLING CORRUPTS. EVEN WHEN DONE FOR THE BEST OF INTENTIONS.
IF ONE KILLING IS JUSTIFIABLE, WHY NOT ANOTHER? AND ANOTHER AFTER THAT?
WWWHEWWWWSSSHH
SSHH-KAAAASSSHHH
CAN MILLIONS BE WIPED OUT OF EXISTENCE IF IT'S FOR THE SUPPOSED GREATER GOOD?
HHHHSSSSSSSSSSSS
THAT WAY LEADS TO THE OBLITERATION OF LIFE...
...AND THE DEATH OF WORLDS.
I TOLD YOU TO TELL LOIS SEE HER SOO
I'M A MAN OF MY WORD.

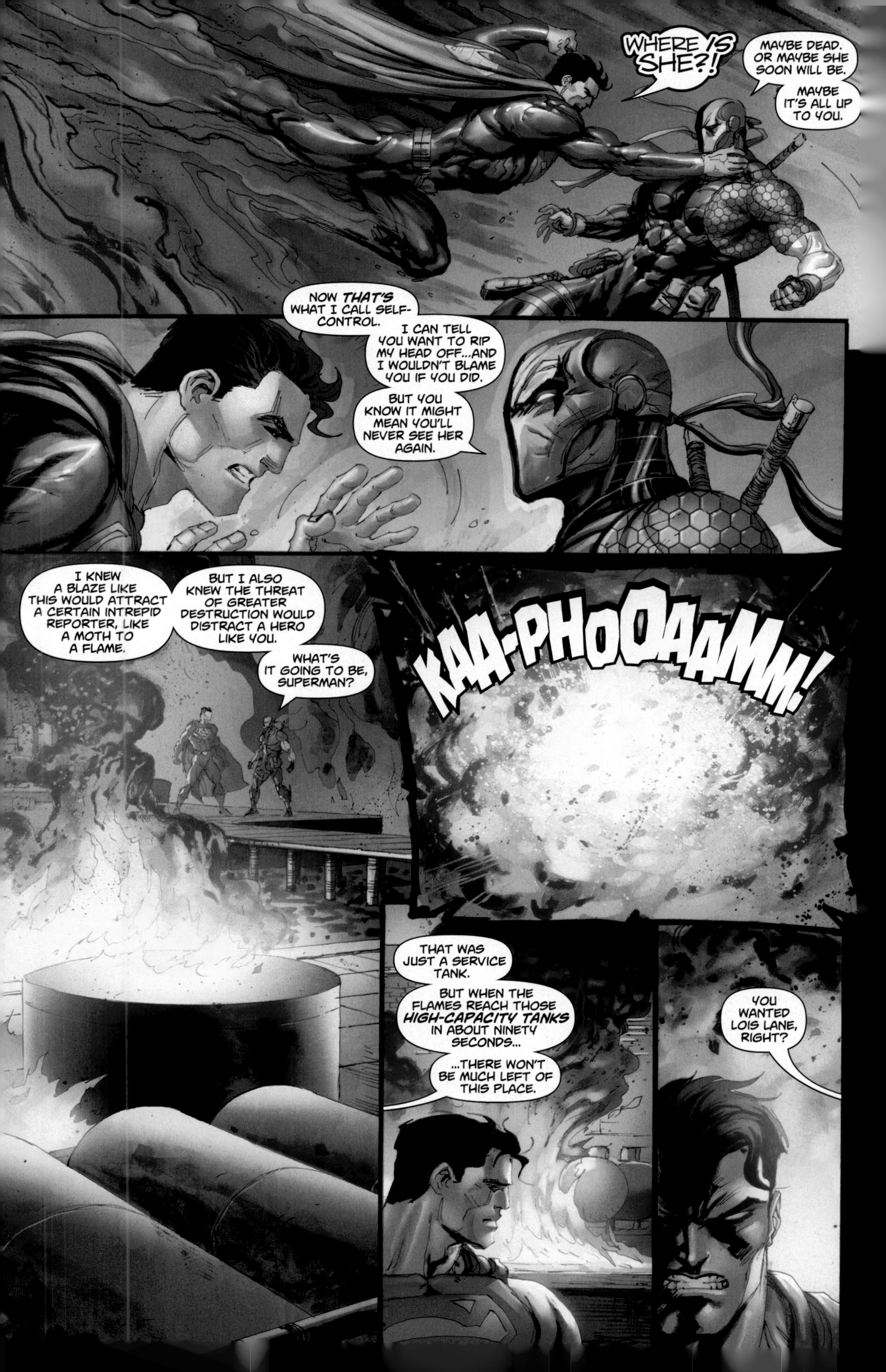
WHERE IS SHE?!
MAYBE DEAD. OR MAYBE SHE SOON WILL BE.
MAYBE IT'S ALL UP TO YOU.
NOW THAT'S WHAT I CALL SELF-CONTROL.
I CAN TELL YOU WANT TO RIP MY HEAD OFF...AND I WOULDN'T BLAME YOU IF YOU DID.
BUT YOU KNOW IT MIGHT MEAN YOU'LL NEVER SEE HER AGAIN.
I KNEW A BLAZE LIKE THIS WOULD ATTRACT A CERTAIN INTREPID REPORTER, LIKE A MOTH TO A FLAME.
BUT I ALSO KNEW THE THREAT OF GREATER DESTRUCTION WOULD DISTRACT A HERO LIKE YOU.
WHAT'S IT GOING TO BE, SUPERMAN?
KAA-PHOOAAMM!
THAT WAS JUST A SERVICE TANK.
BUT WHEN THE FLAMES REACH THOSE HIGH-CAPACITY TANKS IN ABOUT NINETY SECONDS...
...THERE WON'T BE MUCH LEFT OF THIS PLACE.
YOU WANTED LOIS LANE, RIGHT?

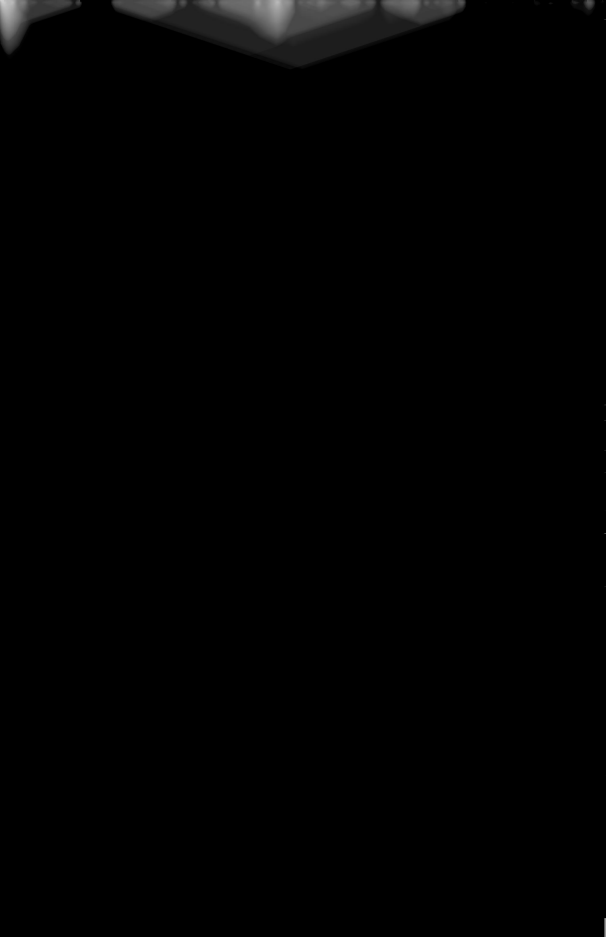

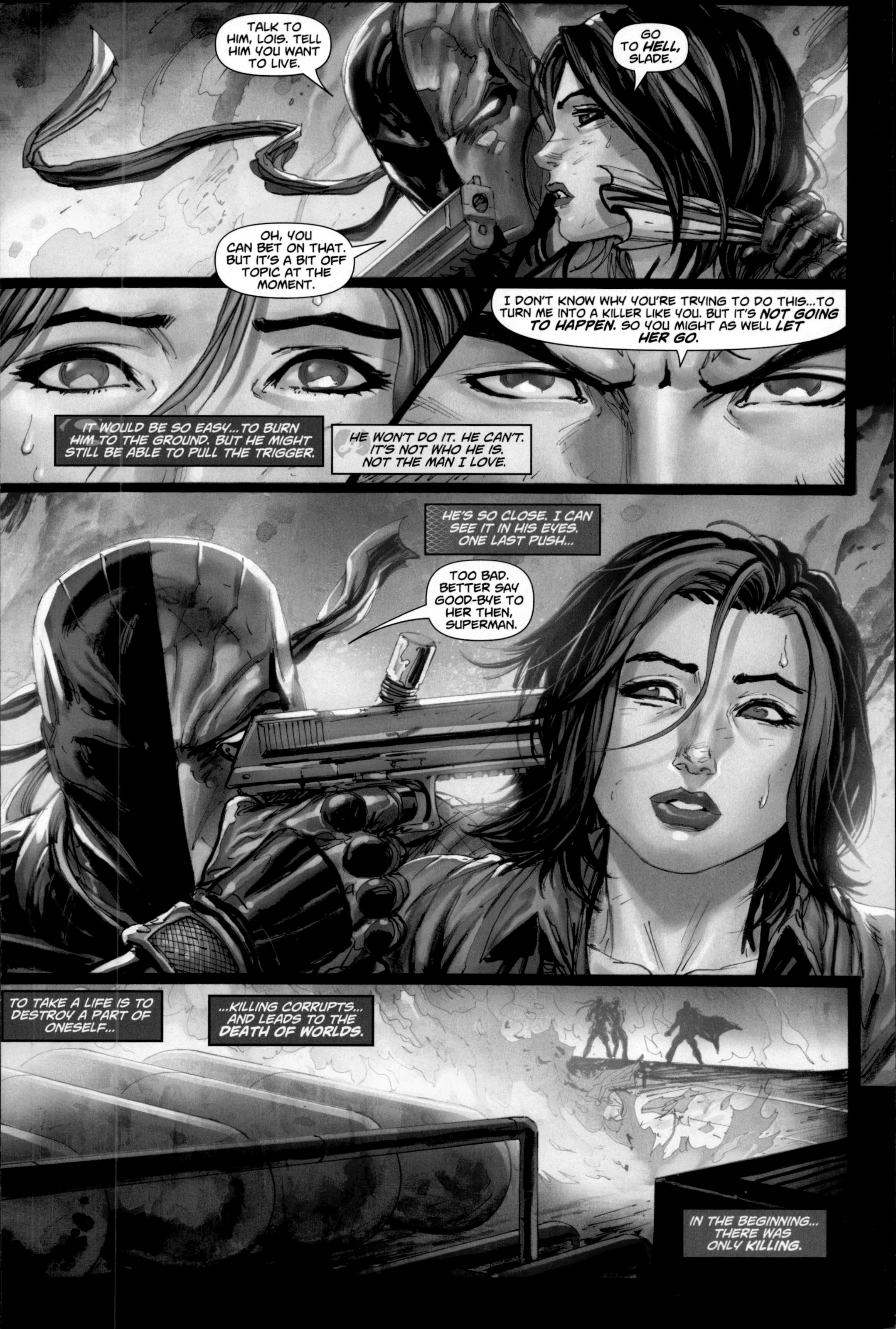

TALK TO HIM, LOIS. TELL HIM YOU WANT TO LIVE.
GO TO HELL, SLADE.
OH, YOU CAN BET ON THAT. BUT IT'S A BIT OFF TOPIC AT THE MOMENT.
I DON'T KNOW WHY YOU'RE TRYING TO DO THIS...TO TURN ME INTO A KILLER LIKE YOU. BUT IT'S NOT GOING TO HAPPEN. SO YOU MIGHT AS WELL LET HER GO.
IT WOULD BE SO EASY...TO BURN HIM TO THE GROUND. BUT HE MIGHT STILL BE ABLE TO PULL THE TRIGGER.
HE WON'T DO IT. HE CAN'T. IT'S NOT WHO HE IS. NOT THE MAN I LOVE.
HE'S SO CLOSE. I CAN SEE IT IN HIS EYES. ONE LAST PUSH...
TOO BAD. BETTER SAY GOOD-BYE TO HER THEN, SUPERMAN.
TO TAKE A LIFE IS TO DESTROY A PART OF ONESELF...
...KILLING CORRUPTS... AND LEADS TO THE DEATH OF WORLDS.
IN THE BEGINNING... THERE WAS ONLY KILLING.

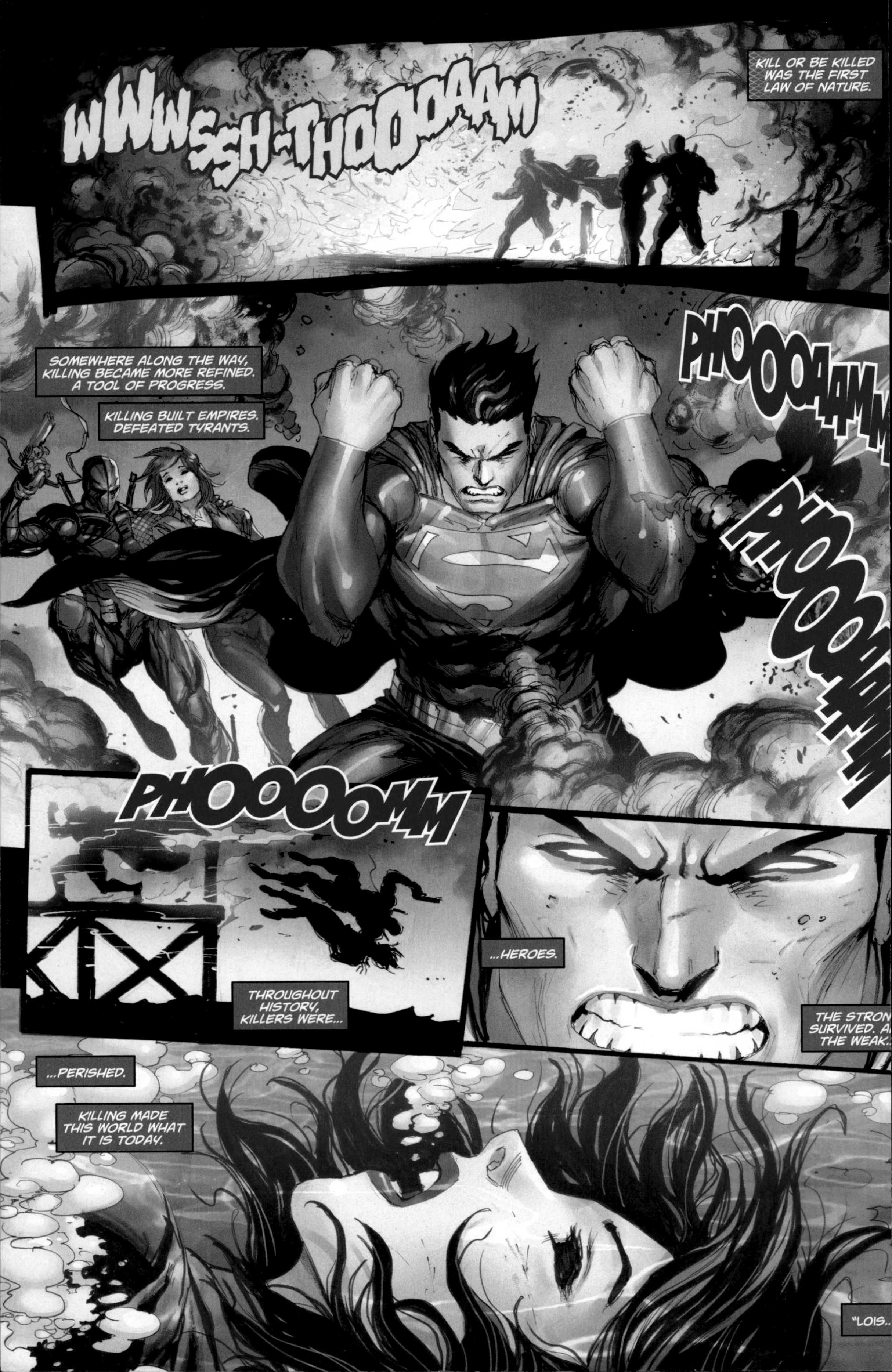
KILL OR BE KILLED WAS THE FIRST LAW OF NATURE.
WWWSSH-THOOOAAM
SOMEWHERE ALONG THE WAY, KILLING BECAME MORE REFINED. A TOOL OF PROGRESS.
KILLING BUILT EMPIRES. DEFEATED TYRANTS.
PHOOOOAAMM
PHOOOOAAMM
PHOOOOOMM
THROUGHOUT HISTORY, KILLERS WERE...
...HEROES.
THE STRON SURVIVED. A THE WEAK...
...PERISHED.
KILLING MADE THIS WORLD WHAT IT IS TODAY.
"LOIS...

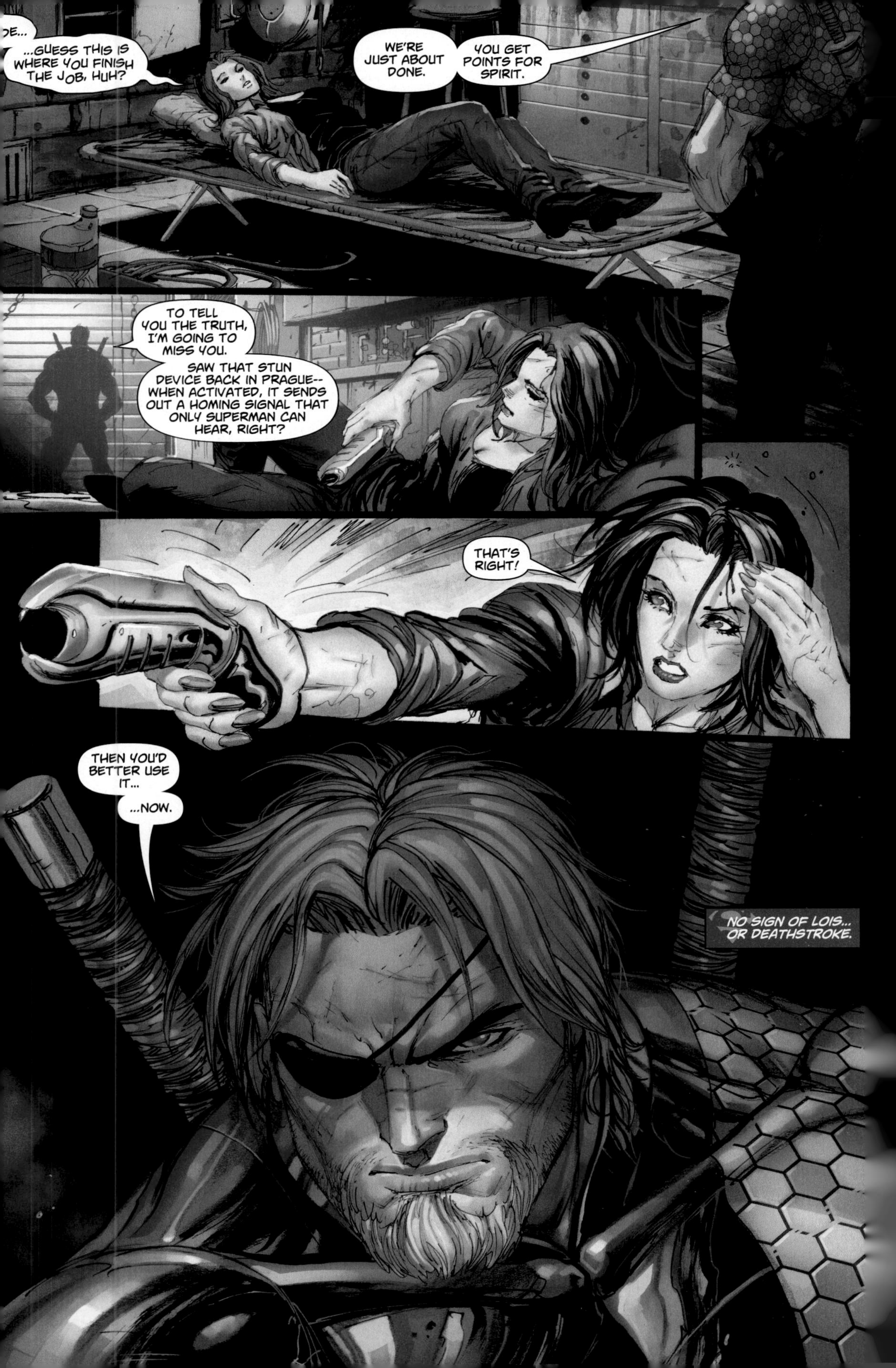
...GUESS THIS IS WHERE YOU FINISH THE JOB, HUH?
WE'RE JUST ABOUT DONE.
YOU GET POINTS FOR SPIRIT.
TO TELL YOU THE TRUTH, I'M GOING TO MISS YOU.
SAW THAT STUN DEVICE BACK IN PRAGUE-- WHEN ACTIVATED, IT SENDS OUT A HOMING SIGNAL THAT ONLY SUPERMAN CAN HEAR, RIGHT?
THAT'S RIGHT!
THEN YOU'D BETTER USE IT...
...NOW.
NO SIGN OF LOIS... OR DEATHSTROKE.

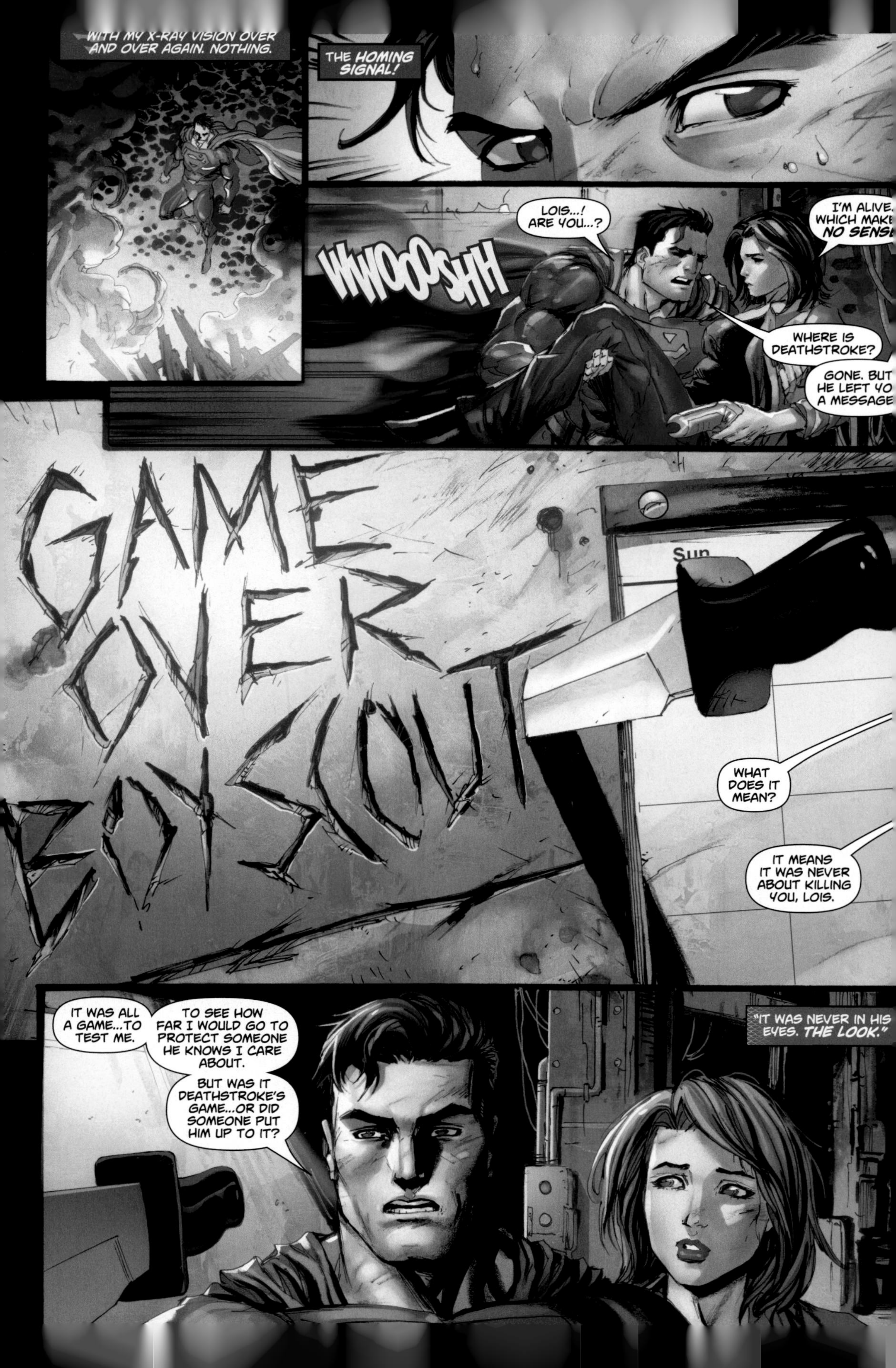
WITH MY X-RAY VISION OVER AND OVER AGAIN. NOTHING.
THE HOMING SIGNAL!
WWOOOSHH
LOIS...! ARE YOU...?
I'M ALIVE. WHICH MAKE NO SENS
WHERE IS DEATHSTROKE?
GONE. BUT HE LEFT YO A MESSAGE
GAME OVER BOY SCOUT
Sun
WHAT DOES IT MEAN?
IT MEANS IT WAS NEVER ABOUT KILLING YOU, LOIS.
IT WAS ALL A GAME...TO TEST ME.
TO SEE HOW FAR I WOULD GO TO PROTECT SOMEONE HE KNOWS I CARE ABOUT.
BUT WAS IT DEATHSTROKE'S GAME...OR DID SOMEONE PUT HIM UP TO IT?
"IT WAS NEVER IN HIS EYES. THE LOOK."

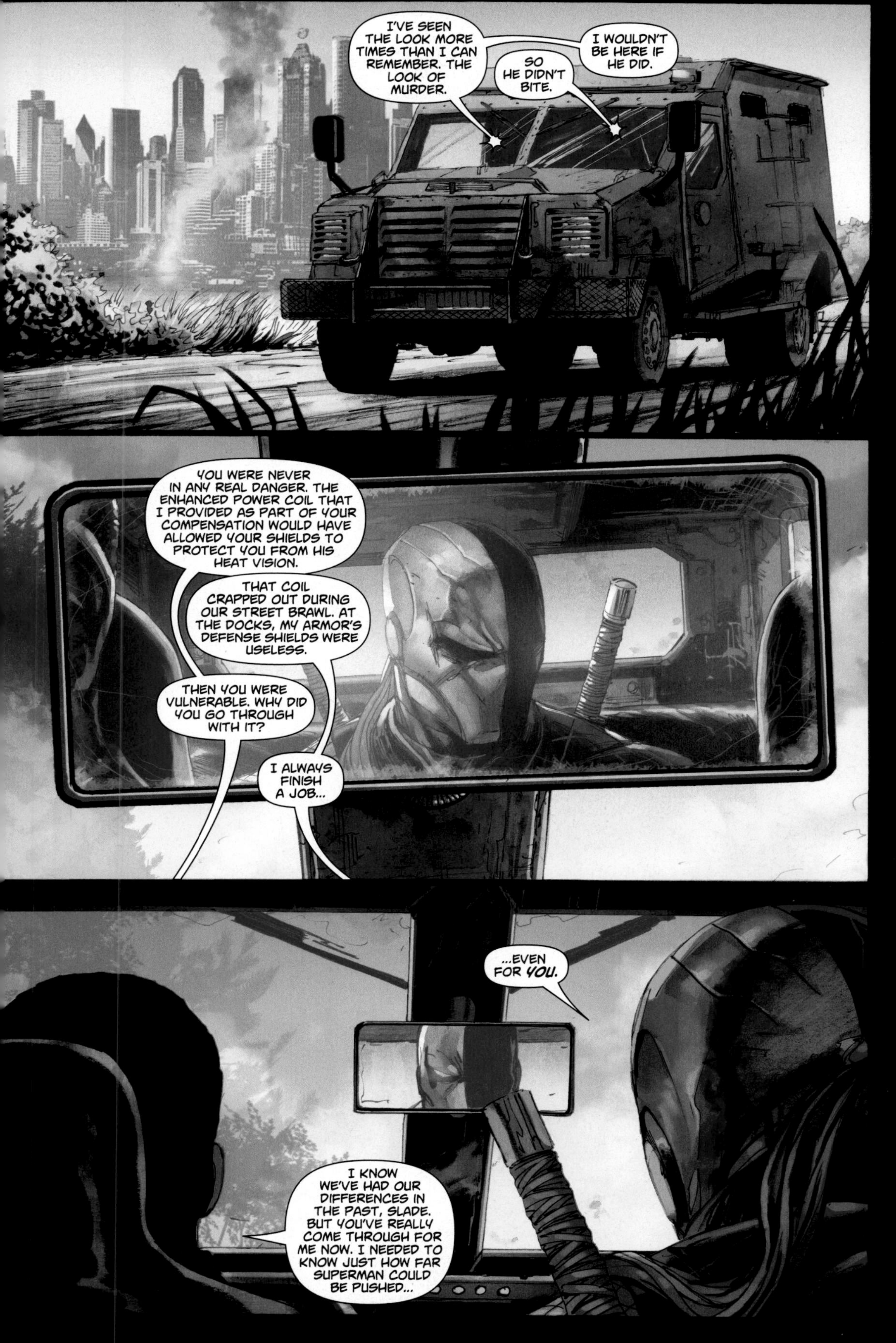
I'VE SEEN THE LOOK MORE TIMES THAN I CAN REMEMBER. THE LOOK OF MURDER.
SO HE DIDN'T BITE.
I WOULDN'T BE HERE IF HE DID.
YOU WERE NEVER IN ANY REAL DANGER. THE ENHANCED POWER COIL THAT I PROVIDED AS PART OF YOUR COMPENSATION WOULD HAVE ALLOWED YOUR SHIELDS TO PROTECT YOU FROM HIS HEAT VISION.
THAT COIL CRAPPED OUT DURING OUR STREET BRAWL. AT THE DOCKS, MY ARMOR'S DEFENSE SHIELDS WERE USELESS.
THEN YOU WERE VULNERABLE. WHY DID YOU GO THROUGH WITH IT?
I ALWAYS FINISH A JOB...
...EVEN FOR *YOU*.
I KNOW WE'VE HAD OUR DIFFERENCES IN THE PAST, SLADE. BUT YOU'VE REALLY COME THROUGH FOR ME NOW. I NEEDED TO KNOW JUST HOW FAR SUPERMAN COULD BE PUSHED...

...IN CASE I NEED TO DO SOME PUSHING MYSELF.
A JOB'S A JOB, WALLER.
I DON'T REALLY GIVE A DAMN ABOUT YOUR REASONS.
KILLING CHANGES YOU.
IT CHANGED ME.
DEEP DOWN I HOPE SUPERMAN IS RIGHT.
BUT WHEN YOU BLINK IN THE PRESENCE OF A PREDATOR...IT CAN BE SUICIDE.

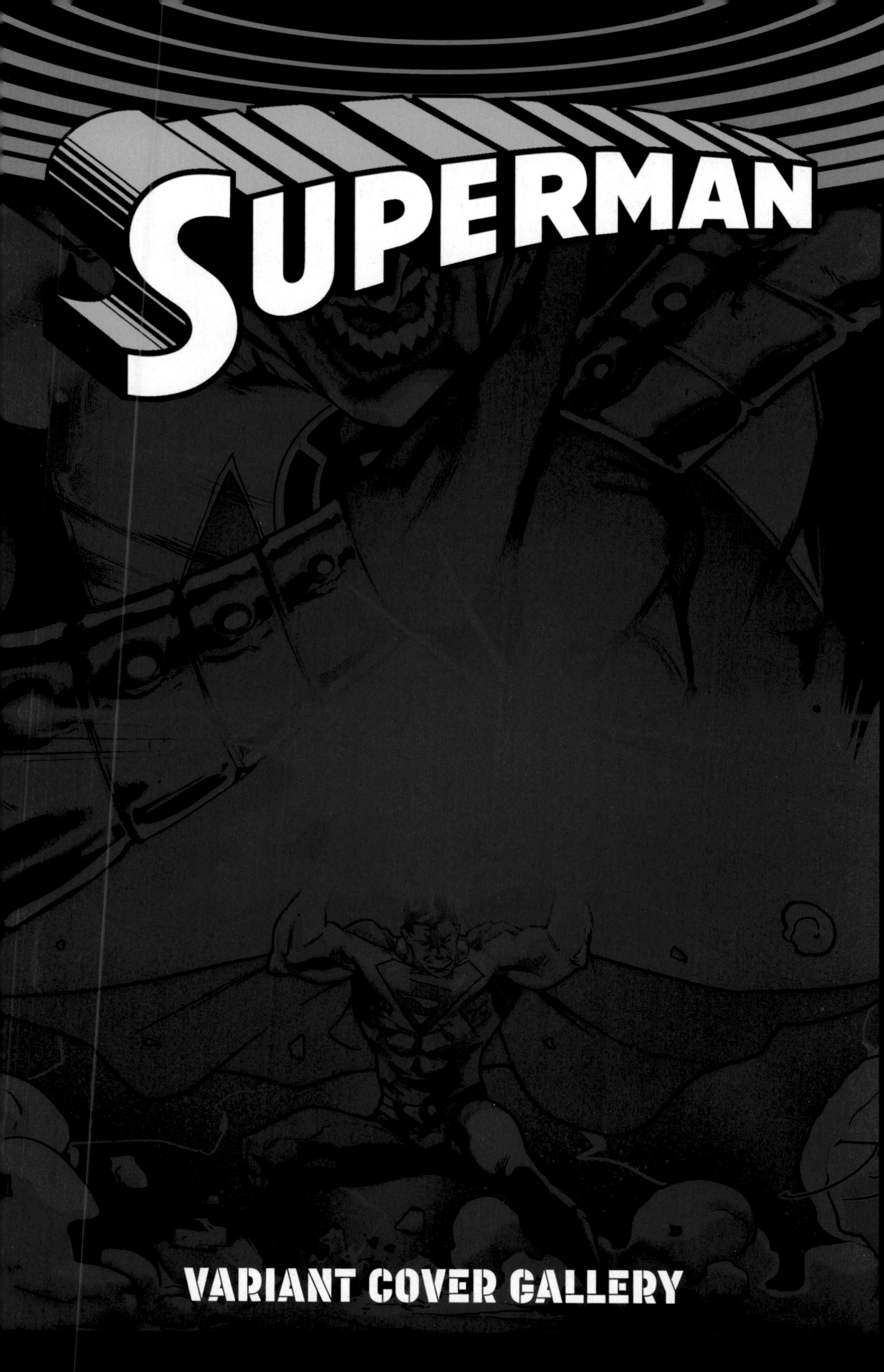
SUPERMAN
VARIANT COVER GALLERY

Variant cover art for SUPERMAN #27 by JORGE JIMENEZ
and ALEJANDRO SANCHEZ

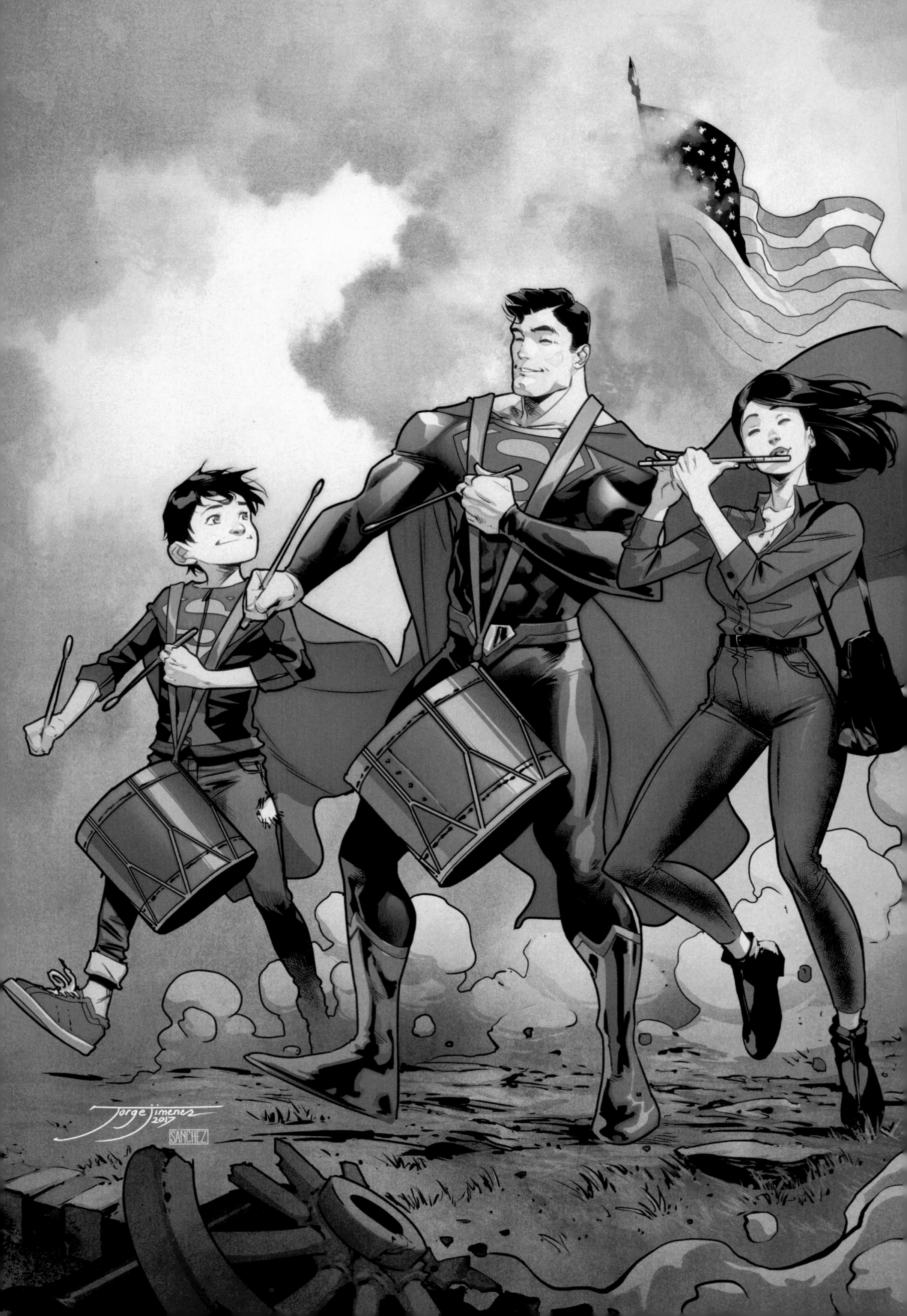
Jorge Jimenez 2017
SANCHEZ

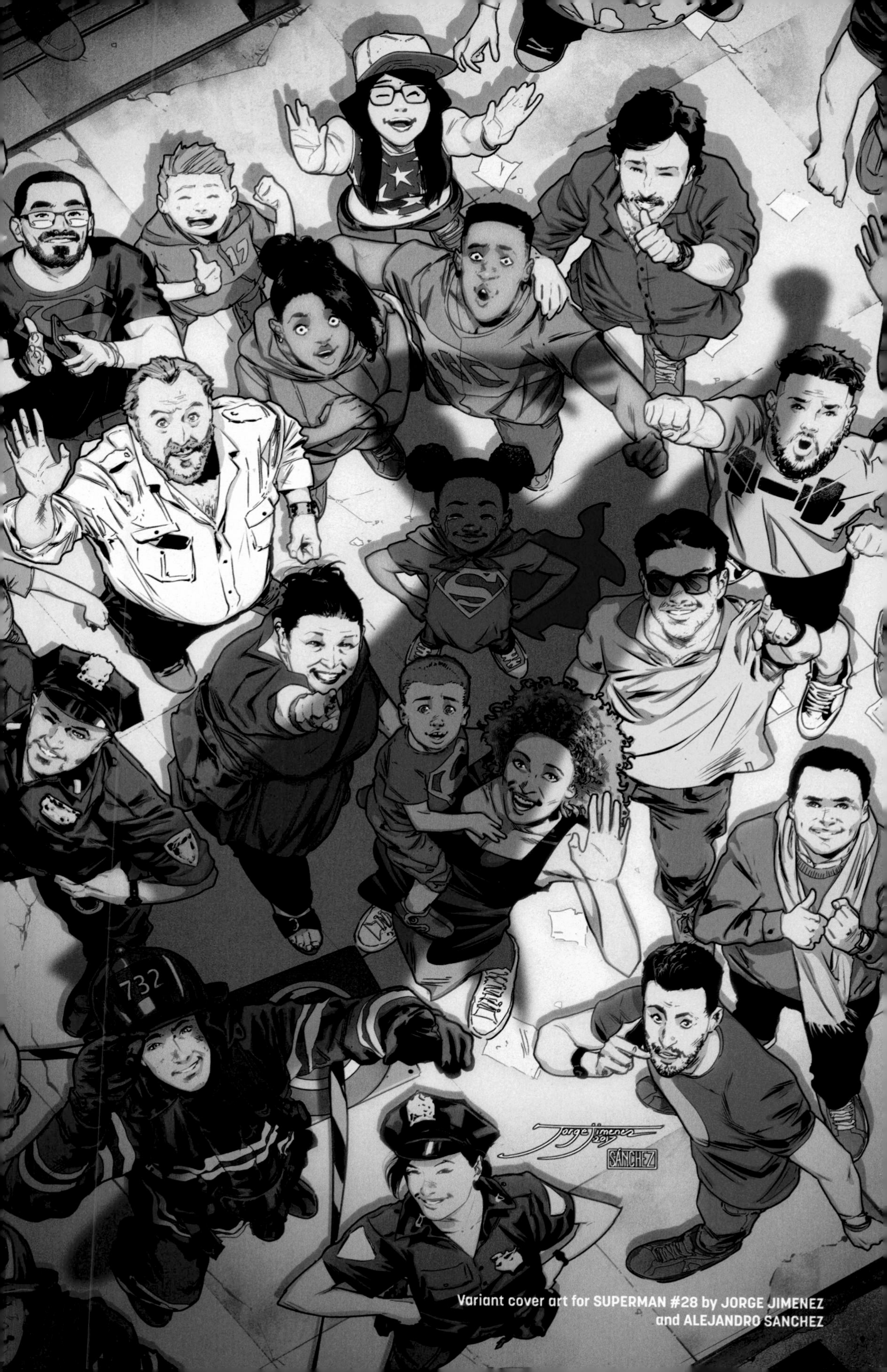

732
Jorge Jimenez 2017
SÁNCHEZ

Variant cover art for SUPERMAN #28 by JORGE JIMENEZ and ALEJANDRO SANCHEZ

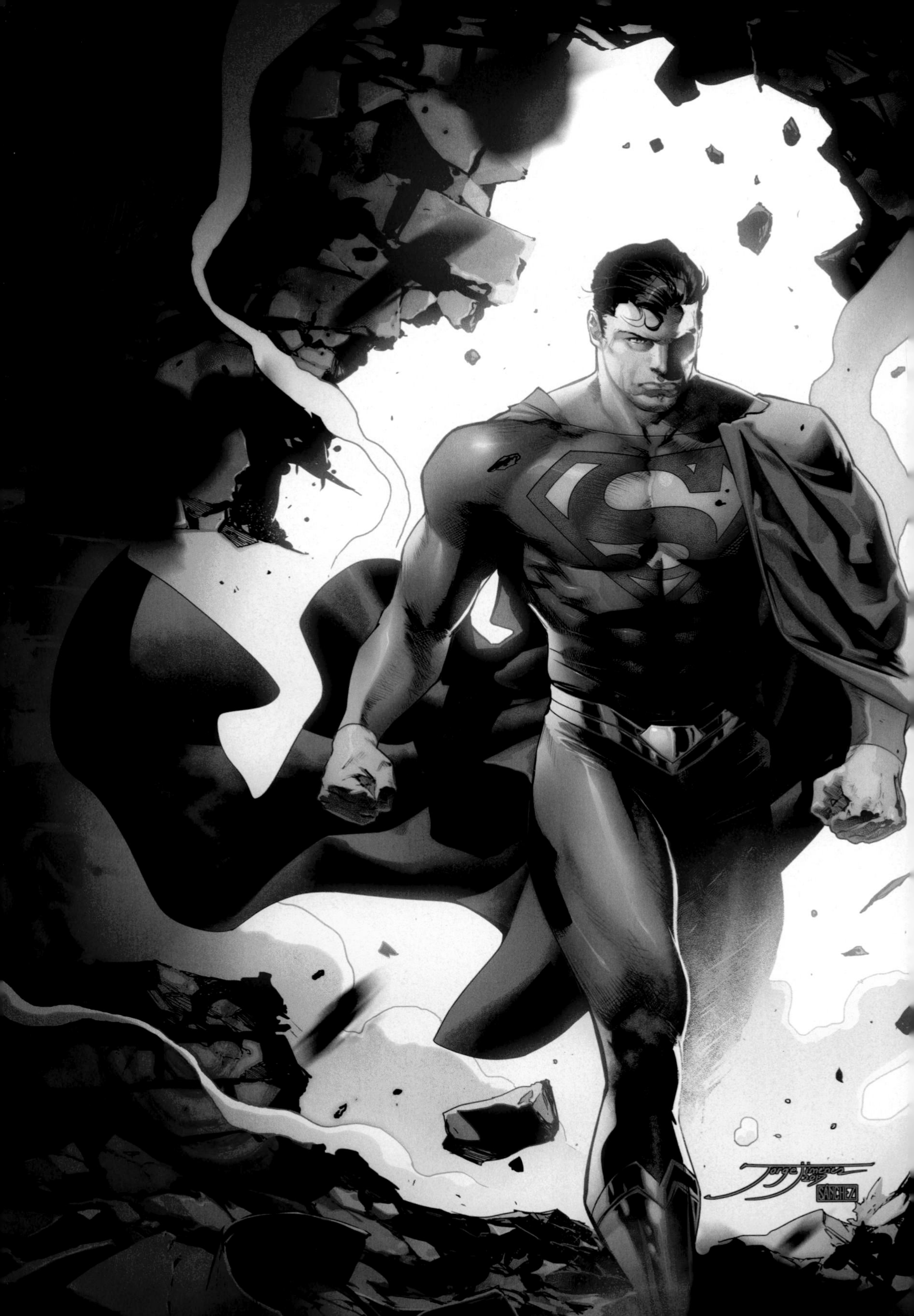

Variant cover art for SUPERMAN #29 by JORGE JIMENEZ and ALEJANDRO SANCHEZ

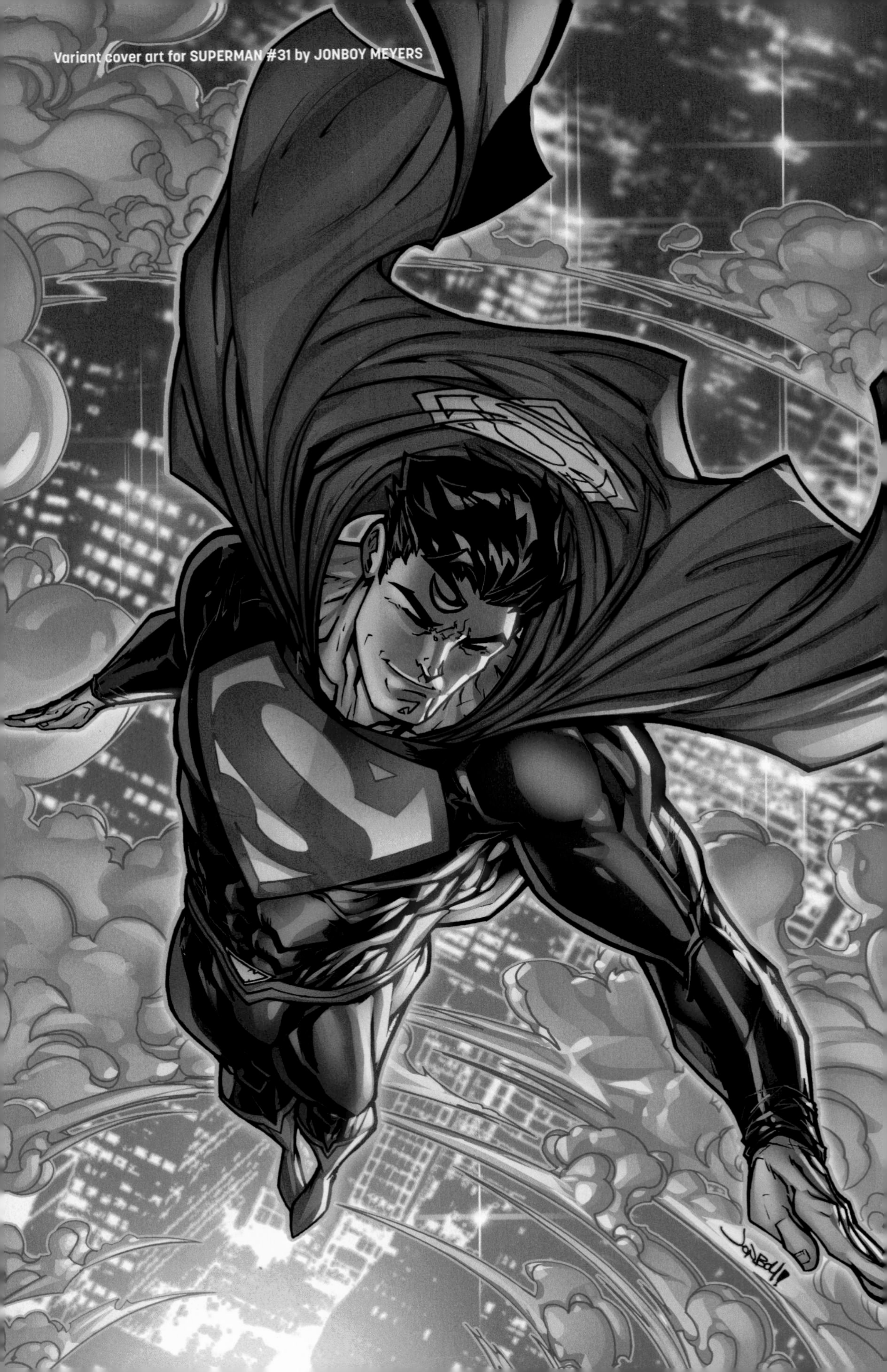
Variant cover art for SUPERMAN #31 by JONBOY MEYERS

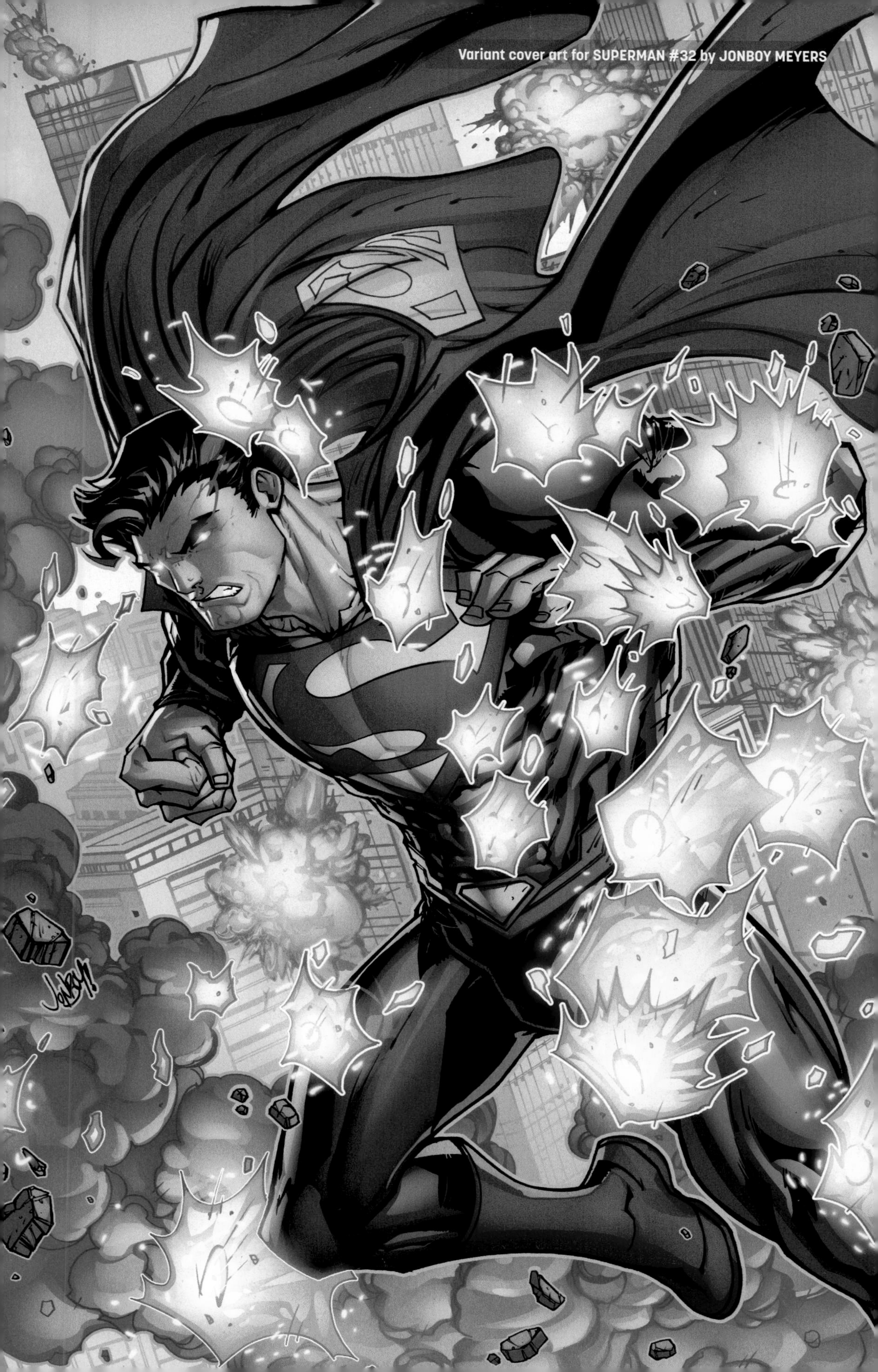

Variant cover art for SUPERMAN #32 by JONBOY MEYERS

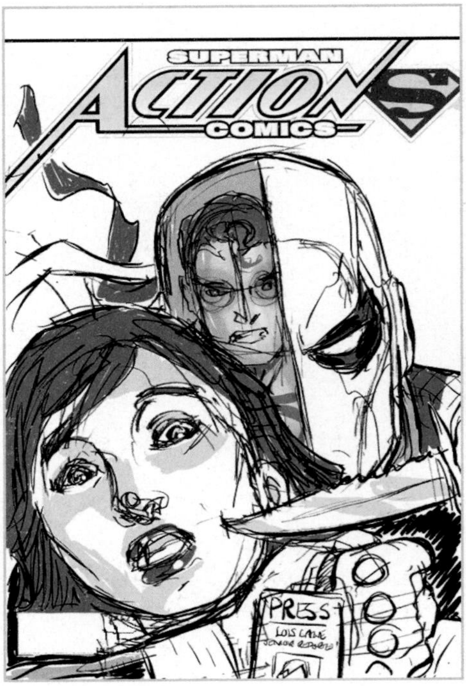
SUPERMAN
ACTION
COMICS
PRESS
LOIS LANE

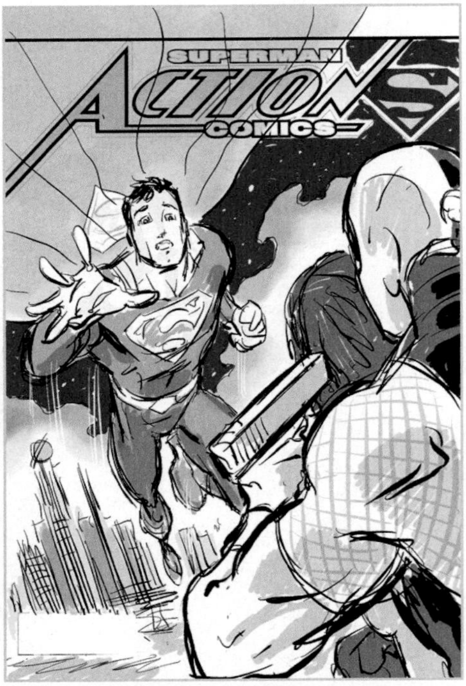
SUPERMAN
ACTION
COMICS

SUPERMAN #31 COVER SKETCHES
by IAN CHURCHILL

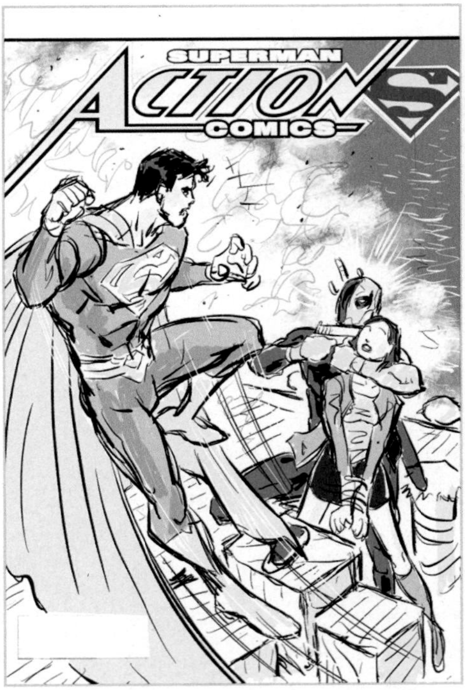
SUPERMAN
ACTION
COMICS

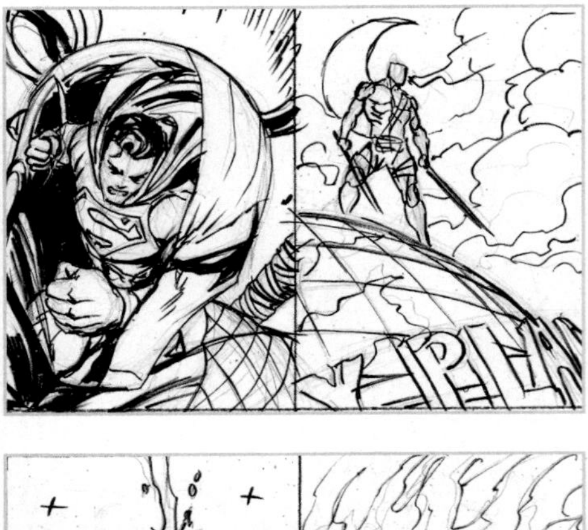

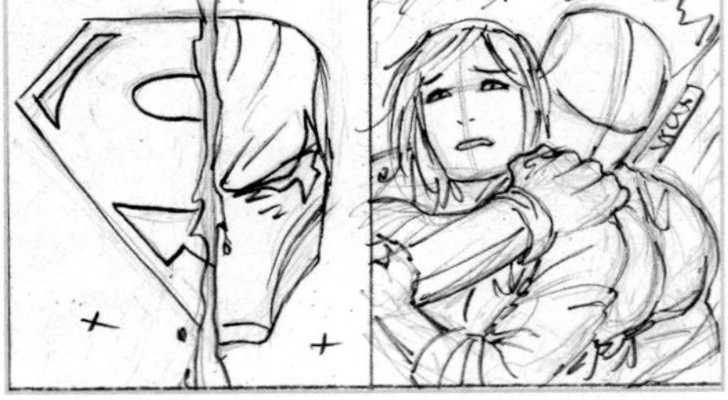

SUPERMAN #32 COVER SKETCHES
by TYLER KIRKHAM